Latin American
Spanish

phrasebooks
and
Roberto Esposto

Latin American Spanish phrasebook
4th edition – October 2003

Published by
Lonely Planet Publications Pty Ltd ABN 36 005 607 983
90 Maribyrnong St, Footscray, Victoria 3011, Australia

Lonely Planet Offices
Australia Locked Bag 1, Footscray, Victoria 3011
USA 150 Linden St, Oakland CA 94607
UK 72-82 Rosebery Ave, London, EC 1R 4RW
France 1 rue du Dahomey, 75011 Paris

Cover illustration
Oi!!! Muy Caliente! by Patrick Marris

ISBN 1 74059 170 4

text © Lonely Planet Publications Pty Ltd 2003
cover illustration © Lonely Planet Publications Pty Ltd 2003

10 9 8 7 6 5 3 2 1

Printed by the Bookmaker International Ltd
Printed in China

acknowledgments

Lonely Planet's Language Products and editor Francesca Coles would like to thank the following *compadres* for bringing this phrasebook to life:

Roberto Esposto (PhD), lecturer in Spanish and Latin American Studies at the University of Queensland, who supplied the translations and transliterations. Roberto wishes to thank his partner Maria Chiaroni for contributing her knowledge of Latin American Spanish gained in Peru and Central America.

Publishing manager Peter D'Onghia and his predecessor Jim Jenkin whose ingenuity gave birth to a new breed of phrasebook.

Commissioning editors Karin Vidstrup Monk and Karina Coates and managing editor Annelies Mertens for her diligent supervision.

Project managers Fabrice Rocher and Charles Rawlings-Way for keeping the Latin American Express on the rails.

Fellow editors Ben Handicott, Quentin Frayne and Emma Koch. Special thanks to editor Piers 'Perspicacity' Kelly for switched on proofing and for sharing the Spanish experience.

Freelance proofers and Spanish language experts Peter and Marta Gibney for careful proofing of the Latin American Spanish.

Layout designer Yvonne Bischofberger for efficient layout and layout managers Adriana Mammarella and Kate McDonald for layout checks. Patrick Marris for the cover and inside illustrations. Series designer Yukiyoshi Kamimura for book and cover design.

Thanks also to cartographer Valentina Kremenchutskaya, managing cartographer Paul Piaia and cartographic designer Wayne Murphy for the language map. *Gracias* to in-house Argentinian Gus Balbontin for his advice, and to layout designer Nick Stebbing and macro-genius David Burnett for production support.

make the most of this phrasebook ...

Anyone can speak another language! It's all about confidence. Don't worry if you can't remember your school language lessons or if you've never learnt a language before. Even if you learn the very basics (on the inside covers of this book), your travel experience will be the better for it. You have nothing to lose and everything to gain when the locals hear you making an effort.

finding things in this book

For easy navigation, this book is in sections. The Tools chapters are the ones you'll thumb through time and again. The Practical section covers basic travel situations like catching transport and finding a bed. The Social section gives you conversational phrases, pick-up lines, the ability to express opinions – so you can get to know people. Food has a section all of its own: gourmets and vegetarians are covered and local dishes feature. Safe Travel equips you with health and police phrases, just in case. Remember the colours of each section and you'll find everything easily; or use the comprehensive Index. Otherwise, check the two-way traveller's Dictionary for the word you need.

being understood

Throughout this book you'll see coloured phrases on the right-hand side of each page. They're phonetic guides to help you pronounce the language. You don't even need to look at the language itself, but you'll get used to the way we've represented particular sounds. The pronunciation chapter in Tools will explain more, but you can feel confident that if you read the coloured phrase slowly, you'll be understood.

communication tips

Body language, ways of doing things, sense of humour – all have a role to play in every culture. 'Local talk' boxes show you common ways of saying things, or everyday language to drop into conversation. 'Listen for ...' boxes supply the phrases you may hear. They start with the phonetic guide (because you'll hear it before you know what's being said) and then lead in to the language and the English translation.

introduction 6

tools 9

practical 37

social 89

food 141

safe travel 175

dictionaries 189

index 251

contents

5

latin american spanish

United States of America

Mexico
Mexico City

Gulf of Mexico

Havana Cuba

Dominican Republic

Santo Domingo

Haiti **Puerto Rico** (US)

San Juan

Caribbean Sea

see enlargement

Venezuela
Caracas

Guyana

Suriname

French Guiana (Fr)

Galápagos Islands ⟩
(Ecuador)

Bogotá

Colombia

Quito
Ecuador

Peru
Lima

Brazil

Bolivia
Sucre

SOUTH PACIFIC

OCEAN

Paraguay
Asunción

Chile

Santiago de Chile

Buenos Aires

Uruguay

Argentina

Montevideo

SOUTH ATLANTIC

OCEAN

Falkland Islands (UK)

Belize

Jamaica

Mexico

Belmopan

Guatemala

Honduras

Guatemala City

Tegucigalpa

San Salvador

Managua

Caribbean Sea

El Salvador

San José

Nicaragua

Panama City

Costa Rica

Panama

Colombia

■ **official language** ■ **widely understood**
For more details see the **introduction**.

You may have thought that Spanish was the same the world over – but think again. Since the Spanish language was first introduced to the Americas following Columbus' discovery of the continent in 1492, it has developed a vast array of colourful characteristics that distinguish it from its European ancestor. Today, the umbrella term 'Latin American Spanish' embraces all manner of unique varieties of Spanish spoken in 19 Latin American nations as well as in parts of the Caribbean and in the southern states of the US.

There are plenty of good reasons to get into Latin American Spanish. Not only is it relatively easy for English speakers to come to grips with, but it's also one of the world's most widely spoken languages. Travellers are easily seduced by its melodic expressiveness and lilting rhythm – there's no doubting the richness of a language that has lent itself to the literary imagination of world-famous authors such as Mario Vargas Llosa, Gabriel García Márquez and Isabel Allende.

at a glance ...

language name:
Latin American Spanish

names in language:
castellano kas·te·*lya*·no
español es·pa·*nyol*

language family: Romance

**approximate number of
speakers:** 300 million

close relatives:
Portuguese, Italian

donations to English:
barbecue, canoe, chili,
chocolate, hammock,
tomato, potato, tobacco
and many more ...

Some say that the differences between Latin American Spanish and the Spanish spoken in Spain can be compared to the contrast between US English and UK English. While speakers of either variety of Spanish will understand each other, both varieties have been subject to very different influences. Many of the first migrants either came from, or passed through, the ports of Andalucia in southern Spain on their way to the New World and brought with them the local speech patterns.

introduction

The fact that Latin Americans do not lisp the letters *c* and *z* is considered evidence of this Andalucian influence. Equally, indigenous languages have left their mark on Latin American Spanish – a fact which is particularly evident in vocabulary to do with flora, fauna and cultural habits.

Latin American Spanish varies slightly from country to country and from region to region. This phrasebook gives some of the main features of regional variations in both accents and vocabulary. Despite this diversity, Latin American Spanish has retained a remarkable unity over time and across a vast geographical area. One exception is Mexico where a number of strong differences in vocabulary and common expressions distinguish it from the rest of Latin America (see Lonely Planet's Mexican Spanish phrasebook).

This book gives you all the practical words and phrases you need to get by as well as all the fun, spontaneous phrases that lead to a better understanding of Latin America and its people. Need more encouragement? Remember, the contact you make using Latin American Spanish will make your travels unique. Local knowledge, new relationships and a sense of satisfaction are on the tip of your tongue, so don't just stand there, say something!

grammatical abbreviations

| **m** masculine | **sg** singular | **pol** polite |
| **f** feminine | **pl** plural | **inf** informal |

country abbreviations

These are the countries where Latin American Spanish is the main language. The abbreviations are those given throughout the book to indicate regional variations:

Arg Argentina	**Cub** Cuba	**Par** Paraguay
Bol Bolivia	**Ecu** Ecuador	**Per** Peru
CAm Central America	**Sal** El Salvador	**Pue** Puerto Rico
	Gua Guatemala	**SAm** South America
Chi Chile	**Hon** Honduras	**Uru** Uruguay
Col Colombia	**Nic** Nicaragua	**Ven** Venezuela
Cos Costa Rica	**Pan** Panama	

TOOLS > pronunciation
pronunciación

Latin American Spanish pronunciation is not difficult as many of the sounds are also found in English. The few sounds that are different aren't hard to produce and you'll probably find that revving up your *eres* (r's) and hissing out your *jotas* (j's) is fun.

Latin American Spanish pronunciation differs from the Castilian Spanish spoken in Spain. The most obvious difference is the lack of the lisping 'th' sound which is found in Castilian Spanish. Pronunciation in Latin America also varies from country to country and from region to region, just as English pronunciation varies from one place to another. In this book we use a generalised system for pronunciation which will allow you to be understood in all parts of Latin America.

vowel sounds

vocales

symbol	english equivalent	spanish example
a	f**a**ther	**a**gua
e	r**e**d	núm**e**ro
ee	b**ee**	d**í**a
o	h**o**t	**o**jo
oo	m**oo**n	g**u**sto

Vowels are pronounced crisply. They don't extend to form vowel sound combinations (diphthongs). Below are four vowel sounds, however, that roughly correspond to diphthongs in English:

symbol	english equivalent	spanish example
ai	**ai**sle	b**ai**lar
ay	s**ay**	s**ei**s
ow	h**ou**se	**au**tobús
oy	b**oy**	h**oy**

pronunciation

9

consonant sounds

symbol	english equivalent	spanish example
b	**b**ig	*barco*
ch	**ch**ili	*chica*
d	**d**in	*dinero*
f	**f**un	*fiesta*
g	**g**o	*gato*
k	**k**ick	*cabeza/queso*
kh	as in the Scottish '**loch**'	*jardín/gente*
l	**l**oud	*lago*
ly	milli**on**	*llamada*
m	**m**an	*mañana*
n	**n**o	*nuevo*
ny	ca**ny**on	*señora*
p	**p**ig	*padre*
r	**r**un, but stronger 'rolled' (especially as the first letter in a word and in all words with *rr*)	*mariposa/ritmo/burro*
s	**s**o	*semana/zarzuela/cinco*
t	**t**in	*tienda*
v	very soft 'v', somewhere between 'v' and 'b'	*severo*
w	**w**in	*guardia*
y	**y**es	*viaje*

regional variations

All transliterations in this book follow the system explained in the tables on pages 9-10. As we've said, pronunciation does vary across Latin America so you may expect to hear some of these variations as part of local accents:

The ly sound is simplified to 'y' (as in 'yes') in much of Latin America. Where this is the case, it drops out altogether before the vowel sounds e and ee. In Argentina, Uruguay and Highland Ecuador ly is pronounced like the 's' in 'measure'.

In much of Latin America s is reduced to just a slight 'h' sound when at the end of a syllable or a word, so *tos* 'cough' may sound like to followed by a barely audible 'h'.

Throughout Latin America there's confusion between the sounds r and l and you may hear one substituted for the other in a random way.

word stress

Latin American Spanish has stress. This means you emphasise one syllable of a word over another. Rule of thumb: when a word ends in *n*, *s* or a vowel, the stress falls on the second-last syllable. Otherwise, the last syllable is stressed. If you see an accent mark over a syllable, it cancels out these rules and you just stress that syllable instead. The stressed syllables are always italicised in our pronunciation guides so you needn't worry about these rules.

plunge in!

Don't worry too much about pronunciation. Just pick up your cue from the people around you. The phonetic guides we've given for every phrase account for the correct sounds and stress.

reading & writing

The relationship between Spanish sounds and their spelling is quite straightforward and consistent. The following rules will help you read any written Spanish you may come across:

c	before *e* or *i* pronounced 's'	**c**erveza, **c**inco
	before *a, o* and *u* pronounced as a 'k'	**c**arro, **c**orto, **c**ubo
h	never pronounced (silent)	**h**aber
q	pronounced as a 'k' and always followed by a *u* which is not pronounced	**q**uince
z	pronounced as an 's'	**z**orro
g	before *e* or *i* pronounced as the as 'ch' in lo**ch** – elsewhere as in 'go'	**g**ente, **g**igante, **g**ato, **g**ordo, **g**uante
gue, gui	the *u* is not pronounced (silent) in these combinations (unless there are two dots over the *u*)	**g**uerra, **g**uinda, **g**üiski

alphabet

a	a	*j*	kho·ta	*r*	er
b	be *lar*·ga	*k*	ka	*rr**	e·re
c	se	*l*	e·le	*s*	e·se
*ch**	che	*ll**	e·lye	*t*	te
d	de	*m*	e·me	*u*	oo
e	e	*n*	e·ne	*v*	be kor·*tal*
f	e·fe	*ñ*	e·nye	*w*	*do*·ble be
g	khe	*o*	o	*x*	e·kees
h	a·che	*p*	pe	*y*	ee *grye*·ga
i	ee	*q*	koo	*z*	se·ta

*The letters *ch*, *ll* and *rr* are no longer officially considered separate letters but they're still sounds in their own right.

a–z phrasebuilder
construyendo frases

This chapter will help you make your own sentences. It's arranged alphabetically for ease of navigation. If you can't find the exact phrase you need in this book, remember that with just a little grammar, a few gestures and a couple of well-chosen words, you'll generally get the message across.

a/an & some

I'd like a leather belt and an alpaca jumper.

Quisiera un cinto de cuero   kee·*sye*·ra oon *seen*·to de *kwe*·ro
y una chompa de alpaca.   ee *oo*·na *chom*·pa de al·*pa*·ka
(lit: I-would-like a belt of
leather and a jumper of alpaca)

Spanish has two words for the article 'a/an': *un* and *una*. The gender of the noun determines which one you use. *Un* and *una* also have plural forms: *unos* and *unas*, meaning 'some'.

masculine	*un* sg	*un huevo* oon *we*·vo	an egg
	unos pl	*unos huevos* *oo*·nos *we*·vos	some eggs
feminine	*una* sg	*una llama* *oo*·na *lya*·ma	a llama
	unas pl	*unas llamas* *oo*·na *lya*·mas	some llamas

adjectives see describing things

articles see **a/an & some** and **the**

be

Spanish has two words for the English verb 'be': *ser* and *estar*.

use *SER* to express	examples	
permanent characteristics of persons/things	*Ángel es muy amable.* an·khel es mooy a·ma·ble	Ángel is very nice.
occupations or nationality	*Pablo es de Puerto Rico.* pa·blo es de pwer·to ree·ko	Pablo is from Puerto Rico.
the time & location of events	*Son las tres.* son las tres	It's 3 o'clock.
possession	*¿De quién es esta mochila?* de kyen es es·ta mo·chee·la	Whose back-pack is this?
use *ESTAR* to express	examples	
temporary characteristics of persons/things	*La comida está fría.* la ko·mee·da es·ta free·a	The meal is cold.
the time & location of persons/things	*Estamos en Buenos Aires.* es·ta·mos en bwe·nos ai·res	We are in Buenos Aires.
the mood of a person	*Estoy contento/a.* m/f es·toy kon·ten·to/a	I'm happy.

Forms of the verb SER

I	am	a journalist	yo	soy	reportero/a m/f
you sg inf	are	from Cuba	tú	eres*	de Cuba
you sg pol	are	an artist	usted	es	artista
he/she	is	an artist	él/ella m/f	es	artista
we	are	single	nosostros/as m/f	somos	solteros/as m/f
you pl pol&inf	are	students	ustedes	son	estudiantes
they	are	students	ellos/as m/f	son	estudiantes

*sos in Arg, Uru & CAm (Also see **you** page 25).

Forms of the verb ESTAR

I	am	well	yo	estoy	bien
you sg inf	are	angry	tú	estás	enojado/a m/f
you sg pol	are	drunk	usted	está	borracho/a m/f
he/she	is	drunk	él/ella	está	borracho/a m/f
we	are	happy	nosotros/as m/f	estamos	contentos/as m/f
you pl pol&inf	are	reading	ustedes	están	leyendo
they	are	reading	ellos/as m/f	están	leyendo

a–z phrasebuilder

describing things

I'm looking for a picturesque route.

Estoy buscando un camino pintoresco.	es·*toy* boos·*kan*·do oon ka·*mee*·no peen·to·*res*·ko
(lit: I-am looking-for a route picturesque)	

When using an adjective to describe a noun, you need to use a different ending depending on whether the noun is masculine or feminine, and singular or plural. Most adjectives have four forms which are easy to remember:

	singular	plural
masculine	*fantástico*	*fantásticos*
feminine	*fantástica*	*fantásticas*

un hotel fantástico	oon o·*tel* fan·*tas*·tee·ko	a fantastic hotel
una comida fantástica	oo·na ko·*mee*·da fan·*tas*·tee·ka	a fantastic meal
unos libros fantásticos	oo·nos *lee*·bros fan·*tas*·tee·kos	some fantastic books
unas tortas fantásticas	oo·nas *tor*·tas fan·*tas*·tee·kas	some fantastic cakes

Adjectives generally come after the noun in Spanish. However, 'adjectives' of quantity (such as 'much', 'a lot', 'little/few', 'too much'), and adjectives expressing possession ('my' and 'your') always precede the noun.

muchos turistas	*moo*·chos too·*rees*·tas	many tourists
primera clase	pree·*me*·ra *kla*·se	first class
mi carro	mee *ka*·ro	my car

diminutives

A distinctive and fun feature of Latin American Spanish is the use of diminutives. These are formed by adding endings such as *-ito/a*, *-cito/a* and *-cillo/a* to words.

They're often used to indicate the smallness of something, eg, *gato* 'cat' becomes *gatito* 'kitten', but they're also a way of expressing how a speaker feels about something.

Diminutives may indicate that a speaker finds something charming, eg, to say *perrito* instead of *perro* 'dog' is akin to saying 'doggy' instead of 'dog' in English. Not surprisingly, many Spanish terms of endearment end in *-ito/a* or *-illo/a*, eg, *palomita* 'darling' is a diminutive of *paloma* 'dove'. Diminutives are used a lot in talking to children too.

Diminutive endings can give a friendly tone to a conversation. For instance, *un momentito* 'just a moment' sounds more light-hearted than *un momento*.

gender

In Spanish , all nouns – words which denote a thing, person or idea – are either masculine or feminine. Dictionaries will tell you what gender a noun is, but here are some handy tips to help you determine gender:

- the gender is masculine when talking about a man and feminine when talking about a female
- words ending in *-o* are usually masculine
- words ending in *-a* are usually feminine
- words ending in *-d*, *-z* or *-ión* are usually feminine

m (masculine) or f (feminine)?

In this book, masculine forms appear before the feminine forms. If you see a word ending in -o/a, it means the masculine form ends in -o, and the feminine form ends in -a (that is, you replace the -o ending with the -a ending to make it feminine). The same goes for the plural endings -os/as. If you see an (a) between brackets on the end of a word, it means you have to add that in order to make that word feminine. In other cases we spell out the whole word.

See also **a/an & some**, **describing things** and **the**.

have

I have two brothers.
Tengo dos hermanos.   ten·go dos er·man·os
(lit: I-have two brothers)

Possession can be indicated in various ways in Spanish. The easiest way is by using the verb *tener*, 'have'.

I	have	a ticket	yo	tengo	un boleto
you sg inf	have	the key	tú	tienes*	la llave
you sg pol	have	the key	usted	tiene	la llave
he/she	has	aspirin	él/ella	tiene	aspirinas
we	have	matches	nosotros/as m/f	tenemos	fósforos
you pl pol&inf	have	cakes	ustedes	tienen	tortas
they	have	problems	ellos/as m/f	tienen	problemas

* *tenés* in Arg, Uru & CAm. (Also see **you** page 25).
See also **my & your** and **somebody's**.

is & are see be

more than one

I'd like two soft drinks.
> *Quisiera dos refrescos.*   kee·*sye*·ra dos re·*fres*·kos
> (lit: I-would-like two soft-drinks)

In general, if the word ends in a vowel, you add *-s* for a plural. If the nouns ends in a consonant (or *y*), you add *-es*:

bed	*cama*	*ka*·ma	beds	*camas*	*ka*·mas
woman	*mujer*	moo·*kher*	women	*mujeres*	moo·*khe*·res

my & your

This is my son.
> *Este es mi hijo.*   *es*·te es mee *ee*·kho
> (lit: this is my son)

There are a number of words for 'my' and 'your' in Spanish. Choose the correct form according to the gender and quantity of the noun.

	singular		plural	
	masculine	feminine	masculine	feminine
	gift	visa	friends	houses
my	*mi regalo*	*mi visa*	*mis amigos*	*mis casas*
your sg inf	*tu regalo*	*tu visa*	*tus amigos*	*tus casas*
your sg pol	*su regalo*	*su visa*	*sus amigos*	*sus casas*
his/her/its	*su regalo*	*su visa*	*sus amigos*	*sus casas*
our	*nuestro regalo*	*nuestra visa*	*nuestros amigos*	*nuestras casas*
your pl pol&inf	*su regalo*	*su visa*	*sus amigos*	*sus casas*
their	*su regalo*	*su visa*	*sus amigos*	*sus casas*

See also **gender** and **more than one**.

negative

Just add the the word *no* before the main verb of the sentence:

I don't live with my family.
No vivo con mi familia.   no *vee*·vo kon mee fa·*mee*·lya
(lit: no live-I with my family)

planning ahead

As in English, you can talk about your plans or future events
by using the verb *ir* (go) followed by the word *a* (to) and the
infinitive of another verb, for example:

Tomorow, I'm going to travel to Guatemala.
Mañana, yo voy a viajar   ma·*nya*·na yo voy a vya·*khar*
a Guatemala.   a gwa·te·*ma*·la
(lit: tomorrow I go-I to travel
to Guatemala)

I	am going	to call	yo	voy	a llamar
you sg inf	are going	to sleep	tú	vas	a dormir
you sg pol	are going	to dance	usted	va	a bailar
he/she	is going	to drink	él/ella	va	a beber
we	are going	to sing	nosotros/as m/f	vamos	a cantar
you pl pol&inf	are going	to eat	ustedes	van	a comer
they	are going	to write	ellos/as m/f	van	a escribir

plural see more than one

pointing something out

To point something out, the easiest phrases to use are *es* (it is), *esto es* (this is) or *eso es* (that is).

Es una guía de Lima.	es *oo*·na *gee*·a de *lee*·ma	It's a guide to Lima.
Esto es mi pasaporte.	es·to es mee pa·sa·*por*·te	This is my passport.
Eso es una empanada.	e·so es *oo*·na em·pa·*na*·da	That is an empanada.

See also **this & that**.

possession see **have**, **my & your** and **somebody's**

questions

When asking a question, simply make a statement, but raise your intonation towards the end of the sentence, as you would in English. The inverted question mark in written Spanish prompts you to do this.

Do you have a car?
  ¿Tienes un carro?   *tye*·nes oon *ka*·ro
  (lit: you-have a car)

question words

	question words	
Who?	¿Quién(es)? sg/pl	kyen/*kye*·nes
Who is it?	¿Quién es?	kyen es
Who are they?	¿Quiénes son ellos?	*kye*·nes son e·lyos
What?	¿Qué?	ke
What are you saying?	¿Qué estás diciendo?	ke es·*tas* dee·*syen*·do
Which?	¿Cuál(es)? sg/pl	kwal/*kwal*·es
Which is the best restaurant?	¿Cuál es el mejor restaurante?	kwal es el me·*khor* res·tow·*ran*·te
Which local dishes do you recommend?	¿Cuáles platos tipicos puedes recomendar?	*kwa*·les *pla*·tos *tee*·pee·kos *pwe*·des re·ko·men·*dar*
When?	¿Cuándo?	*kwan*·do
When does the bus arrive?	¿Cuándo llega el autobús?	*kwan*·do *lye*·ga el ow·to·*boos*
Where?	¿Dónde?	*don*·de
Where can I buy tickets?	¿Dónde puedo comprar boletos?	*don*·de *pwe*·do kom·*prar* bo·*le*·tos
How?	¿Cómo?	*ko*·mo
How do you say that in Spanish?	¿Cómo se dice eso en castellano?	*ko*·mo se *dee*·se e·so en kas·te·*lya*·no
How much?	¿Cuánto?	*kwan*·to
How much is it?	¿Cuánto cuesta?	*kwan*·to *kwes*·ta
How many?	¿Cuántos/as? m/f pl	*kwan*·tos/*kwan*·tas
For how many days?	¿Por cuántos días?	por *kwan*·tos *dee*·as
Why?	¿Por qué?	por ke
Why is the museum closed?	¿Por qué está cerrado el museo?	por ke es·*ta* se·*ra*·do el moo·*se*·o

some see a/an & some

somebody's

In Spanish, ownership is expressed through the word *de* (of).

This is my friend's tent.
  Esta es la carpa de mi amiga.   *es·ta es la kar·pa de mee a·mee·ga*
  (lit: this is the tent of my
    friend)

See also **have** and **my & your**.

this & that

There are three 'distance words' in Spanish, depending on whether something or someone is close (this), away from you (that) or even further away in time or distance (that over there).

masculine	singular	plural
close	*éste* (this)	*éstos* (these)
away	*ése* (that)	*ésos* (those)
further away	*aquél* (that over there)	*aquéllos* (those over there)
feminine	singular	plural
close	*ésta* (this)	*éstas* (these)
away	*ésa* (that)	*ésas* (those)
further away	*aquélla* (that over there)	*aquéllas* (those over there)

See also **pointing something out**.

the

The Spanish articles *el* and *la* both mean 'the'. Whether you use *el* or *la* depends on the gender of the thing, person or idea talked about, which in Spanish will always be either masculine or feminine. The gender is not really concerned with the sex of something, for example, a llama is a feminine noun, even if it's male! There's no rule as to why, say, the sun is masculine but a cloud is feminine.

When talking about plural things, persons or ideas, you use *los* instead of *el* and *las* instead of *la*.

	singular	plural
masculine	el	los
feminine	la	las

el carro m	el *ka·ro*	the car
la tienda f	la *tyen·da*	the shop
los carros m pl	los *ka·ros*	the cars
las tiendas f pl	las *tyen·das*	the shops

See also **gender** and **a/an & some**.

word order

Sentences in Spanish have a basic word order of subject-verb-object, just as English does.

I study business.
   Yo estudio comercio.   yo es·*too*·dyo ko·*mer*·syo
   (lit: I study-I English)

TOOLS

However, the subject pronoun is often omitted: 'Estudio comercio' is enough. Subject pronouns are used if a speaker wishes to emphasise who is the 'doer' of an action.

yes/no questions

It's not impolite to answer questions with a simple *sí* (yes) or *no* (no) in Spanish. There's no way to say 'Yes it is/does', or 'No, it isn't/doesn't'.

See also **questions**.

you

Latin American Spanish has two forms for the singular 'you'. When talking to someone familiar to you or younger than you, use the informal form *tú*, too, rather than the polite form *usted*, oos·te. Use the polite form when you're meeting someone for the first time, talking to someone much older than you or when you're in a formal situation (eg, talking to the police, customs officers etc). All phrases in this book use the form of 'you' that is appropriate to the situation. In Latin American Spanish there's no informal/formal distinction for plural 'you' – you just use *ustedes* oos·te·des.

In many Latin-American countries (particularly in Argentina, Chile, Paraguay and Uruguay and in some Central American countries), you'll hear *vos* instead of *tú*. The form of the verb that goes with *vos* may differ slightly from the form of the verb that goes with *tú* (even when the *vos* is understood from the context). The *vos* verb form that you're likely to hear most is *sos* from the verb *ser* (to be). So, for example, instead of *¿Eres de Australia?* (Are you from Australia?) you may hear *¿Sos de Australia?* In this book we've just used *tú* (and the verb form that goes with it) to keep things simple. You'll be perfectly well understood if you use *tú* – just be aware that locals may use *vos* (and *vos* verb forms) instead.

false friends

Beware of false friends – words which look, and even sound, like an English word but have a different meaning altogether. Using them in the wrong context could confuse, or even amuse, Spanish speakers.

injuria   een·*khoo*·ree·a   insult
   not 'injury' which is *herida,* e·*ree*·da

parientes   pa·*ryen*·tes   relatives
   not 'parents' which is *padres, pa*·dres

éxito   ek·*see*·to   success
   not 'exit' which is *salida,* sa·*lee*·da

Estoy embarazada.   es·*toy* em·ba·ra·*sa*·da   I'm pregnant.
   not 'I'm embarrassed', which is *Estoy avergonzado/a.* m/f
   es·*toy* a·ver·gon·*sa*·do/a

language difficulties
difficultades con el idioma

Do you speak (English)?
¿Habla/Hablas (inglés)? pol/inf   *a*·bla/*a*·blas (een·*gles*)

Does anyone speak (English)?
¿Hay alguien que hable (inglés)?   ai al·*gyen* ke *a*·ble (een·*gles*)

Do you understand?
¿Me entiende/entiendes? pol/inf   me en·*tyen*·de/en·*tyen*·des

I understand.
Entiendo.   en·*tyen*·do

I don't understand.
No entiendo.   no en·*tyen*·do

I speak (Spanish).
Hablo (castellano).   *a*·blo (kas·te·*lya*·no)

I speak a little (Spanish).
Hablo un poco (de castellano).   *a*·blo oon *po*·ko (de kas·te·*lya*·no)

I speak (English).
Hablo (inglés).   *a*·blo (een·*gles*)

speaking of Spanish

In the Spanish-speaking world Spanish is known as both *español* and *castellano*. Latin Americans favour the term *castellano*. The underlying reason for this is probably that *español* is heard more as a nationality than as the name of a language.

How do you pronounce this word?

¿Como se pronuncia esta palabra? ko·mo se pro·*noon*·sya *es*·ta pa·*la*·bra

How do you write 'ciudad'?

¿Como se escribe 'ciudad'? ko·mo se es·*kree*·be syoo·*da*

What does 'entrada' mean?

¿Qué significa 'entrada'? ke seeg·nee·*fee*·ka en·*tra*·da

Could you please …?	*¿Puede …, por favor?*	*pwe*·de … por *fa*·vor
repeat that	*repetirlo*	re·pe·*teer*·lo
speak more slowly	*hablar más despacio*	a·*blar* mas des·*pa*·syo
write it down	*escribirlo*	es·kree·*beer*·lo

tongue twisters

Tongue twisters are known as *trabalenguas* in Spanish. Try exercising your tongue with these two:

From Chile:

Comí chirimoyas, me enchirimoyé. Ahora, para desenchirimoyarme, ¿cómo me desenchirimoyaré?

ko·*mee* chee·ree·mo·yas me en·chee·ree·mo·ye a·o·ra *pa*·ra des·en·chee·ree·mo·*yar* me ko·mo me des·en·chee·ree·mo·ya·*re*

(I ate custard apples, I got myself custard-appled. Now, in order to get un-custard-appled, how shall I un-custard-apple myself?)

From Venezuela:

Poquito a poquito Paquito empaca poquitas copitas en pocos paquetes.

po·*kee*·to a po·*kee*·to pa·*kee*·to em·*pa*·ka po·*kee*·tas ko·*pee*·tas en *po*·kos pa·*ke*·tes

(Little by little Paquito is packing a few small wineglasses in a few boxes.)

cardinal numbers

		los números cardinales
0	*cero*	se·ro
1	*uno*	oo·no
2	*dos*	dos
3	*tres*	tres
4	*cuatro*	kwa·tro
5	*cinco*	seen·ko
6	*seis*	says
7	*siete*	sye·te
8	*ocho*	o·cho
9	*nueve*	nwe·ve
10	*diez*	dyes
11	*once*	on·se
12	*doce*	do·se
13	*trece*	tre·se
14	*catorce*	ka·tor·se
15	*quince*	keen·se
16	*dieciséis*	dye·see·says
17	*diecisiete*	dye·see·sye·te
18	*dieciocho*	dye·see·o·cho
19	*diecinueve*	dye·see·nwe·ve
20	*veinte*	vayn·te
21	*veintiuno*	vayn·tee·oo·no
22	*veintidos*	vayn·tee·dos
30	*treinta*	trayn·ta
40	*cuarenta*	kwa·ren·ta
50	*cincuenta*	seen·kwen·ta
60	*sesenta*	se·sen·ta
70	*setenta*	se·ten·ta
80	*ochenta*	o·chen·ta
90	*noventa*	no·ven·ta
100	*cien*	syen
200	*doscientos*	do·syen·tos

1,000	*mil*	meel
2,000	*dos mil*	dos meel
1,000,000	*un millón*	oon mee·lyon

ordinal numbers

los numeros ordinales

1st	*primero/a* m/f	pree·me·ro/a
2nd	*segundo/a* m/f	se·goon·do/a
3rd	*tercero/a* m/f	ter·se·ro/a
4th	*cuarto/a* m/f	kwar·to/a
5th	*quinto/a* m/f	keen·to/a

fractions

las fracciónes

a quarter	*un cuarto*	oon kwar·to
a third	*un tercio*	oon ter·syo
a half	*medio/a* m/f	me·dee·o/a
three-quarters	*tres cuartos*	tres kwar·tos
all	*todo/a* m/f sg	to·do/a
	todos/as m/f pl	to·dos/as
none	*nada*	na·da

useful amounts

cantidades utiles

How much?	*Cuánto/a?* m/f	kwan·to/a
How many?	*Cuántos/as?* m/f pl	kwan·tos/as
Please give me ...	*Por favor, deme ...*	por fa·vor de·me ...
(just) a little	*(solo) un poco*	(so·lo) oon po·ko
some	*algunos/as* m/f pl	al·goo·nos/as
much	*mucho/a* m/f	moo·cho/a
many	*muchos/as* m/f pl	moo·chos/as
less	*menos*	me·nos
more	*más*	mas

time & dates

la ora & la fecha

telling the time

dando la hora

When telling the time in Spanish, 'It's …' is expressed by *Son las …* followed by a number. However, one o'clock is *Es la una* and 'It's midnight' and 'It's midday' are *Es el mediodía* and *Es la medianoche* respectively. Both the 12-hour and the 24-hour clock are commonly used.

What time is it?	*¿Qué hora es?*	ke o·ra es
It's one o'clock.	*Es la una.*	es la oo·na
It's (ten) o'clock.	*Son las (diez).*	son las (dyes)
Quarter past (two).	*(Las dos) y cuarto.*	(las dos) ee *kwar*·to
Twenty past (two).	*(Las dos) y veinte.*	(las dos) ee *vayn*·te
Half past (two).	*(Las dos) y media.*	(las dos) ee *me*·dya
Twenty to (three).	*(Las tres)*	(las tres)
	menos veinte.	*me*·nos *vayn*·te
Quarter to (three).	*(Las tres)*	(las tres)
	menos cuarto.	*me*·nos *kwar*·to
It's early.	*Es temprano.*	es tem·*pra*·no
It's late.	*Es tarde.*	es *tar*·de
am (in the morning)	*de la mañana*	de la ma·*nya*·na
pm (in the afternoon)	*de la tarde*	de la *tar*·de
in the morning	*por la mañana*	por la ma·*nya*·na
in the afternoon	*por la tarde*	por la *tar*·de
in the evening	*por la tarde*	por la *tar*·de
at night	*por la noche*	por la *no*·che
At what time …?	*¿A qué hora …?*	a ke o·ra …
At one.	*A la una.*	a la oo·na
At (six).	*A las (seis).*	a las (says)
At 7.57 pm.	*A las ocho menos*	a las o·cho *me*·nos
	tres de la tarde.	tres de la *tar*·de

time & dates

31

days of the week

Monday	lunes	*loo*·nes
Tuesday	martes	*mar*·tes
Wednesday	miércoles	*myer*·ko·les
Thursday	jueves	*khwe*·ves
Friday	viernes	*vyer*·nes
Saturday	sábado	*sa*·ba·do
Sunday	domingo	do·*meen*·go

the calendar

el calendario

months

January	enero	e·*ne*·ro
February	febrero	fe·*bre*·ro
March	marzo	*mar*·so
April	abril	a·*breel*
May	mayo	*ma*·yo
June	junio	*khoo*·nyo
July	julio	*khoo*·lyo
August	agosto	a·*gos*·to
September	septiembre	sep·*tyem*·bre
October	octubre	ok·*too*·bre
November	noviembre	no·*vyem*·bre
December	diciembre	dee·*syem*·bre

dates

What date?	¿Qué fecha?	ke *fe*·cha
What's today's date?	¿Qué día es hoy?	ke *dee*·a es oy
It's (18 October).	Es (el dieciocho de octubre).	es (el dye·see·o·cho de ok·*too*·bre)

seasons

summer	verano	ve·*ra*·no
autumn	otoño	o·*to*·nyo
winter	invierno	een·*vyer*·no
spring	primavera	pree·ma·*ve*·ra

present

now	*ahora*	a·o·ra
today	*hoy*	oy
tonight	*esta noche*	es·ta no·che
this ...		
afternoon	*esta tarde*	es·ta tar·de
month	*este mes*	es·te mes
morning	*esta mañana*	es·ta ma·nya·na
week	*esta semana*	es·ta se·ma·na
year	*este año*	es·te a·nyo

past

(three days) ago	*hace (tres días)*	a·se (tres dee·as)
day before yesterday	*anteayer*	an·te·a·yer
last ...		
month	*el mes pasado*	el mes pa·sa·do
night	*anoche*	a·no·che
week	*la semana pasada*	la se·ma·na pa·sa·da
year	*el año pasado*	el a·nyo pa·sa·do
since (May)	*desde (mayo)*	des·de (ma·yo)
yesterday	*ayer*	a·yer
yesterday ...	*ayer por la ...*	a·yer por la ...
afternoon	*tarde*	tar·de
evening	*noche*	no·che
morning	*mañana*	ma·nya·na

time & dates

33

future

day after tomorrow	*pasado mañana*	pa·*sa*·do ma·*nya*·na
in (six days)	*dentro de (seis días)*	*den*·tro de (says *dee*·as)
next ...	*... que viene*	... ke *vye*·ne
month	*el mes*	el mes
week	*la semana*	la se·*ma*·na
year	*el año*	el *a*·nyo
tomorrow	*mañana*	ma·*nya*·na
tomorrow ...	*mañana por la ...*	ma·*nya*·na por la ...
afternoon	*tarde*	*tar*·de
evening	*noche*	*no*·che
morning	*mañana*	ma·*nya*·na
until (June)	*hasta (junio)*	*as*·ta (*khoo*·nyo)

during the day

afternoon	*tarde* f	*tar*·de
dawn	*alba* f	*al*·ba
day	*día* m	*dee*·a
evening	*noche* f	*no*·che
midday	*mediodía* m	me·dyo·*dee*·a
midnight	*medianoche* f	me·dya·*no*·che
morning	*mañana* f	ma·*nya*·na
night	*noche* f	*no*·che
sunrise	*amanecer* m	a·ma·ne·*ser*
sunset	*atardecer* m	a·tar·de·*ser*

How much is it?
¿Cuánto cuesta?   kwan·to kwes·ta

It's free.
Es gratis.   es gra·tees

It's … (pesos).
Cuesta … (pesos).   kwes·ta … (pe·sos)

Can you write down the price?
¿Puede escribir el precio?   pwe·de es·kree·beer el pre·syo

Do you change money here?
¿Se cambia dinero aquí?   se kam·bya dee·ne·ro a·kee

Do you accept …?	*¿Aceptan …?*	a·sep·tan …
credit cards	*tarjetas de crédito*	tar·khe·tas de kre·dee·to
debit cards	*tarjetas de débito*	tar·khe·tas de de·bee·to
travellers cheques	*cheques de viajero*	che·kes de vya·khe·ro

I'd like to …	*Me gustaría …*	me goos·ta·ree·a …
cash a cheque	*cobrar un cheque*	ko·brar oon che·ke
change money	*cambiar dinero*	kam·byar dee·ne·ro
change a travellers cheque	*cambiar un cheque de viajero*	kam·byar oon che·ke de vya·khe·ro
withdraw money	*sacar dinero*	sa·kar dee·ne·ro

What's the …?	*¿Cuál es la …?*	kwal es la …
commission	*comisión*	ko·mee·syon
exchange rate	*tasa de cambio*	ta·sa de kam·byo

I'd like …, please.	*Quisiera …, por favor.*	kee·sye·ra … por fa·vor
a receipt	*un recibo*	oon re·see·bo
my change	*mi cambio*	mee kam·byo
my money back	*que devuelva el dinero*	ke de·vwel·va el dee·ne·ro

There's a mistake in the bill.
Hay un error en la cuenta.   ai oon e·*ror* en la *kwen*·ta

I don't want to pay the full price.
No quiero pagar el precio   no *kye*·ro pa·*gar* el *pre*·syo
íntegro.   *een*·te·gro

Do I need to pay upfront?
¿Hay que pagar por adelantado?   ai ke pa·*gar* por a·de·lan·*ta*·do

Where's the nearest automatic teller machine?
¿Dónde está el cajero   *don*·de es·*ta* el ka·*khe*·ro
automático más cercano?   ow·to·*ma*·tee·ko mas ser·*ka*·no

latin american currencies

Argentina	*peso**	*pe*·so
Bolivia	*boliviano*	bo·lee·*vya*·no
Chile	*peso**	*pe*·so
Colombia	*peso**	*pe*·so
Costa Rica	*colón* (in honour of Columbus)	ko·*lon*
Cuba	*peso**	*pe*·so
Ecuador	*sucre* (named after a general who helped liberate Ecuador from colonial rule)	*soo*·kre
Guatemala	*quetzal* (the name of a native bird)	*ket*·sal
Honduras	*lempira* (the name of a chief of the Lenca tribe who lead the resistance against the Spanish)	lem·*pee*·ra
Nicaragua	*córdoba* (in honour of a Spanish explorer)	*kor*·do·ba
Panama	*dolár/balboa* (the latter named after a Spanish explorer)	do·*lar*/bal·*bo*·a
Paraguay	*guaraní* (an Amerindian people)	gwa·ra·*nee*
Peru	*nuevo sol* (lit: new sun)	*nwe*·vo sol
Uruguay	*peso**	*pe*·so
Venezuela	*bolivár* (named after Simón Bolivár who freed several countries from Spanish rule)	bo·lee·*var*

*The word *peso* literally means 'weight'.

getting around

desplazándose

What time does the ... leave?	¿A qué hora sale ...?	a ke o·ra sa·le ...
boat	el barco	el bar·ko
bus (city)	el autobús	el ow·to·boos
(Col)	la chiva	la chee·va
(Arg)	el colectivo	el ko·lek·tee·vo
(Cub)	la guagua	la gwa·gwa
(Bol, Chi)	el micro	el mee·kro
bus (intercity)	el ómnibus	el om·nee·boos
(Arg)	el micro	el mee·kro
ferry	la ferry	la fe·ree
metro	el subterráneo	el soob·te·ra·ne·o
(Arg)	el subte	el soob·te
plane	el avión	el a·vyon
train	el tren	el tren
tram	el tranvía	el tran·vee·a

listen for ...

el (vwe·lo) es·ta kan·se·la·do El (vuelo) está cancelado.	The (flight) is cancelled.
el (om·nee·boos) es·ta re·tra·sa·do El (ómnibus) está retrasado.	The (bus) is delayed.
es·ta kom·ple·to Está completo.	It's full.

What time's the ... bus?	¿A qué hora es el ... autobús?	a ke o·ra es el ... ow·to·boos
first	primer	pree·mer
last	último	ool·tee·mo
next	próximo	prok·see·mo

When's the next flight to (Machala)?

¿Cuándo sale el próximo   kwan·do sa·le el prok·see·mo
vuelo para (Machala)?   vwe·lo pa·ra (ma·cha·la)

Can you tell me when we get to (San Miguel)?

¿Me puede decir cuándo   me pwe·de de·seer kwan·do
lleguemos a (San Miguel)?   lye·ge·mos a (san mee·gel)

I want to get off here.

Quiero bajarme aquí.   kye·ro ba·khar·me a·kee

Is this seat free?

¿Está libre este asiento?   es·ta lee·bre es·te a·syen·to

That's my seat.

Ése es mi asiento.   e·se es mee a·syen·to

For phrases about getting through customs and immigration, see **border crossing**, page 49.

buying tickets

Where can I buy a ticket?
*¿Dónde puedo comprar
un boleto?*
don·de pwe·do kom·prar
oon bo·le·to

Do I need to book?
¿Tengo que reservar?
ten·go ke re·ser·var

Can I get a stand-by ticket?
*¿Puede ponerme en la lista
de espera?*
pwe·de po·ner·me en la lees·ta
de es·pe·ra

How much is it?
¿Cuánto cuesta?
kwan·to kwes·ta

How long does the trip take?
¿Cuánto se tarda?
kwan·to se tar·da

Is it a direct route?
¿Es un viaje directo?
es oon vya·khe dee·rek·to

What time do I have to check in?
*¿A qué hora tengo que facturar
mi equipaje?*
a ke o·ra ten·go ke fak·too·rar
mee e·kee·pa·khe

I'd like to ... my ticket, please.	*Quisiéra ... mi boleto, por favor.*	kee·sye·ra ... mee bo·le·to por fa·vor
cancel	*cancelar*	kan·se·lar
change	*cambiar*	kam·byar
confirm	*confirmar*	kon·feer·mar

A ... ticket to (Lima), please.	*Un boleto ... a (Lima), por favor.*	oon bo·le·to ... a (lee·ma) por fa·vor
1st-class	*de primera clase*	de pree·me·ra kla·se
2nd-class	*de segunda clase*	de se·goon·da kla·se
child's	*infantil*	een·fan·teel
one-way	*de ida*	de ee·da
return	*de ida y vuelta*	de ee·da ee vwel·ta
student's	*de estudiante*	de es·too·dyan·te

I'd like a/an ...	*Quisiéra un*	kee·*sye*·ra oon
seat.	*asiento ...*	a·*syen*·to ...
aisle	*de pasillo*	de pa·*see*·lyo
(non-)smoking	*de (no)*	de (no)
	fumadores	foo·ma·*do*·res
window	*junto a la*	*khoon*·to a la
	ventana	ven·*ta*·na
Is there (a) ...?	*¿Hay ... ?*	ai ...
air-conditioning	*aire*	*ai*·re
	acondicionado	a·kon·dee·syo·*na*·do
blanket	*una frazada*	*oo*·na fra·*sa*·da
toilet	*baños*	*ba*·nyos
video	*vídeo*	*vee*·de·o

luggage

el equipaje

My luggage hasn't arrived.
| *Mi equipage no ha* | mee e·kee·*pa*·khe no a |
| *llegado.* | lye·*ga*·do |

My luggage has	*Mi equipaje ha*	mee e·kee·*pa*·khe a
been ...	*sido ...*	*see*·do ...
damaged	*dañado*	da·*nya*·do
lost	*perdido*	per·*dee*·do
stolen	*robado*	ro·*ba*·do

I'd like ...	*Quisiera ...*	kee·*sye*·ra ...
a luggage locker	*un casillero de*	oon ka·see·*lye*·ro de
	consigna	kon·*seeg*·na
some coins	*unas monedas*	*oo*·nas mo·*ne*·das
some tokens	*unas fichas*	*oo*·nas *fee*·chas

bus, tram & metro

el autobús, el tranvía & el subteráneo

Which bus goes to (the centre of town)?
¿Qué autobús va al   ke ow·to·*boos* va al
(centro de la cuidad)?   (*sen*·tro de la syoo·*da*)

Which bus goes to (Cochabamba)?
¿Qué ómnibus va a   ke *om*·nee·boos va a
(Cochabamba)?   (ko·cha·*bam*·ba)

This/That one.
Éste/Ése.   *es*·te/*es*·e

Tram number (three).
El tranvía número   el tran·*vee*·a *noo*·me·ro
(tres).   (tres)

How many stops to (the museum)?
¿Cuantas paradas hay hasta   *kwan*·tas pa·*ra*·das ai *as*·ta
(el museo)?   (el moo·*se*·o)

Do you stop at (the market)?
¿Tiene parada en   *tye*·ne pa·*ra*·da en
(el mercado)?   (el mer·*ka*·do)

bussing it

The most common way to get around Latin America is by bus.
Throughout Latin America the general name for a bus station
is *una estación de autobúses* although in Argentina, it's known
as *una terminal de ómnibuses*. In Venezuela and Colombia
you'll find the term *una terminal terrestre* (lit: land terminal) or
una terminal de pasajeros (lit: passenger terminal). Travelling
by bus can be slow and crowded but it's often a great way to
meet local people – just pull out your phrasebook and get
chatting.

train

What station is this?
  ¿Cuál es esta estación?   kwal es *es*·ta es·ta·*syon*

What's the next station?
  ¿Cuál es la próxima   kwal es la *prok*·see·ma
  estación?   es·ta·*syon*

Does this train stop at (Veracruz)?
  ¿Para el tren en (Veracruz)?   *pa*·ra el tren en (ve·ra·*kroos*)

Do I need to change trains?
  ¿Tengo que cambiar de tren?   *ten*·go ke kam·*byar* de tren

Which carriage is …?	*¿Cuál es el coche …?*	kwal es el *ko*·che …
1st class	*de primera clase*	de pree·*me*·ra *kla*·se
for (Buenos Aires)	*para (Buenos Aires)*	para (*bwe*·nos *ai*·res)
for dining	*comedor*	ko·me·*dor*

boat

Where do we get on the boat?
  ¿Donde subimos al barco?   *don*·de soo·*bee*·mos al *bar*·ko

Are there life jackets?
  ¿Hay chalecos salvavidas?   ai cha·*le*·kos sal·va·*vee*·das

What's the sea like today?
  ¿Cómo está el mar hoy?   *ko*·mo es·*ta* el mar oy

I feel seasick.
  Estoy mareado/a. m/f   es·*toy* ma·re·*a*·do/a

barge/ferry	**(CAm)** *panga* f	*pan*·ga
canoe	*canoa* f	ka·*no*·a
dugout canoe	*cayuco* m	ka·*yoo*·ko
port	*puerto* m	*pwer*·to
raft	*balsa* f	*bal*·sa
wharf	*embarcadero* m	em·bar·ka·*de*·ro
	(Per, CAm) *malecón* m	ma·le·*kon*

taxi

I'd like a taxi …	Quisiera un taxi …	kee·sye·ra oon tak·see …
at (9am)	a las (nueve de la mañana)	a las (nwe·ve de la ma·nya·na)
now	ahora	a·o·ra
tomorrow	mañana	ma·nya·na

Is this taxi free?
¿Está libre este taxi?   es·ta lee·bre es·te tak·see

How much is it (to the airport)?
¿Cuánto cuesta ir (al aeropuerto)?   kwan·to kwes·ta eer (al a·e·ro·pwer·to)

Please put the meter on.
Por favor, ponga el taxímetro.   por fa·vor pon·ga el tak·see·me·tro

Please take me to (this address).
Por favor, lléveme a (esta dirección).   por fa·vor lye·ve·me a (es·ta dee·rek·syon)

typical addresses

avenue	avenida f	a·ve·nee·da
	(Per) paseo m	pa·se·o
	(Arg) rambla f	ram·bla
lane	callejón m	ka·lye·khon
street	calle f	ka·lye

Please …	Por favor, …	por fa·vor …
slow down	vaya más despacio	va·ya mas des·pa·syo
wait here	espere aquí	es·pe·re a·kee

Stop …	Pare …	pa·re …
at the corner	en la esquina	en la es·kee·na
here	aquí	a·kee

transport

43

car & motorbike

car & motorbike hire

I'd like to hire a/an ...	Quisiera alquilar ...	kee·sye·ra al·kee·lar ...
4WD	un todo terreno	oon to·do te·re·no
automatic (car)	un carro automático	oon ka·ro ow·to·ma·tee·ko
car	un carro	oon ka·ro
(SAm)	un auto	oon ow·to
manual (car)	un carro manual	oon ka·ro man·wal
motorbike	una moto	oo·na mo·to

with ...	con ...	kon ...
air-conditioning	aire acondicionado	ai·re a·kon·dee·syo·na·do
a driver	un chofer	oon cho·fer

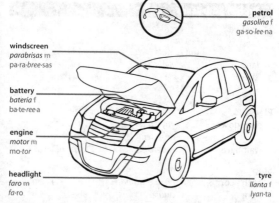

petrol
gasolina f
ga·so·lee·na

windscreen
parabrisas m
pa·ra·bree·sas

battery
batería f
ba·te·ree·a

engine
motor m
mo·tor

headlight
faro m
fa·ro

tyre
llanta f
lyan·ta

PRACTICAL

How much for	¿Cuánto cuesta	kwan·to kwes·ta
... hire?	alquilar por ...?	al·kee·lar por ...
daily	día	dee·a
hourly	hora	o·ra
weekly	semana	se·ma·na

on the road

What's the ...	¿Cuál es el límite	kwal es el lee·mee·te
speed limit?	de velocidad ...?	de ve·lo·see·da ...
city	en la ciudad	en la syoo·da
country	en el campo	en el kam·po

Is this the road to (Tegucigalpa)?

| ¿Se va a (Tegucigalpa) por | se va a (te·goo·see·gal·pa) por |
| esta carretera? | es·ta ka·re·te·ra |

(How long) Can I park here?

| ¿(Por cuánto tiempo) | (por kwan·to tyem·po) |
| Puedo aparcar aquí? | pwe·do a·par·kar a·kee |

Where's a petrol station?

| ¿Dónde hay una | don·de ai oo·na |
| gasolinera? | ga·so·lee·ne·ra |

gas guzzlers

The word *gasolinera* for 'petrol station' is the standard term that will be understood throughout Latin America but you may come across some other country-specific terms:

Argentina:	estación f de servicio	es·ta·syon de ser·vee·syo
Bolivia:	surtidor m	soor·tee·dor
Chile:	bencinera f	ben·see·ne·ra
Colombia and Central America:	bomba f	bom·ba
Peru:	grifo m	gree·fo

Please fill it up.
Lleno, por favor. — *lye*·no por fa·*vor*

I'd like (20) litres.
Quiero (veinte) litros. — *kye*·ro (*vayn*·te) *lee*·tros

Where do I pay?
¿Dónde se paga? — *don*·de se *pa*·ga

diesel	*diesel*	*dee*·sel
leaded (regular)	*gasolina con plomo*	ga·so·*lee*·na kon *plo*·mo
petrol (gas)	*gasolina*	ga·so·*lee*·na
(Arg)	*nafta*	*naf*·ta
(Chi)	*bencina*	ben·*see*·na
unleaded	*gasolina sin plomo*	ga·so·*lee*·na seen *plo*·mo

Please check the ...	*Por favor, revise ...*	por fa·*vor* re·*vee*·se ...
oil	*el nivel del aceite*	el nee·*vel* del a·*say*·te
tyre pressure	*la presión de las llantas*	la pre·*syon* de las *lyan*·tas
water	*el nivel del agua*	el nee·*vel* del *a*·gwa

road signs

Acceso	ak·*se*·so	**Entrance**
Aparcamiento	a·par·ka·*myen*·to	**Parking**
Ceda el Paso	se·da el *pa*·so	**Give way**
Dirección Única	dee·rek·*syon* oo·nee·ka	**One-way**
Peaje	pe·*a*·khe	**Toll**
Peligro	pe·*lee*·gro	**Danger**
Prohibido Aparcar	pro·ee·*bee*·do a·par·*kar*	**No Parking**
Prohibido el Paso	pro·ee·*bee*·do el *pa*·so	**No Entry**
Pare	*pa*·re	**Stop**
Stop	e·*stop*	**Stop**
Salida de Autopista	sa·*lee*·da de ow·to·*pees*·ta	**Exit Freeway**

PRACTICAL

46

problems

I need a mechanic.
Necesito un   ne·se·*see*·to oon
mecánico.   me·*ka*·nee·ko

The car has broken down (in Granada).
El carro se ha averiado   el *ka*·ro se a a·ve·*rya*·do
(en Granada).   (en gra·*na*·da)

I had an accident.
Tuve un accidente.   *too*·ve oon ak·see·*den*·te

The motorbike won't start.
No arranca la moto.   no a·*ran*·ka la *mo*·to

The battery is flat.
La batería está   la ba·te·*ree*·a es·*ta*
descargada.   des·kar·*ga*·da

I have a flat tyre.
Tengo un pinchazo.   *ten*·go oon peen·*cha*·so

I've lost my car keys.
He perdido las llaves   e per·*dee*·do las *lya*·ves
de mi carro.   de mee *ka*·ro

I've locked the keys inside.
Dejé las llaves   de·*khe* las *lya*·ves
encerradas dentro.   en·se·*ra*·das *den*·tro

I've run out of petrol.
Me quedé sin gasolina.   me ke·*de* seen ga·so·*lee*·na

Can you fix it (today)?
¿Puede arreglarlo (hoy)?   *pwe*·de a·re·*glar*·lo (oy)

How long will it take?
¿Cuánto tardará?   *kwan*·to tar·da·*ra*

listen for ...

de ke *mar*·ka es
  ¿De qué marca es?   **What make/model is it?**

ten·go ke pe·*deer* e·se re·*pwes*·to
  Tengo que pedir ese repuesto.   **I have to order that part.**

bicycle

Where can I ...?	¿Dónde se puede ...?	don·de se pwe·de ...
hire a bicycle	alquilar una bicicleta	al·kee·lar oo·na bee·see·kle·ta
buy a second-hand bike	comprar una bicicleta de segunda mano	kom·prar oo·na bee·see·kle·ta de se·goon·da ma·no

How much is it per ...?	¿Cuánto cuesta por ...?	kwan·to kwes·ta por ...
afternoon	una tarde	oo·na tar·de
day	un día	oon dee·a
hour	hora	o·ra
morning	una mañana	oo·na ma·nya·na

I have a puncture.

Se me pinchó una rueda. se me peen·cho oo·na rwe·da

---

trucking it

In rural areas of Latin America, where bus services are infrequent, drivers of pick-up trucks and other vehicles transport others in need of a ride for a fare similar to a bus fare. We don't recommend hitchhiking per se, but if you find yourself in a situation where this informal taxi service is your only option, these phrases might come in handy:

Could you give me a ride in your (pick-up)?

¿Me podría llevar en su (pick-up)? me po·dree·a lye·var en soo (peek·oop)

How much do I owe you?

¿Cuánto le debo? kwan·to le de·bo

Are you waiting for more people?

¿Está esperando a más gente? es·ta es·pe·ran·do a mas khen·te

I'm here …	Estoy aquí …	es·toy a·kee …
in transit	en tránsito	en tran·see·to
on business	de negocios	de ne·go·syos
on holiday	de vacaciones	de va·ka·syo·nes

I'm here for …	Estoy aquí por …	es·toy a·kee por …
(four) days	(cuatro) días	(kwa·tro) dee·as
(two) weeks	(dos) semanas	(dos) se·ma·nas
(three) months	(tres) meses	(tres) me·ses

I have a … permit.	Tengo un permiso de …	ten·go oon per·mee·so de …
residency	residencia	re·see·den·sya
study	estudios	es·too·dyos
work	trabajo	tra·ba·kho

I have a visa.
Tengo un visado.   *ten·*go oon vee·*sa·*do

I have nothing to declare.
No tengo nada que declarar.   no *ten·*go *na·*da ke de·kla·*rar*

I have something to declare.
Tengo algo que declarar.   *ten·*go *al·*go ke de·kla·*rar*

I didn't know I had to declare it.
No sabía que tenía que declararlo.   no sa·*bee·*a ke te·*nee·*a ke de·kla·*rar·*lo

Do you have this form in English?
¿Tiene ese formulario en inglés?   *tye·*ne e·*se* for·moo·*la·*ryo en een·*gles*

Where's (the bank)?
¿Dónde está (el banco)?   don·de es·ta (el ban·ko)

I'm looking for (the public toilets).
Busco (los baños).   boos·ko (los ba·nyos)

Which way's (the post office)?
¿Por dónde se va (a correos)?   por don·de se va (a ko·re·os)

How can I get there?
¿Cómo puedo ir?   ko·mo pwe·do eer

How far is it?
¿A cuánta distancia está?   a kwan·ta dees·tan·sya es·ta

Can you show me (on the map)?
¿Me lo podría indicar   me lo po·dree·a een·dee·kar
(en el mapa)?   (en el ma·pa)

What's the address?
¿Cuál es la dirección?   kwal es la dee·rek·syon

It's …	Está …	es·ta …
behind …	detrás de …	de·tras de …
far away	lejos	le·khos
here	aquí	a·kee
in front of …	adelante de …	a·de·lan·te de …
left	a la izquierda	a la ees·kyer·da
near	cerca	ser·ka
next to …	al lado de …	al la·do de …
on the corner	en la esquina	en la es·kee·na
opposite …	frente a …	fren·te a …
right	a la derecha	a la de·re·cha
straight ahead	todo derecho	to·do de·re·cho
there	ahí	a·ee
	(Arg) acá	a·ka

Turn ...	Doble ...	do·ble ...
left/right	a la izquierda/ derecha	a la ees·kyer·da/ de·re·cha
at the corner	en la esquina	en la es·kee·na
at the traffic lights	en el semáforo	en el se·ma·fo·ro

It's ...	Está a ...	es·ta a ...
(100) metres	(cien) metros	(syen) me·tros
(two) kilometres	(dos) kilómetros	(dos) kee·lo·me·tros
(five) minutes	(cinco) minutos	(seen·ko) mee·noo·tos

by bus	en autobús	en ow·to·boos
on foot	a pie	a pye
by taxi	en taxi	en tak·see
by train	en tren	en tren

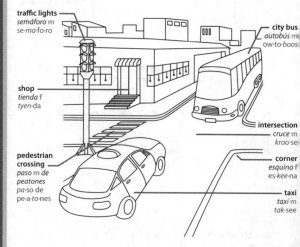

traffic lights
semáforo m
se·ma·fo·ro

city bus
autobús m
ow·to·boos

shop
tienda f
tyen·da

intersection
cruce m
kroo·se

pedestrian crossing
paso m de peatones
pa·so de pe·a·to·nes

corner
esquina f
es·kee·na

taxi
taxi m
tak·see

finding accommodation

buscar alojamiento

Where's a …?	¿Dónde hay …?	don·de ai …
bed and breakfast	una pensión con desayuno	oo·na pen·syon kon de·sa·yoo·no
cabin	una cabaña	oo·na ka·ba·nya
camping ground	un terreno de cámping	oon te·re·no de kam·peen
guesthouse	una pensión	oo·na pen·syon
	una casa de huéspedes	oo·na ka·sa de wes·pe·des
(Arg, Chi)	una hostería	oo·na os·te·ree·a
hotel	un hotel	oon o·tel
youth hostel	un albergue juvenil	oon al·ber·ge khoo·ve·neel

Can you recommend somewhere …?	¿Puede recomendar algún sitio …?	pwe·de re·ko·men·dar al·goon see·tyo …
cheap	barato	ba·ra·to
good	bueno	bwe·no
luxurious	de lujo	de loo·kho
nearby	cercano	ser·ka·no
romantic	romántico	ro·man·tee·ko

What's the address?
¿Cuál es la dirección? kwal es la dee·rek·syon

For more on asking and giving directions, see **directions**, page 51.

accommodation

booking ahead & checking in

hacer una reserva & registrándose

Do you have a … room?	*¿Tiene una habitación …?*	tye·ne oo·na a·bee·ta·*syon* …
double	*dòble*	*do*·ble
single	*individual*	een·dee·vee·*dwal*
twin	*con dos camas*	kon dos *ka*·mas

How much is it per …?	*¿Cuánto cuesta por …?*	*kwan*·to *kwes*·ta por …
night	*noche*	*no*·che
person	*persona*	per·*so*·na
week	*semana*	se·*ma*·na

I'd like to book a room, please.
Quisiera reservar una habitación.
kee·*sye*·ra re·ser·*var* oo·na a·bee·ta·*syon*

I have a reservation.
Tengo una reserva.
ten·go oo·na re·*ser*·va

My name's …
Me llamo …
me *lya*·mo …

For (three) nights/weeks.
Para (tres) noches/semanas.
pa·ra (tres) *no*·ches/se·*ma*·nas

From (July 2) to (July 6).
   Desde (el dos de julio)   des·de (el dos de *khoo*·lyo)
   hasta (el seis de julio).   *as*·ta (el says de *khoo*·lyo)

Can I see it?
   ¿Puedo verla?   *pwe*·do *ver*·la

It's fine. I'll take it.
   OK. La alquilo.   o·*kay* la al·*kee*·lo

Do I need to pay upfront?
   ¿Necesito pagar por   ne·se·*see*·to pa·*gar* por
   adelantado?   a·de·lan·*ta*·do

Can I pay by ...?   *¿Puedo pagar*   *pwe*·do pa·*gar*
         con ...?   kon ...
   credit card   *tarjeta de*   tar·*khe*·ta de
         crédito   *kre*·dee·to
   travellers   *cheques de*   *che*·kes de
    cheque   *viajero*   vya·*khe*·ro

For other methods of payment, see **money**, page 35.

requests & queries

peticiones & preguntas

When/Where's breakfast served?
   ¿Cuándo/Dónde se sirve   *kwan*·do/*don*·de se *seer*·ve
   el desayuno?   el de·sa·*yoo*·no

Please wake me at (seven).
   Por favor, despiérteme   por fa·*vor* des·*pyer*·te·me
   a (las siete).   a (las *sye*·te)

Can I get another ...?
   ¿Puede darme otro/a ...? m/f   *pwe*·de *dar*·me *o*·tro/a ...

Can I use the ...?	¿Puedo usar ...?	pwe·do oo·sar ...
kitchen	la cocina	la ko·see·na
laundry	la lavandería	la la·van·de·ree·a
telephone	el teléfono	el te·le·fo·no

Do you have a/an ...?	¿Hay ...?	ai ...
elevator	ascensor	a·sen·sor
laundry service	servicio de lavandería	ser·vee·syo de la·van·de·ree·a
message board	tablón de anuncios	ta·blon de a·noon·syos
(CAm)	pizarra de anuncios	pee·sa·ra de a·noon·syos
(Chi)	diario mural	dya·ryo moo·ral
safe	una caja fuerte	oo·na ka·kha fwer·te
swimming pool	piscina	pee·see·na
(SAm)	pileta	pee·le·ta

Do you ... here?	¿Aquí ...?	a·kee ...
arrange tours	organizan paseos guiados	or·ga·nee·san pa·se·os gee·a·dos
change money	cambian dinero	kam·byan dee·ne·ro

listen for ...

la lya·ve es·ta en re·sep·syon La llave está en recepción.	The key is at reception.
lo syen·to es·ta kom·ple·to Lo siento, está completo.	I'm sorry, we're full.
por kwan·tas no·ches ¿Por cuántas noches?	For how many nights?
soo pa·sa·por·te por fa·vor Su pasaporte, por favor.	Your passport, please.

Can I leave a message for someone?
*¿Puedo dejar un
mensaje para alguien?*
pwe·do de·khar oon
men·sa·khe pa·ra al·gyen

Is there a message for me?
*¿Hay algún mensaje
para mí?*
ai al·goon men·sa·khe
pa·ra mee

I'm locked out of my room.
*Cerré la puerta y se me
olvidaron las llaves
dentro.*
se·re la pwer·ta ee se me
ol·vee·da·ron las lya·ves
den·tro

The (bathroom) door is locked.
*La puerta (del baño) está
cerrada con llave.*
la pwer·ta (del ba·nyo) es·ta
se·ra·da kon lya·ve

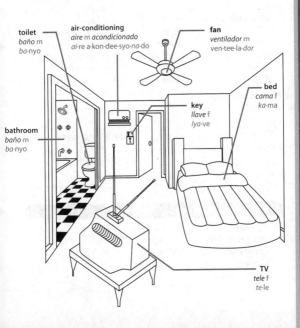

toilet
baño m
ba·nyo

air-conditioning
aire m *acondicionado*
ai·re a·kon·dee·syo·na·do

fan
ventilador m
ven·tee·la·dor

bathroom
baño m
ba·nyo

key
llave f
lya·ve

bed
cama f
ka·ma

TV
tele f
te·le

accommodation

57

complaints

The room is too ...	La habitación es demasiado ...	la a·bee·ta·*syon* es de·ma·*sya*·do ...
cold	fría	*free*·a
dark	oscura	os·*koo*·ra
dirty	sucia	*soo*·sya
expensive	cara	*ka*·ra
light/bright	luminosa	loo·mee·*no*·sa
noisy	ruidosa	rwee·*do*·sa
small	pequeña	pe·*ke*·nya
The ... doesn't work.	No funciona ...	no foon·*syo*·na ...
air-conditioning	el aire acondicionado	el *ai*·re a·kon·dee·syo·*na*·do
fan	el ventilador	el ven·tee·la·*dor*
heater	la estufa	la es·*too*·fa
toilet	el baño	el *ba*·nyo
window	la ventana	la ven·*ta*·na

The room smells.
La habitación huele mal.   la a·bee·ta·*syon* *we*·le mal

The toilet smells.
El baño huele mal.   el *ba*·nyo *we*·le mal

There's no hot water.
No hay agua caliente.   no ai *a*·gwa ka·*lyen*·te

This ... isn't clean.
Éste/a ... no está limpio/a. m/f   es·te/a ... no es·*ta* leem·pyo/a

---

a knock at the door ...

Who is it?	¿Quién es?	kyen es
Just a moment.	Un momento.	oon mo·*men*·to
Come in.	Adelante.	a·de·*lan*·te
Come back later, please.	¿Puede volver más tarde, por favor?	*pwe*·de vol·*ver* mas *tar*·de por fa·*vor*

checking out

What time is checkout?
¿A qué hora hay que dejar   a ke o·ra ai ke de·*khar*
libre la habitación?   *lee*·bre la a·bee·ta·*syon*

Can I have a late checkout?
¿Puedo dejar libre la   pwe·do de·*khar lee*·bre la
habitación más tarde?   a·bee·ta·*syon* mas *tar*·de

How much extra to stay until (6 o'clock)?
¿Cuánto más cuesta   *kwan*·to mas *kwes*·ta
quedarse hasta (las seis)?   ke·*dar*·se *as*·ta (las says)

Can I leave my luggage here?
¿Puedo dejar el   pwe·do de·*khar* el
equipaje aquí?   e·kee·*pa*·khe a·*kee*

I'm leaving now.
Me voy ahora.   me voy a·*o*·ra

There's a mistake in the bill.
Hay un error en la cuenta.   ai oon e·*ror* en la *kwen*·ta

Can you call a taxi for me (for 11 o'clock)?
¿Me puede pedir un   me *pwe*·de pe·*deer* oon
taxi (para las once)?   *tak*·see (*pa*·ra las *on*·se)

Could I have   *¿Me puede dar*   me *pwe*·de dar
my ..., please?   *..., por favor?*   ... por fa·*vor*
  deposit   *mi depósito*   mee de·*po*·see·to
  passport   *mi pasaporte*   mee pa·sa·*por*·te
  valuables   *mis objetos*   mees ob·*khe*·tos
     de valor   de va·*lor*

I'll be back ...   *Volveré ...*   vol·ve·*re* ...
  in (three) days   *en (tres) días*   en (tres) *dee*·as
  on (Tuesday)   *el (martes)*   el (*mar*·tes)

I had a great stay, thank you.
 Tuve una estancia muy *too*·ve *oo*·na es·*tan*·sya mooy
 agradable, gracias. a·gra·*da*·ble *gra*·syas

You've been terrific.
 Fueron muy amables. *fwe*·ron mooy a·*ma*·bles

I'll recommend it to my friends.
 Se lo recomendaré a se lo re·ko·men·da·*re* a
 mis amigos. mees a·*mee*·gos

camping

acampar

Where's the nearest …?	*¿Dónde está …?*	*don*·de es·*ta* …
campsite	*el terreno de cámping más cercano*	el te·*re*·no de *kam*·peen mas ser·*ka*·no
shop	*la tienda más cercana*	la *tyen*·da mas ser·*ka*·na
Where are the nearest …?	*Donde están …?*	*don*·de es·*tan* …
showers	*las duchas más cercanas*	las *doo*·chas mas ser·*ka*·nas
toilets	*los baños más cercanos*	los *ba*·nyos mas ser·*ka*·nos
Do you have …?	*¿Tiene …?*	*tye*·ne …
electricity	*electricidad*	e·lek·tree·see·*da*
shower facilities	*duchas*	*doo*·chas
a site	*un lugar*	oon loo·*gar*
tents for hire	*carpas para alquilar*	*kar*·pas *pa*·ra al·kee·*lar*

How much is	¿Cuánto vale	kwan·to va·le
it per …?	por …?	por …
caravan	caravana	ka·ra·va·na
person	persona	per·so·na
tent	carpa	kar·pa
vehicle	vehículo	ve·ee·koo·lo

Can I …?	¿Se puede …?	se pwe·de …
camp here	acampar aquí	a·kam·par a·kee
park next to	estacionar al lado	es·ta·syo·nar al la·do
my tent	de mi carpa	de mee kar·pa

Who do I ask to stay here?
¿Con quién tengo que hablar — kon kyen ten·go ke a·blar
para quedarme aquí? — pa·ra ke·dar·me a·kee

Is it coin-operated?
¿Funciona con monedas? — foon·syo·na kon mo·ne·das

Is the water drinkable?
¿Se puede beber el agua? — se pwe·de be·ber el a·gwa

Could I borrow (a mallet)?
¿Me podría prestar — me po·dree·a pres·tar
(un mazo)? — (oon ma·so)

For more words related to camping, see the **dictionary**.

renting

alquilar

I'm here about (the room) for rent.
Vengo por (la habitación) — ven·go por (la a·bee·ta·syon)
que anuncian para alquilar. — ke a·noon·syan pa·ra al·kee·lar

Do you have	¿Tiene … para	tye·ne … pa·ra
a/an … for rent?	alquilar?	al·kee·lar
apartment	un departamento	oon de·par·ta·men·to
cabin	una cabaña	oo·na ka·ba·nya
house	una casa	oo·na ka·sa
room	una habitación	oo·na a·bee·ta·syon
villa	un chalet	oon cha·le

furnished	*amueblado/a* m/f	a·mwe·*bla*·do/a
partly	*parcialmente*	par·syal·*men*·te
furnished	*amueblado/a* m/f	a·mwe·*bla*·do/a
unfurnished	*sin amueblar*	seen a·mwe·*blar*

staying with locals

hospedárse con la gente de la zona

Can I stay at your place?
¿Me podría quedar en su/tu casa? pol/inf — me po·*dree*·a ke·*dar* en soo/too *ka*·sa

Is there anything I can do to help?
¿Puedo ayudar en algo? — *pwe*·do a·yoo·*dar* en *al*·go

I have my own …	*Tengo mi propio/a …* m/f	*ten*·go mee *pro*·pyo/a …
mattress	*colchón* m	kol·*chon*
sleeping bag	*bolsa* f *de dormir*	*bol*·sa de dor·*meer*

Can I …?	*¿Puedo …?*	*pwe*·do …
bring anything for the meal	*traer algo para la comida*	tra·*er al*·go *pa*·ra la ko·*mee*·da
do the dishes	*lavar los platos*	la·*var* los *pla*·tos
set/clear the table	*poner/quitar la mesa*	po·*ner*/kee·*tar* la *me*·sa
take out the rubbish	*sacar la basura*	sa·*kar* la ba·*soo*·ra

Thanks for your hospitality.
Gracias por su/tu hospitalidad. pol/inf — *gra*·syas por soo/too os·pee·ta·lee·*da*

If you're dining with your hosts, see **eating out**, page 146 for more phrases.

looking for ...

Where's (a supermarket)?
¿Dónde hay   *don*·de ai
(un supermercado)?   (oon soo·per·mer·*ka*·do)

Where can I buy (bread)?
¿Dónde puedo comprar (pan)?   *don*·de *pwe*·do kom·*prar* (pan)

For asking and giving directions, see **directions**, page 51 and for types of shops, see the **dictionary**.

shop till you drop

In Latin America the generic term for 'general store' is *una tienda*. Look out for some of these regional variations:

Argentina:
   un almacén   oon al·ma·*sen*
Central America, Colombia, Bolivia, Ecuador and Peru:
   una tienda de abarrrotes   oo·na *tyen*·da de a·ba·ro·tes
Central America:
   una bodega   oo·na bo·*de*·ga
Costa Rica and Chile:
   una pulpería   oo·na pool·pe·*ree*·a
Venezuela:
   un abasto   oon a·*bas*·to

making a purchase

I'd like to buy …
Quisiera comprar … kee·*sye*·ra kom·*prar* …

I'm just looking.
Sólo estoy mirando. so·lo es·*toy* mee·*ran*·do

How much is this?
¿Cuánto cuesta esto? *kwan*·to *kwes*·ta es·to

Can you write down the price?
¿Puede escribir el precio? *pwe*·de es·kree·*beer* el *pre*·syo

Do you have any others?
¿Tiene otros? *tye*·ne o·tros

Can I look at it?
¿Puedo verlo? *pwe*·do *ver*·lo

---

market hopping

Markets or *mercados* are a colourful feature of Latin American life and you'll find a vast array of comestibles and consumables there. Smaller, open-air street markets are known as *ferias*. If it's vibrant folk art you're after, the place to visit is a *mercado de artesanía* or craft market.

Could I have it wrapped?
¿Me lo podría envolver? me lo po·*dree*·a en·vol·*ver*

Does it have a guarantee?
¿Tiene garantía? *tye*·ne ga·ran·*tee*·a

Can I have it sent overseas?
¿Pueden enviarlo por correo a otro país? *pwe*·den en·*vyar*·lo por ko·*re*·o a o·tro pa·*ees*

Can you order it for me?
¿Me lo puede pedir? me lo *pwe*·de pe·*deer*

Can I pick it up later?
¿Puedo recogerlo más tarde? *pwe*·do re·ko·*kher*·lo mas *tar*·de

al·go mas	¿Algo más?	**Anything else?**
kwan·tos/as	¿Cuántos/as	**How many**
kye·re	quiere? m/f pl	**would you like?**
no no te·ne·mos	No, no tenemos	**No, we don't**
neen·goo·no	ninguno.	**have any.**

Do you have change?
¿Tiene cambio? tye·ne *kam*·byo

It's faulty.
Es defectuoso. es de·fek·*two*·so

I don't like it.
No me gusta. no me *goos*·ta

Do you accept ...?	¿Aceptan ...?	a·sep·tan ...
American dollars	dólares americanos	do·la·res a·me·ree·ka·nos
credit cards	tarjetas de crédito	tar·khe·tas de kre·dee·to
debit cards	tarjetas de débito	tar·khe·tas de de·bee·to
travellers cheques	cheques de viajero	che·kes de vya·khe·ro

Could I have a ..., please?	¿Podría darme ..., por favor?	po·dree·a dar·me ... por fa·vor
bag	una bolsa	oo·na bol·sa
receipt	un recibo	oon re·see·bo

I'd like ..., please.	Quisiera ..., por favor.	kee·sye·ra ... por fa·vor
my change	mi cambio	mee kam·byo
my money back	que me devuelva el dinero	ke me de·vwel·va el dee·ne·ro
to return this	devolver esto	de·vol·ver es·to

bargaining

That's too expensive.
Es muy caro. es mooy *ka*·ro

The price is very high.
Cuesta demasiado. *kwes*·ta de·ma·*sya*·do

Can you lower the price (a little)?
¿Podría bajar po·*dree*·a ba·*khar*
(un poco) el precio? (oon *po*·ko) el *pre*·syo

Do you have something cheaper?
¿Tiene algo más barato? *tye*·ne *al*·go mas ba·*ra*·to

I'll give you …
Le/La daré … m/f le/la da·*re* …

What's your final price?
¿Cuál es su precio final? kwal es soo *pre*·syo fee·*nal*

local talk

bargain	*ganga* f	*gan*·ga
bargain hunter	*cazador* m *de ofertas*	ka·sa·*dor* de o·*fer*·tas
rip-off	*estafa* f	es·*ta*·fa
specials	*saldos* m pl	*sal*·dos
sale	*venta* f	*ven*·ta

clothes

la ropa

Can I try it on?
¿Me lo puedo probar? me lo *pwe*·do pro·*bar*

My size is (medium).
Uso la talla (mediana). *oo*·so la *ta*·lya (me·*dya*·na)

It doesn't fit.
No me queda bien. no me *ke*·da byen

For different types of clothing, see the **dictionary**.

PRACTICAL

repairs

Can I have my ...	¿Puede reparar	pwe·de re·pa·*rar*
repaired here?	mi ... aquí?	mee ... a·*kee*
backpack	mochila	mo·*chee*·la
camera	cámara	*ka*·ma·ra
When will my	¿Cuándo estarán	*kwan*·do es·ta·*ran*
... be ready?	listos mis ...?	*lees*·tos mees ...
(sun)glasses	anteojos (de sol)	an·te·o·khos (de sol)
shoes	zapatos	sa·*pa*·tos

hairdressing

I'd like (a) ...	Quisiera ...	kee·*sye*·ra ...
blow wave	un secado a mano	oon se·*ka*·do a *ma*·no
colour	un tinte de pelo	oon *teen*·te de *pe*·lo
haircut	un corte de pelo	oon *kor*·te de *pe*·lo
highlights	reflejos	re·*fle*·khos
my beard	que me recorte	ke me re·*kor*·te
trimmed	la barba	la *bar*·ba
shave	que me afeite	ke me a·*fay*·te
trim	que me recorte	ke me re·*kor*·te
	el pelo	el *pe*·lo

Don't cut it too short.

No me lo corte   no me lo *kor*·te
demasiado corto.   de·ma·*sya*·do *kor*·to

Shave it all off!

¡Aféitelo todo!   a·*fay*·te·lo *to*·do

Please use a new blade.

Por favor, use una   por fa·*vor* oo·se oo·na
cuchilla nueva.   koo·*chee*·lya *nwe*·va

I should never have let you near me!

¡No debía haberle/haberla   no de·*bee*·a a·*ber*·le/a·*ber*·la
dejado tocarme! m/f   de·*kha*·do to·*kar*·me

books & reading

Is there a/an (English-language) …?	¿Hay alguna … (en inglés)?	ai al·*goo*·na … (en een·*gles*)
bookshop	librería	lee·bre·*ree*·a
entertainment guide	guía de espectáculos	*gee*·a de es·pek·*ta*·koo·los
section	sección	sek·*syon*

Do you have a book by (Gabriel García Márquez)?
¿Tiene un libro de
(Gabriel García Márquez)?
tye·ne oon *lee*·bro de
(ga·*bryel* gar·*see*·a *mar*·kes)

I like (Isabel Allende).
Me gusta
(Isabel Allende).
me *goos*·ta
(ee·sa·*bel* a·*lyen*·de)

Do you have Lonely Planet guidebooks?
¿Tiene guías de Lonely Planet?
tye·ne *gee*·as de *lon*·lee *pla*·net

music

I'd like (a) …	Quisiera …	kee·*sye*·ra …
blank tape	una cinta virgen	*oo*·na *seen*·ta *veer*·khen
CD	un cómpact	oon *kom*·pak
headphones	unos auriculares	*oo*·nos ow·ree·koo·*la*·res

I heard a singer called (Omara Portuondo).
Escuché un cantante
que se llama
(Omara Portuondo).
es·koo·*che* oon kan·*tan*·te
ke se *lya*·ma
(o·ma·*ra* por·*twon*·do)

I heard a band called (Maná).
Escuché un grupo
que se llama (Maná).
es·koo·*che* oon *groo*·po
ke se *lya*·ma (ma·*na*)

What's his/her best recording?
¿Cuál es su mejor disco?
kwal es soo me·*khor* *dees*·ko

Can I listen to this?
¿Puedo escuchar este?
pwe·do es·koo·*char* *es*·te

photography

I need ... film for this camera.	*Necesito un carrete de película ... para esta cámara.*	ne·se·*see*·to oon ka·*re*·te de pe·*lee*·koo·la ... *pa*·ra es·ta *ka*·ma·ra
APS	*APS*	a pe *e*·se
B&W	*en blanco y negro*	en *blan*·ko ee *ne*·gro
colour	*en color*	en ko·*lor*
slide	*para diapositivas*	para dya·po·see·*tee*·vas
(400) speed	*de sensibilidad (cuatro cientos)*	de sen·see·bee·lee·*da* (*kwa*·tro *syen*·tos)
Can you ... ?	*¿Puede ...?*	*pwe*·de ...
load my film	*cargar el carrete*	kar·*gar* el ka·*re*·te
develop this film	*revelar este carrete*	re·ve·*lar* es·te ka·*re*·te

How much is it to develop this film?
¿Cuánto cuesta revelar este carrete?
kwan·to *kwes*·ta re·ve·*lar* es·te ka·*re*·te

When will it be ready?
¿Cuándo estará listo?
kwan·do es·ta·*ra* lees·to

I need passport photos taken.
Necesito fotos de pasaporte.
ne·se·*see*·to *fo*·tos de pa·sa·*por*·te

I'm not happy with these photos.
No estoy contento/a con estas fotos. m/f
no es·*toy* kon·*ten*·to/a kon es·tas *fo*·tos

For more photographic equipment, see the **dictionary**.

souvenirs

alpaca jumper	*chompa* f *de alpaca*	*chom*·pa de al·*pa*·ka
basketwork	*cestería* f	ses·te·*ree*·a
cigars	*cigarros* m pl	see·*ga*·ros
coffee	*café* m	ka·*fe*
earrings	*pendientes* m pl	pen·*dyen*·tes
(Arg, CAm)	*aritos* m pl	a·*ree*·tos
(Uru)	*caravanas* f pl	ka·ra·*va*·nas
(Nic)	*chapas* f pl	*cha*·pas
hammock	*hamaca* f	a·*ma*·ka
jewellery	*joyería* f	kho·ye·*ree*·a
leather belt	*cinto* m *de cuero*	*seen*·to de *kwe*·ro
leather boots	*botas* f pl *de cuero*	*bo*·tas de *kwe*·ro
leather handbag	*cartera* f *de cuero*	kar·*te*·ra de *kwe*·ro
necklace	*collar* m	ko·*lyar*
Panamanian appliqué textile	*mola* f	*mo*·la
panpipes	*zampoña* f	sam·*po*·nya
Peruvian hat	*chullo* m	*choo*·lyo
pottery	*alfarería* f	al·fa·re·*ree*·a
ring	*anillo* m	a·*nee*·lyo
rug	*alfombra* f	al·*fom*·bra
silverware	*plata* f	*pla*·ta
weaving	*tejido* m	te·*khee*·do
woodcarving	*talla* f *de madera*	*ta*·lya de ma·*de*·ra

post office

correos

I want to send a …	*Quisiera enviar …*	kee·*sye*·ra en·*vyar* …
fax	*un fax*	oon faks
letter	*una carta*	*oo*·na *kar*·ta
parcel	*un paquete*	oon pa·*ke*·te
(Arg)	*una*	*oo*·na
	encomienda	en·ko·*myen*·da
postcard	*una postal*	*oo*·na pos·*tal*
I want to buy …	*Quisiera comprar …*	kee·*sye*·ra kom·*prar* …
an aerogram	*un aerograma*	oon a·e·ro·*gra*·ma
an envelope	*un sobre*	oon *so*·bre
stamps	*unos sellos*	*oo*·nos *se*·lyos

airmail	*correo* m *aéreo*	ko·*re*·o a·*e*·re·o
customs	*declaración* f	de·kla·ra·*syon*
declaration	*de aduana*	de a·*dwa*·na
domestic	*nacional*	na·syo·*nal*
express mail	*correo* m *urgente*	ko·*re*·o oor·*khen*·te
fragile	*frágil*	*fra*·kheel
international	*internacional*	een·ter·na·syo·*nal*
mailbox	*buzón* m	boo·*son*
postcode	*código* m *postal*	*ko*·dee·go pos·*tal*
(Arg)	*característica* f	ka·rak·te·*rees*·tee·ka
registered mail	*correo* m	ko·*re*·o
	certificado	ser·tee·fee·*ka*·do
regular mail	*correo* m *normal*	ko·*re*·o nor·*mal*
surface mail	*por vía terrestre*	por *vee*·a te·*res*·tre

Please send it by airmail (to England).

Por favor, mándelo por vía aérea (a Inglaterra). por fa·*vor* man·de·lo por *vee*·a a·e·re·a (a een·gla·*te*·ra)

Please send it by surface mail (to Buenos Aires).

Por favor, mándelo por vía terrestre (a Buenos Aires). por fa·*vor* man·de·lo por *vee*·a te·*res*·tre (a *bwe*·nos *ai*·res)

It contains …

Contiene … kon·*tye*·ne …

Where's the poste restante section?

¿Dónde está la lista de correos? *don*·de es·*ta* la *lees*·ta de ko·*re*·os

Is there any mail for me?

¿Hay alguna carta para mí? ai al·*goo*·na *kar*·ta *pa*·ra mee

---

listen for …

a·*don*·de lo *man*·da
¿Adónde lo manda? **Where are you sending it?**

por ko·*re*·o oor·*khen*·te o nor·*mal*
¿Por correo urgente o normal? **By express post or regular post?**

phone

el teléfono

What's your phone number?

¿Cuál es su número de teléfono? kwal es soo *noo*·me·ro de te·*le*·fo·no

Where's the nearest public phone?

¿Dónde está la cabina telefónica más cercana? *don*·de es·*ta* la ka·*bee*·na te·le·*fo*·nee·ka mas ser·*ka*·na

I want to make a (reverse-charge/collect) call to Singapore.

Quiero hacer una llamada (a cobro revertido) a Singapur. *kye*·ro a·*ser* oo·na lya·*ma*·da (a *ko*·bro re·ver·*tee*·do) a seen·ga·*poor*

I want …	Quiero …	kye·ro …
to buy a phone card	comprar una tarjeta telefónica	kom·prar oo·na tar·khe·ta te·le·fo·nee·ka
to speak for (three) minutes	hablar por (tres) minutos	a·blar por (tres) mee·noo·tos

How much does … cost?	¿Cuánto cuesta …?	kwan·to kwes·ta …
a (three)-minute call	una llamada de (tres) minutos	oo·na lya·ma·da de (tres) mee·noo·tos
each extra minute	cada minuto extra	ka·da mee·noo·to ek·stra

The number is …
El número es …   el *noo*·me·ro es …

What's the area code for (Lima)?
¿Cuál es el prefijo de (Lima)?   kwal es el pre·*fee*·kho de (*lee*·ma)

What's the country code for (Chile)?
¿Cuál es el prefijo de (Chile)?   kwal es el pre·*fee*·kho de (*chee*·le)

It's engaged.
Está ocupada.   es·*ta* o·koo·*pa*·da

The connection's bad.
Es mala conexión.   es *ma*·la ko·nek·*syon*

I've been cut off.
Me han cortado (la comunicación).   me an kor·*ta*·do (la ko·moo·nee·ka·*syon*)

Hello. (making a call)
¡Hola!   o·la

Hello. (answering a call)
¿Diga?   dee·ga

It's … (when identifying yourself)
Habla …   a·bla …

Can I speak to (Pedro)?
¿Está (Pedro)?   es·ta pe·dro

Can I leave a message?
¿Puedo dejar un   pwe·do de·khar oon
mensaje?   men·sa·khe

Please tell him/her I called.
Dile/Dila que llamé,   dee·le/dee·la ke lya·me
por favor. m/f   por fa·vor

I'll call back later.
Ya llamaré más tarde.   ya lya·ma·re mas tar·de

My number is …
Mi número es …   mee noo·me·ro es …

I don't have a contact number.
No tengo número de   no ten·go noo·me·ro de
contacto.   kon·tak·to

listen for …

de par·te de kyen
¿De parte de quién?   **Who's calling?**

kon kyen kye·re a·blar
¿Con quién quiere   **Who do you want to**
hablar?   **speak to?**

lo syen·to pe·ro a·o·ra no es·ta
Lo siento, pero ahora   **I'm sorry he's/she's**
no está.   **not here.**

lo syen·to tye·ne el noo·me·ro e·kee·vo·ka·do
Lo siento, tiene el   **Sorry, wrong number.**
numero equivocado.

oon mo·men·to
Un momento.   **One moment.**

see a·kee es·ta
Sí, aquí está.   **Yes, he's/she's here.**

mobile/cell phone

I'd like a/an ...	*Quisiera ...*	kee·*sye*·ra ...
adaptor plug	*un adaptador*	oon a·dap·ta·*dor*
charger for	*un cargador*	oon kar·ga·*dor*
my phone	*para mi*	*pa*·ra mee
	teléfono	te·*le*·fo·no
mobile/cell	*un móvil para*	oon *mo*·veel *pa*·ra
phone for hire	*alquilar*	al·kee·*lar*
prepaid mobile/	*un móvil*	oon *mo*·veel
cell phone	*pagado por*	pa·*ga*·do por
	adelantado	a·de·lan·*ta*·do
SIM card for	*una tarjeta*	*oo*·na tar·*khe*·ta
your network	*SIM para su red*	seem *pa*·ra soo re

What are the rates?
¿Cuáles son las tarifas? kwa·les son las ta·*ree*·fas

(30c) per (30) seconds.
(Treinta centavos) por (*trayn*·ta sen·*ta*·vos) por
(treinta) segundos. (*trayn*·ta) se·*goon*·dos

the internet

Where's the local Internet cafe?
¿Dónde hay un cibercafé *don*·de ai oon see·ber·ka·*fe*
cercano? ser·*ka*·no

I'd like to ...	*Quisiera ...*	kee·*sye*·ra ...
get Internet	*usar el*	oo·*sar* el
access	*Internet*	een·ter·*net*
check my email	*revisar mi*	re·vee·*sar* mee
	correo	ko·*re*·o
	electrónico	e·lek·*tro*·nee·ko
use a printer	*usar una*	oo·*sar* *oo*·na
	impresora	eem·pre·*so*·ra
use a scanner	*usar un escáner*	oo·*sar* oon es·*ka*·ner

How much per ...?	¿Cuánto cuesta por ...?	kwan·to kwes·ta por ...
CD	cómpact	kom·pak
(10) minutes	(diez) minutos	(dyes) mee·noo·tos
hour	hora	o·ra
page	página	pa·khee·na

Do you have ...?	¿Tiene ...?	tye·ne ...
PCs	PC	pe se
Macs	MacIntosh	ma·keen·tosh
a Zip drive	unidad de Zip	oo·nee·da de seep

How do I log on?

¿Cómo me conecto al sistema?

ko·mo me ko·nek·to al sees·te·ma

I need help with the computer.

Necesito ayuda con la computadora.

ne·se·see·to a·yoo·da kon la kom·poo·ta·do·ra

It's crashed.

Se ha quedado colgado.

se a ke·da·do kol·ga·do

I've finished.

He terminado.

e ter·mee·na·do

---

return to sender

In Latin America dwellings may not be numbered and addresses are sometimes short descriptive passages. Be prepared to decipher an exotic address like the following:

*Marirosa Ferrer Botero
la casa azul en la
esquina de Avenida de
la Paz y Calle 12
cerca de la farmacia
una manzana al norte de
la catedral
Tegucigalpa Honduras*

Marirosa Ferrer Botero
the blue house on the
corner of Avenida de
la Paz and 12th Street
near the pharmacy
one block north of
the cathedral
Tegucigalpa Honduras

If you're having trouble finding your way to such an address, try using the **dictionary** to translate the various elements, or ask for help using the phrases in **directions**, page 51.

Where can I …?	¿Dónde puedo …?	don·de pwe·do …
I'd like to …	Me gustaría …	me goos·ta·ree·a …
arrange a transfer	organizar una transferencia	or·ga·nee·sar oo·na trans·fe·ren·sya
cash a cheque	cobrar un cheque	ko·brar oon che·ke
change a travellers cheque	cambiar un cheque de viajero	kam·byar oon che·ke de vya·khe·ro
change money	cambiar dinero	kam·byar dee·ne·ro
get a cash advance	obtener un adelanto	ob·te·ner oon a·de·lan·to
use internet banking	usar la banca por internet	oo·sar la ban·ka por een·ter·net
withdraw money	sacar dinero	sa·kar dee·ne·ro
Where's the nearest …?	¿Dónde está …?	don·de es·ta …
automatic teller machine	el cajero automático más cercano	el ka·khe·ro ow·to·ma·tee·ko mas ser·ka·no
foreign exchange office	la oficina de cambio más cercana	la o·fee·see·na de kam·byo mas ser·ka·na

What time does the bank open?

¿A qué hora abre el banco?	a ke o·ra a·bre el ban·ko

The automatic teller machine took my card.

El cajero automático se ha tragado mi tarjeta.	el ka·khe·ro ow·to·ma·tee·ko se a tra·ga·do mee tar·khe·ta

I've forgotten my PIN.

Me he olvidado del NPI.	me e ol·vee·da·do del e·ne pe ee

Can I use my credit card to withdraw money?

¿Puedo usar mi tarjeta de crédito para sacar dinero?	pwe·do oo·sar mee tar·khe·ta de kre·dee·to pa·ra sa·kar dee·ne·ro

What's the exchange rate?
¿Cuál es la tasa de cambio?   kwal es la *ta*·sa de *kam*·byo

What's the commission?
¿Cuál es la comisión?   kwal es la ko·mee·*syon*

What's the charge for that?
¿Cuánto hay que pagar por eso? *kwan*·to ai ke pa·*gar* por *e*·so

Can I have smaller notes?
¿Me lo puede dar en   me lo *pwe*·de dar en
billetes más pequeños?   bee·*lye*·tes mas pe·*ke*·nyos

Has my money arrived yet?
¿Ya ha llegado mi dinero?   ya a lye·*ga*·do mee dee·*ne*·ro

How long will it take to arrive?
¿Cuánto tiempo tardará   *kwan*·to *tyem*·po tar·da·*ra*
en llegar?   en lye·*gar*

For other useful phrases, see **money**, page 35.

---

listen for ...

ai oon pro·*ble*·ma kon soo *kwen*·ta
Hay un problema   **There's a problem**
con su cuenta.   **with your account.**

no po·*de*·mos a·*ser e*·so
No podemos hacer eso.   **We can't do that.**

pwe·de es·kree·*beer*·lo
¿Puede escribirlo?   **Could you write it down?**

por fa·*vor* feer·me a·*kee*
Por favor firme aquí.   **Please sign here.**

en ...	En ...	In ...
(*kwa*·tro) dee·as	(cuatro) días	(four)
la·bo·*ra*·bles	laborables	working days
(*kwa*·tro) dee·as (**SAm**)	(cuatro) días	
a·bee·les	hábiles	
soo ...	Su ...	Your ...
ee·den·tee·fee·ka·*syon*	identificación	ID
pa·sa·*por*·te	pasaporte	passport

PRACTICAL

78

I'd like a/an …	*Quisiera …*	kee·*sye*·ra …
audio set	*un equipo audio*	oon e·*kee*·po ow·dyo
catalogue	*un catálogo*	oon ka·*ta*·lo·go
guide (person)	*un/una guía* m/f	oon/*oo*·na *gee*·a
guidebook in English	*una guía turística en inglés*	*oo*·na *gee*·a too·*rees*·tee·ka en een·*gles*
(local) map	*un mapa (de la zona)*	oon *ma*·pa (de la *so*·na)

Do you have information on … sights?	*¿Tiene información sobre los lugares … de interés?*	*tye*·ne een·for·ma·*syon so*·bre los loo·*ga*·res … de een·te·*res*
cultural	*culturales*	kool·too·*ra*·les
local	*locales*	lo·*ka*·les
religious	*religiosos*	re·lee·*khyo*·sos
unique	*únicos*	*oo*·nee·kos

I'd like to see …
Me gustaría ver … — me goos·ta·*ree*·a ver …

What's that?
¿Qué es eso? — ke es *e*·so

Who made it?
¿Quién lo hizo? — kyen lo *ee*·so

How old is it?
¿De cuándo es? — de *kwan*·do es

Could you take a photograph of me?
¿Me puede sacar una foto? — me *pwe*·de sa·*kar oo*·na *fo*·to

Can I take photographs (of you)?
¿(Le/Te) Puedo sacar fotos? pol/inf — (le/te) *pwe*·do sa·*kar fo*·tos

I'll send you the photograph.
Le/Te mandaré la foto. pol/inf — le/te man·da·*re* la *fo*·to

getting in

What time does it open/close?
 ¿A qué hora abre/cierra? a ke o·ra a·bre/sye·ra

What's the admission charge?
 ¿Cuánto cuesta la entrada? kwan·to kwes·ta la en·tra·da

It costs (100 pesos).
 Cuesta (cien pesos). kwes·ta (syen pe·sos)

Is there a discount for …?	*¿Hay descuentos para …?*	ai des·kwen·tos pa·ra …
children	*niños*	nee·nyos
families	*familias*	fa·mee·lyas
groups	*grupos*	groo·pos
pensioners	*pensionados*	pen·syo·na·dos
	(Arg) *jubilados*	khoo·bee·la·dos
students	*estudiantes*	es·too·dyan·tes

what's in a name?

Many Latin American place names are linked to historical events. *Argentina* comes from the Latin *argentum* 'silver' allegedly because the first Europeans to arrive observed the indigenous people wearing silver jewellery. *Bolivia* is named after Simón Bolívar, the famous revolutionary general who helped liberate many Latin American countries from Spanish rule and became the country's first president. *Costa Rica* means 'rich coast' and was named by Christopher Columbus for the precious metals that the land was expected to yield. *Honduras* literally means 'depths' and was named by Columbus for the deep waters off the country's north coast. *Colombia* was named after Columbus himself, though not until the 19th century.

tours

Can you recommend a …?	*¿Puede recomendar algún …?*	pwe·de re·ko·men·*dar* al·*goon* …
boat trip	*paseo en barca*	pa·*se*·o en *bar*·ka
tour	*recorrido*	re·ko·*ree*·do
When's the next …?	*¿Cuándo es la próxima …?*	*kwan*·do es la *prok*·see·ma …
daytrip	*excursión de un día*	ek·skoor·*syon* de oon *dee*·a
excursion	*excursión*	ek·skoor·*syon*
Is … included?	*¿Incluye …?*	een·*kloo*·ye …
accommodation	*alojamiento*	a·lo·kha·*myen*·to
equipment	*equipo*	e·*kee*·po
food	*comida*	ko·*mee*·da
transport	*transporte*	trans·*por*·te

Can we hire a guide?
  ¿Podemos alquilar un guía?
  po·*de*·mos al·kee·*lar* oon *gee*·a

The guide will pay.
  El guía va a pagar.
  el *gee*·a va a pa·*gar*

The guide has paid.
  El guía ha pagado.
  el *gee*·a a pa·*ga*·do

Do I need to take (lunch) with me?
  ¿Necesito llevar (el almuerzo)?
  ne·se·*see*·to lye·*var* (el al·*mwer*·so)

How long is the tour?
¿Cuánto dura el
recorrido?
kwan·to doo·ra el
re·ko·ree·do

What time should I be back?
¿A qué hora tengo que volver?
a ke o·ra ten·go ke vol·ver

Be back here at (four).
Vuelva a (las cuatro).
vwel·va a (las kwa·tro)

I'm with them.
Voy con ellos.
voy kon e·lyos

I've lost my group.
He perdido mi grupo.
e per·dee·do mee groo·po

signs

Abierto	a·*byer*·to	**Open**
Baños	*ba*·nyos	**Toilets**
Caliente	ka·*lyen*·te	**Hot**
Cerrado	se·*ra*·do	**Closed**
Entrada	en·*tra*·da	**Entry**
Frío	*free*·o	**Cold**
Información	een·for·ma·*syon*	**Information**
No Tocar	no to·*kar*	**Don't Touch**
Prohibido	pro·ee·*bee*·do	**No**
Tomar Fotos	to·*mar* fo·tos	**Photography**
Prohibido	pro·ee·*bee*·do	**No Flash**
Usar el Flash	oo·*sar* el flash	**Photography**
Reservado	re·ser·*va*·do	**Reserved**
Salida	sa·*lee*·da	**Exit**
Salida de	sa·*lee*·da de	**Emergency**
Emergencia	e·mer·*khen*·sya	**Exit**
Servicios	ser·*vee*·syos	**Toilets**

I'm attending a …	Asisto a …	a·*sees*·to a …
conference	un congreso	oon kon·*gre*·so
course	un curso	oon koor·so
meeting	una reunión	oo·na re·oo·*nyon*
trade fair	una feria de muestras	oo·na *fe*·rya de *mwes*·tras

I'm here with …	Estoy aquí con …	es·*toy* a·*kee* kon …
my company	mi compañía	mee kom·pa·*nyee*·a
my colleague(s)	mi(s) colega(s)	mee(s) ko·*le*·ga(s)
(two) others	otros (dos)	o·tros (dos)

I'm alone.
Estoy solo/a. m/f   es·*toy* so·lo/a

I'm staying at the (Hotel Libertad), room (82).
Me estoy alojando en el (Hotel Libertad), habitación (ochenta y dos).
me es·*toy* a·lo·*khan*·do en el (o·tel lee·ber·*ta*) a·bee·ta·*syon* (o·*chen*·ta ee dos)

I'm here for (two) days/weeks.
Estoy aquí por (dos) días/semanas.
es·*toy* a·*kee* por (dos) *dee*·as/se·*ma*·nas

I have an appointment with (Mr Gonzáles).
Tengo una cita con (el Señor Gonzáles).
ten·go oo·na *see*·ta kon (el se·*nyor* gon·*sa*·les)

Here's my business card.
Aquí tiene mi tarjeta de visita.
a·*kee* tye·ne mee tar·*khe*·ta de vee·*see*·ta

Let me introduce you to my colleague.
¿Puedo presentarle a mi colega?
pwe·do pre·sen·*tar*·le a mee ko·*le*·ga

That went very well.
Eso salió muy bien.
e·so sa·*lyo* mooy byen

Shall we go for a drink/meal?
¿Vamos a tomar/comer algo?
va·mos a to·*mar*/ko·*mer* al·go

Where's the ...?	¿Dónde está ...?	don·de es·ta ...
business centre	el servicio secretarial	el ser·vee·syo se·kre·ta·ryal
conference	el congreso	el kon·gre·so
meeting	la reunión	la re·oo·nyon
I need ...	Necesito ...	ne·se·see·to ...
a computer	una computadora	oo·na kom·poo·ta·do·ra
a connection to the Net	una conexión al Internet	oo·na ko·nek·syon al een·ter·net
an interpreter	un/una intérprete m/f	oon/oo·na een·ter·pre·te
more business cards	más tarjetas de visita	mas tar·khe·tas de vee·see·ta
some space to set up	espacio para disponer	es·pa·syo pa·ra dees·po·ner
to send an email/fax	enviar un email/fax	en·vyar oon ee·mayl/faks
I'm expecting a ...	Estoy esperando ...	es·toy es·pe·ran·do ...
call	una llamada	oo·na lya·ma·da
fax	un fax	oon faks

don't worry, don't hurry

The attitude towards time is more relaxed in Latin American countries than in the English-speaking world. Latin Americans do differentiate, however, between formal and social occasions and are usually more punctual for the former.

When arranging a business meeting, try adding the expres–sion *en punto* (equivalent to the English 'sharp') to the time expression, eg, *a las once en punto* means 'at 11 o'clock sharp'.

For social occasions, it's common to show up at least half an hour later than the designated time. If you don't want to be kept waiting, you could ask, when arranging to meet, if the appointed time is *a la hora inglesa* (lit: on English time) meaning promptly, or *a la hora latina* (lit: on Latin American time), ie, approximately half an hour later than specified.

I have a disability.
Soy discapacitado/a. m/f — soy dees·ka·pa·see·*ta*·do/a

I need assistance.
Necesito asistencia. — ne·se·*see*·to a·sees·*ten*·sya

I have a hearing aid.
Llevo audífono. — *lye*·vo ow·*dee*·fo·no

I'm deaf.
Soy sordo/a. m/f — soy *sor*·do/a

What services do you have for people with a disability?
¿Qué servicios tienen para — ke ser·*vee*·syos *tye*·nen *pa*·ra
discapacitados? — dees·ka·pa·see·*ta*·dos

Is there wheelchair access?
¿Hay acceso para silla — ai ak·*se*·so *pa*·ra *see*·lya
de ruedas? — de *rwe*·das

Is there a lift?
¿Hay ascensor? — ai a·sen·*sor*

How many steps are there?
¿Cuántos escalones hay? — *kwan*·tos es·ka·*lo*·nes ai

How wide is the entrance?
¿Cuánto es de ancha la — *kwan*·to es de *an*·cha la
entrada? — en·*tra*·da

Are guide dogs permitted?
¿Se permite la entrada — se per·*mee*·te la en·*tra*·da
a los perros guía? — a los *pe*·ros *gee*·a

Is there somewhere I can sit down?
¿Hay algún sitio dónde me — ai al·*goon see*·tyo *don*·de me
pueda sentar? — *pwe*·da sen·*tar*

Could you call me a disabled taxi please?

¿Me podría llamar a un taxi para discapacitados?

me po·*dree*·a lya·*mar* a oon tak·*see pa*·ra dees·ka·pa·see·*ta*·dos

Could you help me cross this street?

¿Me puede ayudar a cruzar la calle?

me *pwe*·de a·yoo·*dar* a kroo·*sar* la *ka*·lye

Braille library	*biblioteca* f *Braille*	bee·blyo·*te*·ka *brai*·e·le
disabled person	*persona* f *discapacitada*	per·*so*·na dees·ka·pa·see·*ta*·da
guide dog	*perro* m *guía*	*pe*·ro *gee*·a
ramp	*rampa* f	*ram*·pa
space (to move around)	*espacio* m *(para moverse)*	es·*pa*·syo (*pa*·ra mo·*ver*·se)
wheelchair	*silla* f *de ruedas*	*see*·lya de *rwe*·das

gender rules

When you see an m it means masculine, so the article you use should be either *un* or *el* . When you see an f it means feminine, so the article should be either *una* or *la*.

Where an -*o* ending and an -*a* ending mark masculine and feminine forms respectively we've used a slash. For example, the two forms of the word 'beautiful' *lindo* and *linda* are written *lindo/a*.

Where the only difference between masculine and feminine forms is the addition of an -*a* ending for the feminine form, we've used brackets. Hence the two forms of the word 'doctor', *doctor* and *doctora*, are abbreviated to *doctor(a)*.

Also see **gender** in the **a–z phrasebuilder**, page 17.

Is there a/an ...?	¿Hay ...?	ai ...
baby change room	una sala en la que pueda cambiarle el pañal al bebé	oo·na sa·la en la ke pwe·da kam·byar·le el pa·nyal al be·be
child-minding service	servicio de cuidado de niños	ser·vee·syo de kwee·da·do de nee·nyos
children's menu	menú infantil	me·noo een·fan·teel
creche	guardería	gwar·de·ree·a
(English-speaking) babysitter	niñera (de habla inglesa)	nee·nye·ra (de a·bla een·gle·sa)
family discount	descuento familiar	des·kwen·to fa·mee·lyar
highchair	trona	tro·na
park	un parque	oon par·ke
playground nearby	un parque infantil cercano	oon par·ke een·fan·teel ser·ka·no
theme park	un parque de atracciones	oon par·ke de a·trak·syo·nes
toyshop	una juguetería	oo·na khoo·ge·te·ree·a
I need a ...	Necesito ...	ne·se·see·to ...
baby seat	un asiento de seguridad para bebés	oon a·syen·to de se·goo·ree·da pa·ra be·bes
booster seat	un asiento de seguridad para niños	oon a·syen·to de se·goo·ree·da pa·ra nee·nyos
potty	una bacinica (SAm) una pelela	oo·na ba·see·nee·ka oo·na pe·le·la
stroller	un cochecito	oon ko·che·see·to

Do you mind if I breast-feed here?

¿Le molesta que dé   le mo·*les*·ta ke de
de pecho aquí?   de *pe*·cho a·*kee*

Are children allowed?

¿Se admiten niños?   se ad·*mee*·ten *nee*·nyos

Is this suitable for (two)-year-old children?

¿Es apto para niños de   es *ap*·to *pa*·ra *nee*·nyos de
(dos) años?   (dos) *a*·nyos

kids' talk

When's your birthday?

¿Cuándo es tu   *kwan*·do es too
cumpleaños?   koom·ple·*a*·nyos

Do you go to school or kindergarten?

¿Vas al colegio o   vas al ko·*le*·khyo o
a la guardería?   a la gwar·de·*ree*·a

What grade are you in?

¿En qué grado estás?   en ke *gra*·do es·*tas*

Do you like school?

¿Te gusta el colegio?   te *goos*·ta el ko·*le*·khyo

Do you like sport?

¿Te gusta el deporte?   te *goos*·ta el de·*por*·te

What do you do after school?

¿Qué haces después del   ke *a*·ses des·*pwes* del
colegio?   ko·*le*·khyo

Do you learn English?

¿Aprendes inglés?   a·*pren*·des een·*gles*

I come from very far away.

Vengo de muy lejos.   *ven*·go de mooy *le*·khos

Show me how to play.

Dime cómo se juega.   *dee*·me *ko*·mo se *khwe*·ga

Well done!

¡Muy bien!   mooy byen

basics

lo básico

Yes.	*Sí.*	see
No.	*No.*	no
Please.	*Por favor.*	por fa·*vor*
Thank you (very much).	*(Muchas) Gracias.*	(*moo*·chas) *gra*·syas
You're welcome.	*De nada.*	de *na*·da
(CAm)	*Con mucho gusto.*	kon *moo*·cho *goo*·sto
Sorry. (condolence)	*Lo siento.*	lo *syen*·to
Sorry. (apology)	*Perdón.*	per·*don*

Excuse me. (regret)
Perdón.   per·*don*

Excuse me. (for attention or apology)
Discúlpe.   dees·*kool*·pe
Con permiso. **(CAm)**   kon per·*mee*·so

greetings

saludos

Latin Americans are cordial yet polite when dealing with others and will expect you to reciprocate. Never address a stranger without extending a greeting such as *buenos días* (good morning) or *buenas tardes* (good afternoon). These are shortened to *buenos* and *buenas* in Central America and the Andean countries.

Hello./Hi.	*¡Hola!*	*o*·la
(Chi)	*¿Qué hubo?*	ke *oo*·bo
Good day.	*Buen día.*	bwen *dee*·a
Good morning.	*Buenos días.*	*bwe*·nos *dee*·as
Good afternoon. (until 8pm)	*Buenas tardes.*	*bwe*·nas *tar*·des
Good evening/night.	*Buenas noches.*	*bwe*·nas *no*·ches

meeting people

89

See you later.	*Hasta luego.*	as·ta *lwe*·go
Goodbye.	*¡Adiós!*	a·*dyos*
Bye.	*Chao./Chaucito.*	chow/chow·*see*·to

getting friendly

Spanish has two forms for the singular 'you'. With people you know well, with your peers and with children, use the informal form *tú*. When addressing strangers, older people, or people that you've just met, use the polite form *usted*. Once your new-found friends feel it's time to switch to *tú* they may say:

Let's use the tú form.

Hablemos de tú.   a·*ble*·mos de too

Also see **you** in the **a–z phrasebuilder**.

How are you?

¿Cómo está? pol	*ko*·mo es·*ta*
¿Cómo estás? inf	*ko*·mo es·*tas*
¿Cómo están? pl pol&inf	*ko*·mo es·*tan*

Fine, thank you.

Bien, gracias.   byen *gra*·syas

And you?

¿Y usted/tú? pol/inf   ee oos·*te*/too

What's your name?

| *¿Cómo se llama usted?* pol | *ko*·mo se *lya*·ma oos·*te* |
| *¿Cómo te llamas?* inf | *ko*·mo te *lya*·mas |

My name is …

Me llamo …   me *lya*·mo …

I'd like to introduce you to …

Quisiera presentarle/te   kee·*sye*·ra pre·sen·*tar*·le/te
a … pol/inf   a …

I'm pleased to meet you.

Mucho gusto.   moo·cho *goos*·to

SOCIAL

90

titles & addressing people

Women are mostly addressed as *Señora* regardless of age or marital status, though some older unmarried women may prefer to be called *Señorita*. Men are usually addressed as *Señor*. Professional titles are important too and should be used before the surname when addressing someone directly.

Mr	*Señor*	se·*nyor*
Ms/Mrs	*Señora*	se·*nyo*·ra
Miss	*Señorita*	se·nyo·*ree*·ta

Architect
Arquitecto/a m/f   ar·kee·*tek*·to/a

Doctor (holder of a PhD or medical doctor)
Doctor/Doctora m/f   dok·*tor*/dok·*to*·ra

Graduate
Licenciado/a m/f   lee·sen·*sya*·do/a

Engineer
Ingeniero/a m/f   een·khe·*nye*·ro/a

Lawyer
Abogado/a m/f   a·bo·*ga*·do/a

Professor (teacher or university lecturer or professor)
Profesor/Profesora m/f   pro·fe·*sor*/pro·fe·*so*·ra

Master (teacher or skilled musician or craftsman)
Maestro/a m/f   ma·*es*·tro/a

hey mate!

Friends may call each other *tío* tee·o (lit: uncle) or *tía* tee·a (lit: aunt). It's a bit like saying 'bloke' or 'sheila' in Australian slang. Guys may call each other *colega* ko·*le*·ga (lit: colleague) or may be addressed, or address one another, as *hombre* om·bre (lit: man). Women may be addressed, or address one another, as *mujer* moo·*kher* (lit: woman). In the Southern Cone countries of Argentina, Paraguay and Uruguay you may also hear the term *che* che used to address a man or boy.

making conversation

Do you live here?
¿Vive/Vives aquí? pol/inf
vee·ve/vee·ves a·kee

Where are you going?
¿Adónde va/vas? pol/inf
a·don·de va/vas

What are you doing?
¿Qué hace/haces? pol/inf
ke a·se/a·ses

Are you waiting (for a bus)?
¿Está/Estás esperando
(un autobús)? pol/inf
es·ta/es·tas es·pe·ran·do
(oon ow·to·boos)

Can I have a light, please?
¿Tiene/Tienes fuego,
por favor? pol/inf
tye·ne/tye·nes fwe·go
por fa·vor

What's this called?
¿Cómo se llama esto?
ko·mo se lya·ma es·to

What a beautiful baby!
¡Qué niño/a más lindo/a! m/f
ke nee·nyo/a mas leen·do/a

That's (beautiful), isn't it?
Qué (precioso), ¿no?
ke (pre·syo·so) no

Are you here on holiday?
¿Está/Estás aquí de
vacaciones? pol/inf
es·ta/es·tas a·kee de
va·ka·syo·nes

How long are you here for?
¿Cuánto tiempo le va a
quedar? pol
kwan·to tyem·po le va a
ke·dar
¿Cuánto tiempo te vas a
quedar? inf
kwan·to tyem·po te vas a
ke·dar

I'm here for (four) weeks/days.
Estoy aquí por (cuatro)
semanas/días.
es·toy a·kee por (kwa·tro)
se·ma·nas/dee·as

Do you like it here?
¿Le/Te gusta esto? pol/inf
le/te goos·ta es·to

I love it here.
Me encanta esto.
me en·kan·ta es·to

SOCIAL

92

I'm here …	Estoy aquí …	es·toy a·kee …
for a holiday	de vacaciones	de va·ka·syo·nes
on business	en viaje de negocios	en vya·khe de ne·go·syos
to study	estudiando	es·too·dyan·do
with my family	con mi familia	kon mee fa·mee·lya
with my partner	con mi pareja m&f	kon mee pa·re·kha

This is my …	Éste/a es mi … m/f	es·ta/e es mee …
child	hijo/a m/f	ee·kho/a
colleague	colega m&f	ko·le·ga
friend	amigo/a m/f	a·mee·go/a
husband	esposo	es·po·so
partner (intimate)	pareja m&f	pa·re·kha
wife	esposa	es·po·sa

local talk

Hey!	¡Eh, tú!	e too
What's up?	¿Qué onda?	ke on·da
What's happening?	¿Qué pasó?	ke pa·so
It's/I'm OK.	Está/Estoy bien.	es·ta/es·toy byen
Listen (to this)!	¡Escucha (esto)!	es·koo·cha (es·to)
Look!	¡Mira!	mee·ra
How cool!	¡Qué bárbaro!	ke bar·ba·ro
(Arg)	¡Se pasa!	se pa·sa
(Ven)	¡Chévere!	che·ve·re
Just joking.	Te estoy tomando el pelo.	te es·toy to·man·do el pe·lo
(Arg)	Te estoy cargando.	te es·toy kar·gan·do
No problem.	No hay drama.	no ai dra·ma
Maybe.	Quizás.	kee·sas
No way!	¡De ningún modo!	de neen·goon mo·do
Sure.	Macanudo.	ma·ka·noo·do

nationalities

Where are you from?
¿De dónde es/eres? pol/inf   de *don*·de es/*e*·res

I'm from ...   *Soy de ...*   soy de ...
  Australia   *Australia*   ow·*stra*·lya
  Germany   *Alemania*   a·le·*ma*·nya
  Scotland   *Escocia*   es·*ko*·sya
  the USA   *Los Estados*   los es·*ta*·dos
        Unidos   oo·*nee*·dos

For more countries, see the **dictionary**.

age

la edad

How old ...?   *¿Cuántos años ...?*   *kwan*·tos *a*·nyos ...
  are you   *tiene/tienes* pol/inf   *tye*·ne/*tye*·nes
  is your   *tiene su/tu*   *tye*·ne soo/too
    daughter   *hija* pol/inf   *ee*·kha
  is your son   *tiene su/tu*   *tye*·ne soo/too
        hijo pol/inf   *ee*·kho

I'm ... years old.
  Tengo ... años.   *ten*·go ... *a*·nyos
He's/She's ... years old.
  Tiene ... años.   *tye*·ne ... *a*·nyos
Too old!
  ¡Demasiado viejo/a! m/f   de·ma·*sya*·do *vye*·kho/a
I'm younger than I look.
  Soy más joven de lo que   soy mas *kho*·ven de lo ke
  parezco.   pa·*res*·ko

For your age, see **numbers**, page 29.

occupations & studies

What's your occupation?
¿A qué le dedica? pol — a ke le de·dee·ka
¿A qué te dedicas? inf — a ke te de·dee·kas

I'm self-employed.
Soy trabajador/ — soy tra·ba·kha·*dor/*
trabajadora — tra·ba·kha·*do*·ra
autónomo/a. m/f — ow·*to*·no·mo/a

I'm a/an ... *Soy ...* soy ...
  architect *arquitecto/a* m/f ar·kee·*tek*·to/a
  mechanic *mecánico/a* m/f me·*ka*·nee·ko/a
  writer *escritor/* es·kree·*tor/*
  escritora m/f es·kree·*to*·ra

I work in ... *Trabajo en ...* tra·*ba*·kho en ...
  communications *comunicaciones* ko·moo·nee·ka·*syo*·nes
  education *enseñanza* en·se·*nyan*·sa
  hospitality *hostelería* os·te·le·*ree*·a

I'm ... *Estoy ...* es·*toy* ...
  retired *jubilado/a* m/f khoo·bee·*la*·do/a
  unemployed *desempleado/a* m/f des·em·ple·*a*·do/a

What are you studying?
¿Qué estudia/estudias? pol/inf ke es·*too*·dya/es·*too*·dyas

I'm studying ... *Estudio ...* es·*too*·dyo ...
  business *economía* e·ko·no·*mee*·a
  languages *idiomas* ee·*dyo*·mas
  science *ciencias* *syen*·syas

I'm studying at …	Estudio en …	es·too·dyo en …
college	un instituto	oon een·stee·too·to
school	un colegio	oon ko·le·khyo
trade school	un instituto	oon een·stee·too·to
	técnico	tek·nee·ko
university	una	oo·na
	universidad	oo·nee·ver·see·da

For more occupations and studies, see the **dictionary**.

family

la familia

Do you have (a brother)?
¿Tiene/Tienes   tye·ne/tye·nes
(hermano)? pol/inf   (er·ma·no)

I have (a partner).
Tengo (pareja). m&f   ten·go (pa·re·kha)

Do you live with (your family)?
¿Vive/Vives con (su/tu   vee·ve/vee·ves kon (soo/too
familia)? pol/inf   fa·mee·lya)

I live with (my sister).
Vivo con (mi hermana).   vee·vo kon (mee er·ma·na)

This is (my mother).
Ésta es (mi madre).   es·ta es (mee ma·dre)

Are you married?
¿Está casado/a? m/f pol   es·ta ka·sa·do/a
¿Estás casado/a? m/f inf   es·tas ka·sa·do/a

I live with someone.
Vivo con alguien.   vee·vo kon al·gyen

I'm single.
Soy soltero/a. m/f   soy sol·te·ro/a

I'm …	Estoy …	es·toy …
married	casado/a m/f	ka·sa·do/a
separated	separado/a m/f	se·pa·ra·do/a

For more kinship terms, see the **dictionary**.

farewells

Tomorrow is my last day here.
Mañana es mi   ma·*nya*·na es mee
último día aquí.   ool·tee·mo *dee*·a a·kee

Here's my …	*Ésta es mi …*	es·ta es mee …
What's your …?	*¿Cuál es tu …?*	kwal es too …
(email) address	*dirección*	dee·rek·*syon*
	(de email)	(de *ee*·mayl)
fax number	*número de fax*	*noo*·me·ro de faks
mobile number	*número de*	*noo*·me·ro de
	móvil	mo·veel
work number	*número de*	*noo*·mero de
	teléfono en el	te·*le*·fo·no en el
	trabajo	tra·*ba*·kho

If you ever visit (Scotland) come and visit us.
Si algún día visitas   see al·*goon* dee·a vee·*see*·tas
(Escocia) ven a vernos.   (es·*ko*·sya) ven a *ver*·nos

If you ever visit (the USA) you can stay with me.
Si algún día visitas (los   see al·*goon* dee·a vee·*see*·tas (los
Estados Unidos) te puedes   es·*ta*·dos oo·*nee*·dos) te *pwe*·des
quedar conmigo.   ke·*dar* kon·*mee*·go

body language

Personal space boundaries vary from culture to culture and in Latin America they're set closer than in Anglo-Saxon countries. You'll probably find that people stand closer to you when talking than you're used to. Casual touching on the arm or shoulder during conversation is not outside the norm so don't be taken aback if it happens to you. You'll observe good friends greeting each other with an *abrazo* a·*bra*·so (hug) or *beso be*·so (kiss) and and it's quite usual to see people of the same sex walking down the street arm-in-arm.

I want to come and visit you.
   Quiero venir a visitarte.   kye·ro ve·*neer* a vee·see·*tar*·te

I'll send you copies of the photos.
   Te enviaré copias de   te en·vya·*re* ko·pyas de
   las fotos.   las *fo*·tos

It's been great meeting you.
   Me ha encantado conocerte.   me a en·kan·*ta*·do ko·no·*ser*·te

I'll miss you.
   Te voy a echar de menos.   te voy a e·*char* de *me*·nos

Keep in touch!
   ¡Nos mantendremos en   nos man·ten·*dre*·mos en
   contacto!   kon·*tak*·to

---

melting pot

Latin American Spanish reflects the rich ethnic mix of the region. A good example of this are the few words coined to refer to people with respect to their heritage. These terms aren't racially loaded labels and are used by people to refer to themselves and their background.

   criollo/a m/f   kree·o·lo/a
     person born in Latin America of Spanish ancestry. On the Caribbean Coast, a person of mixed African and European ancestry.

   ladino/a m/f   la·*dee*·no/a
     Spanish-speaking person of mixed Indian and European ancestry

   mestizo/a m/f   mes·*tee*·so/a
     person of mixed ancestry (usually Spanish and Indian)

   zambo/a m/f   *sam*·bo/a
     person of mixed African and Indian ancestry

Avoid using the term *indio/a* m/f 'Indian' which can be offensive to indigenous people. *Indígena* een·*dee*·khe·na is the preferred option.

common interests

los intereses en común

What do you do in your spare time?
¿Qué te gusta hacer en tu   ke te *goos*·ta a·*ser* en too
tiempo libre?   *tyem*·po *lee*·bre

Do you like ...?   *¿Te gusta/*   te *goos*·ta/
                       gustan ...? sg/pl   *goos*·tan ...
I (don't) like ... *(No) Me gusta/*   (no) me *goos*·ta/
                        gustan ... sg/pl   *goos*·tan ...
  board games *los juegos* m pl   los *khwe*·gos
                             de tablero   de ta·*ble*·ro
  cooking   *cocinar*   ko·see·*nar*
  films   *el cine* sg   el *see*·ne
  travelling   *viajar*   vya·*khar*

For more hobbies and types of sports, see **sport**, page 125, and the **dictionary**.

---

like it or not

In Spanish, in order to say you like something, you say *me gusta* (lit: me it-pleases). If what you're referring to is plural, use *me gustan* (lit: me they-please). If you're referring to an activity, eg, cooking or travelling, use *me gusta* followed by the verb.

I like that song.
Me gusta esta canción.   me *goos*·ta *es*·ta kan·*syon*

I like soap operas.
Me gustan las telenovelas. me *goos*·tan las te·le·no·*ve*·las

I like dancing.
Me gusta bailar.   me *goos*·ta bai·*lar*

music

Do you like to …?	Te gusta …?	te *goos*·ta …
dance	*bailar*	bai·*lar*
go to concerts	*ir a conciertos*	eer a kon·*syer*·tos
listen to music	*escuchar*	es·koo·*char*
	música	*moo*·see·ka
play an	*tocar un*	to·*kar* oon
instrument	*instrumento*	een·stroo·*men*·to
sing	*cantar*	kan·*tar*

What bands do you like?
  ¿Qué grupos te gustan?   ke *groo*·pos te *goos*·tan

What music do you like?
  ¿Qué música te gusta?   ke *moo*·see·ka te *goos*·ta

classical music	*música* f *clásica*	*moo*·see·ka *kla*·see·ka
electronic music	*música* f	*moo*·see·ka
	electrónica	e·lek·*tro*·nee·ka
merengue	*merengue* m	me·*ren*·ge
pop	*música* f *pop*	*moo*·see·ka pop
R&B	*rhythm and blues* m	*ree*·dem en bloos
rock	*música* f *rock*	*moo*·see·ka rok
salsa	*salsa* f	*sal*·sa
tango	*tango* m	*tan*·go
traditional	*música* f	*moo*·see·ka
music	*folclórica*	fol·*klo*·ree·ka
world music	*música* f *étnica*	*moo*·see·ka *et*·nee·ka

Planning to go to a concert? See **buying tickets**, page 39 and **going out**, page 109.

---

idiosyncratic interests

Here's a quirky Latin American equivalent of the English saying 'To each his own'.

Cada perico a su estaca, cada changa a su mecate.
ka·da pe·*ree*·ko a soo es·*ta*·ka ka·da *chan*·ga a soo me·*ka*·te
(lit: each parrot on its perch, each monkey on its rope)

cinema & theatre

el cine & el teatro

I feel like going to a …	Tengo ganas de ir a …	ten·go ga·nas de eer a …
ballet	un ballet	oon ba·le
comedy	una comedia	oo·na ko·me·dya
film	una película	oo·na pe·lee·koo·la
play	una obra	oo·na o·bra

What's showing at the cinema (tonight)?
¿Qué película dan en el cine (esta noche)?
ke pe·lee·koo·la dan en el see·ne (es·ta no·che)

Is it in English/Spanish?
¿Es en inglés/castellano?
es en een·gles/kas·te·lya·no

Does it have (English) subtitles?
¿Tiene subtítulos (en inglés)?
tye·ne soob·tee·too·los (en een·gles)

I want to sell this ticket.
Quiero vender esta entrada.
kye·ro ven·der es·ta en·tra·da

Are those seats taken?
¿Están libres estos asientos?
es·tan lee·bres es·tos a·syen·tos

Have you seen …?
¿Has visto …?
as vees·to …

Who's in it?
¿Quién actúa?
kyen ak·too·a

It stars …
Actúa …
ak·too·a …

Did you like (the film)?
Te gustó (la película)?
te goos·to (la pe·lee·koo·la)

I thought it was …	Pienso que fue …	pyen·so ke fwe …
crap	una porquería	oo·na por·ke·ree·a
excellent	excelente	ek·se·len·te
long	larga	lar·ga

animated films	*películas* f pl *de dibujos animados*	pe·*lee*·koo·las de dee·*boo*·khos a·nee·*ma*·dos
comedies	*comedias* f pl	ko·*me*·dyas
documentaries	*documentales* m pl	do·koo·men·*ta*·les
drama	*drama* m	*dra*·ma
film noir	*cine* m *negro*	*see*·ne *ne*·gro
(Latin American) cinema	*cine* m (*latino-americano*)	*see*·ne (la·tee·no·a·me·ree·*ka*·no)
horror movies	*cine* m *de terror*	*see*·ne de te·*ror*
sci-fi	*cine* m *de ciencia ficción*	*see*·ne de *syen*·sya feek·*syon*
short films	*cortos* m pl	*kor*·tos
thrillers	*cine* m *de suspenso*	*see*·ne de soos·*pen*·so

reading

la lectura

What kind of books do you read?
¿Qué tipo de libros lees?   ke *tee*·po de *lee*·bros *le*·es

Which (Latin American) author do you recommend?
¿Qué autor (latino-americano) recomiendas?   ke ow·*tor* (la·tee·no·a·me·ree·*ka*·no) re·ko·*myen*·das

Have you read (Pablo Neruda)?
¿Has leído a (Pablo Neruda)?   as le·*ee*·do a (*pa*·blo ne·*roo*·da)

On this trip I'm reading (One Hundred Years of Solitude).
En este viaje estoy leyendo (Cien años de soledad).   en *es*·te *vya*·khe es·*toy* ley·*en*·do (syen *a*·nyos de so·le·*da*)

I'd recommend (Jorge Luís Borges).
Recomiendo a (Jorge Luís Borges).   re·ko·*myen*·do a (*khor*·khe loo·*ees* bor·khes)

Where can I exchange books?
¿Dónde puedo cambiar libros?   *don*·de *pwe*·do kam·*byar* *lee*·bros

For more on books, see **shopping**, page 68.

feelings & opinions

feelings

los sentimientos

Feelings are described with either nouns or adjectives: the nouns use 'have' in Spanish (eg, 'I have hunger') and the adjectives use 'be' (like in English).

I'm (not) …	(No) Tengo …	(no) ten·go …
Are you …?	¿Tiene(s)…? pol/inf	tye·ne(s) …
cold	frío	free·o
hot	calor	ka·lor
hungry	hambre	am·bre

I'm (not) …	(No) Estoy …	(no) es·toy …
Are you …?	¿Está(s) …? pol/inf	es·ta(s) …
annoyed	enojado/a m/f	e·no·kha·do/a
embarrassed	avergonzado/a m/f	a·ver·gon·sa·do/a
tired	cansado/a m/f	kan·sa·do/a

opinions

opiniones

Did you like it?
¿Le/Te gustó? pol/inf   le/te goos·to

What did you think of it?
¿Qué pensó/pensaste   ke pen·so/pen·sas·te
de eso? pol/inf   de e·so

I thought it was …	Pienso que fue …	pyen·so ke fwe …
It's …	Es …	es …
beautiful	bonito/a m/f	bo·nee·to/a
bizarre	raro/a m/f	ra·ro/a
crap	un coñazo	oon ko·nya·so
entertaining	entretenido/a m/f	en·tre·te·nee·do/a
excellent	fantástico/a m/f	fan·tas·tee·ko/a
full-on	total	to·tal

mixed emotions

Generally, *un poco*, *bastante* and *muy* are used to qualify feelings.

a little	*un poco*	oon *po*·ko
I'm a little sad.	*Estoy un poco triste.*	es·*toy* oon *po*·ko *trees*·te
quite	*bastante*	bas·*tan*·te
I'm quite disappointed.	*Estoy bastante decepcionado/a.* m/f	es·*toy* bas·*tan*·te de·sep·syo·*na*·do/a
very	*muy*	mooy
I feel very lucky.	*Me siento muy afortunado/a.* m/f	me *syen*·to mooy a·for·too·*na*·do/a

politics & social issues

la política & los temas sociales

The political scene is notoriously volatile in many Latin American countries and politics are the subject of much conversation and debate. People will probably be interested to hear your opinions but be tactful as passions can run high on certain issues.

Who do you vote for?
   ¿A quién vota/votas? pol/inf   a kyen *vo*·ta/*vo*·tas

I support the ... party.	*Apoyo al partido ...*	a·*po*·yo al par·*tee*·do ...
I'm a member of the ... party.	*Soy miembro del partido ...*	soy *myem*·bro del par·*tee*·do ...
communist	*comunista*	ko·moo·*nees*·ta
conservative	*conservador*	kon·ser·va·*dor*
green	*verde*	*ver*·de
labour	*laborista*	la·bo·*rees*·ta
liberal (progressive)	*progre*	*pro*·gre
social democratic	*socialdemócrata*	so·syal·de·*mo*·kra·ta
socialist	*socialista*	so·sya·*lees*·ta

Do you agree with it?
¿Está/Estás de acuerdo con eso? pol/inf — es·*ta*/es·*tas* de a·*kwer*·do kon *e*·so

I (don't) agree with …
(No) Estoy de acuerdo con … — (no) es·*toy* de a·*kwer*·do kon …

Are you against …?
¿Está/Estás en contra de …? pol/inf — es·*ta*/es·*tas* en *kon*·tra de …

Are you in favour of …?
¿Está/Estás a favor de …? pol/inf — es·*ta*/es·*tas* a fa·*vor* de …

How do people feel about …?
¿Cómo se siente la gente de …? — *ko*·mo se *syen*·te la *khen*·te de …

abortion	*aborto* m	a·*bor*·to
corruption	*corrupción* f	ko·roop·*syon*
crime	*crimen* m	*kree*·men
discrimination	*discriminación* f	dees·kree·mee·na·*syon*
drugs	*drogas* f pl	*dro*·gas
the economy	*economía* f	e·ko·no·*mee*·a
education	*educación* f	e·doo·ka·*syon*
the environment	*medio* m *ambiente*	*me*·dyo am·*byen*·te
equal opportunity	*igualdad* f *de oportunidades*	ee·gwal·*da* de o·por·too·nee·*da*·des
euthanasia	*eutanasia* f	e·oo·ta·*na*·sya
globalisation	*globalización* f	glo·ba·lee·sa·*syon*
human rights	*derechos* m pl *humanos*	de·*re*·chos oo·*ma*·nos
immigration	*inmigración* f	een·mee·gra·*syon*
party politics	*política* f *de partido*	po·*lee*·tee·ka de par·*tee*·do
privatisation	*privatización* f	pree·va·tee·sa·*syon*
racism	*racismo* m	ra·*sees*·mo
sexism	*sexismo* m	sek·*sees*·mo
social welfare	*estado* m *del bienestar*	es·*ta*·do del byen·es·*tar*
terrorism	*terrorismo* m	te·ro·*rees*·mo
unemployment	*desempleo* m	des·em·*ple*·o

feelings & opinions

the environment

Is there a/an (environmental) problem here?
  ¿Aquí hay un problema (con   a·kee ai oon pro·ble·ma (kon
  el medio ambiente)?   el me·dyo am·byen·te)

conservation	conservación f	kon·ser·va·syon
deforestation	deforestación f	de·fo·res·ta·syon
drought	sequía f	se·kee·a
ecosystem	ecosistema m	e·ko·sees·te·ma
hunting	caza f	ka·sa
hydroelectricity	hidroelectricidad f	ee·dro·e·lek·tree·see·da
irrigation	irrigación f	ee·ree·ga·syon
ozone layer	capa f de ozono	ka·pa de o·so·no
pesticides	pesticidas f pl	pes·tee·see·das
pollution	contaminación f	kon·ta·mee·na·syon
recycling programme	programa m de reciclaje	pro·gra·ma de re·see·kla·khe
toxic waste	residuos m pl tóxicos	re·see·dwos tok·see·kos
water supply	suministro m de agua	soo·mee·nees·tro de a·gwa

Is this a protected ...?	¿Es este/a ... protegido/a? m/f	es es·te/a ... pro·te·khee·do/a
forest	un bosque m	oon bos·ke
park	un parque m	oon par·ke
species	una especie f	oo·na es·pe·sye

local talk

Absolutely!	¡Por supuesto!	por soo·pwes·to
Come off it!	¡No me jodas!	no me kho·das
Exactly!	¡Exactamente!	ek·sak·ta·men·te
How interesting!	¡Qué interesante!	ke een·te·re·san·te
In your dreams!	¡Anda ya!	an·da ya
No way!	¡Ni hablar!	nee a·blar
Sure!	¡Claro!	kla·ro
That's not true!	¡Eso no es verdad!	e·so no es ver·da

where to go

adónde ir

What's there to do in the evenings?

¿Qué se puede hacer por las noches?		ke se *pwe*·de a·*ser* por las *no*·ches

What's on …? | ¿Qué hay …? | ke ai …
locally	*en la zona*	en la *so*·na
this weekend	*este fin de semana*	*es*·te feen de se·*ma*·na
today	*hoy*	oy
tonight	*esta noche*	*es*·ta *no*·che

Where are the …? | ¿Dónde hay …? | *don*·de ai …
clubs	*clubs nocturnos*	kloobs nok·*toor*·nos
gay venues	*lugares gay*	loo·*ga*·res gay
places to eat	*lugares donde comer*	loo·*ga*·res *don*·de ko·*mer*
pubs	*bares*	*ba*·res

Is there a local … guide? | ¿Hay una guía de … de la zona? | ai *oo*·na *gee*·a de … de la *so*·na
entertainment	*espectáculos*	es·pek·*ta*·koo·los
film	*cine*	*see*·ne
music	*música*	*moo*·see·ka

put on your dancing shoes

In dance-crazy Latin America the general term for a dance club is *discoteca*. Dance clubs are also known by these regional terms:

Argentina:	*boliche* m	bo·*lee*·che
Colombia:	*salseadero* m	sal·se·a·*de*·ro
	rumbeadero m	room·be·a·*de*·ro
Ecuador:	*salsoteca* f	sal·so·*te*·ka

going out

Come on!	*¡Venga, vamos!*	*ven·ga va·mos*
This place is great!	*¡Es un lugar bárbaro!*	*es oon loo·gar bar·ba·ro*

I feel like going to …	*Tengo ganas de ir …*	*ten·go ga·nas de eer …*
a bar	*a un bar*	a oon bar
a cafe	*a una cafetería*	a oo·na ka·fe·te·ree·a
a concert	*a un concierto*	a oon kon·syer·to
a nightclub	*a una discoteca*	a oo·na dees·ko·te·ka
a party	*a una fiesta*	a oo·na fyes·ta
a restaurant	*a un restaurante*	a oon res·tow·ran·te
a salsa dance club	*a una salsoteca*	a oo·na sal·so·te·ka
a tango club	*a un club de tango*	a oon kloob de tan·go
the movies	*al cine*	al see·ne
the theatre	*al teatro*	al te·a·tro

What's the cover charge?
   ¿Cuánta cuesta entrar?   kwan·ta kwes·ta en·trar

It's free.
   Es gratis.   es gra·tees

Am I likely to be harassed for being gay?
   ¿Me van a molestar por ser   me van a mo·les·tar por ser
   homosexual?   o·mo·sek·swal

invitations

What are you doing …?	*¿Qué haces/ hacen …?* sg/pl	ke a·ses/ a·sen …
right now	*ahora*	a·o·ra
this evening	*esta noche*	es·ta no·che
this weekend	*este fin de semana*	es·te feen de se·ma·na

Would you like to go for a …?	*¿Te/Les gustaría ir a …?* sg/pl	te/les goos·ta·ree·a eer a …
coffee	*tomar un café*	to·mar oon ka·fe
drink	*tomar unos tragos*	to·mar oo·nos tra·gos
meal	*comer*	ko·mer
walk	*pasear*	pa·se·ar

I feel like going …	*Tengo ganas de …*	ten·go ga·nas de …
dancing	*ir a bailar*	eer a bai·lar
out somewhere	*salir*	sa·leer
out to lunch	*ir a almorzar*	eer a al·mor·sar
out to dinner	*ir a cenar*	eer a se·nar

Do you know a good restaurant?
   ¿Conoces/Conocen un   ko·no·ses/ko·no·sen oon
   buen restaurante? sg/pl   bwen res·tow·ran·te

Do you want to come to the (Inti-Illimani) concert with me?
   ¿Quieres/Quieren venir   kye·res/kye·ren ve·neer
   conmigo al concierto   kon·mee·go al kon·syer·to
   (de Inti-Illimani)? sg/pl   (de een·tee ee·lyee·ma·nee)

We're having a party.
Vamos a dar una fiesta.   *va*·mos a dar *oo*·na *fyes*·ta

You should come.
¿Por qué no vienes/vienen? **sg/pl**   por ke no *vye*·nes/*vye*·nen

responding to invitations

Sure!
¡Por supuesto!   por soo·*pwes*·to

Yes, I'd love to.
Me encantaría.   me en·kan·ta·*ree*·a

Yes, let's go.
Sí, vamos.   see *va*·mos

No, I'm afraid I can't.
Lo siento pero no puedo.   lo *syen*·to *pe*·ro no *pwe*·do

What about tomorrow?
¿Qué tal mañana?   ke tal ma·*nya*·na

Sorry, I can't sing/dance.
Lo siento, no sé cantar/bailar.   lo *syen*·to no se kan·*tar*/bai·*lar*

party animals

Latin Americans know how to let down their hair and *pasarlo guay* pa·*sar*·lo gway (have a good time). Here are some expressions which all mean 'going out drinking and partying' to help you get a slice of the action:

ir de copas	eer de *ko*·pas
ir de farra	eer de *fa*·ra
ir de rumba	eer de *room*·ba
ir de juerga	eer de *khwer*·ga
ir de fiesta	eer de *fyes*·ta
ir de pachanga	eer de pa·*chan*·ga

arranging to meet

What time shall we meet?
¿A qué hora quedamos? — a ke o·ra ke·*da*·mos

Where will we meet?
¿Dónde quedamos? — *don*·de ke·*da*·mos

Let's meet at (eight o'clock).
Quedamos a (las ocho). — ke·*da*·mos a (las o·cho)

Let's meet at the entrance.
Quedamos en la entrada. — ke·*da*·mos en la en·*tra*·da

I'll pick you up.
Paso a recogerte/ — *pa*·so a re·ko·*kher*·te/
recogerles. sg/pl — re·ko·*kher*·les

I'll be coming later.
Iré más tarde. — ee·*re* mas *tar*·de

Where will you be?
¿Dónde estarás/estarán? sg/pl — *don*·de es·ta·*ras*/es·ta·*ran*

If I'm not there by (nine), don't wait for me.
Si no estoy a (las nueve), — see no es·*toy* a (las *nwe*·ve)
no me esperes/esperen. sg/pl — no me es·*pe*·res/es·*pe*·ren

OK!
¡OK! — o·key

I'll see you then.
Nos vemos. — nos *ve*·mos

See you later/tomorrow.
Hasta luego/mañana. — *as*·ta *lwe*·go/ma·*nya*·na

I'm looking forward to it.
Tengo muchas ganas de ir. — *ten*·go *moo*·chas *ga*·nas de eer

Sorry I'm late.
Siento llegar tarde. — *syen*·to lye·*gar tar*·de

Never mind.
No importa. — no eem·*por*·ta

111

drugs

las drogas

I don't take drugs.
No consumo ningún no kon·*soo*·mo neen·*goon*
tipo de drogas. *tee*·po de *dro*·gas

I have … occasionally.
Tomo … de vez en cuando. *to*·mo … de ves en *kwan*·do

Do you want to have a smoke?
¿Nos fumamos un porro? nos foo·*ma*·mos oon *po*·ro

I'm high.
Estoy volado/a. m/f es·*toy* vo·*la*·do/a

latin american rhythms

Latin America has a profusion of musical styles. Pre-Colombian, Latin, Caribbean and African styles mesh to create a rich variety of rhythms, dances, regional styles and songs.

Música Andina *moo*·see·ka an·*dee*·na
Well known in the West, Andean music incorporates woodwind instruments of pre-Columbian origin such as the *quena* (reed flute), the *zampoña* (pan flute), the *caja* (tamourine-like drums) and the ukulele-like *charango*.

Música de Los Llanos *moo*·see·ka de los *lya*·nos
A Venezuelan and Colombian song style accompanied by a *cuatro* (harp) and maracas.

Música Criolla *moo*·see·ka kree·o·la
With its roots in Spain and Africa, the main instruments of Creole music are guitars and a *cajón* (wooden box drum).

Reggae *re*·gay
The reggae influence is strongly felt along the Caribbean coast of Central America.

Salsa *sal*·sa
This immensely popular dance style originated in New York but spread through the Caribbean in the 1960s.

Tango *tan*·go
Argentina is the birthplace of this musical style and it remains hugely popular today. A visit to a *club de tango* in Buenos Aires is an unforgettable experience.

asking someone out

Would you like to do something (tonight)?
¿Quieres hacer algo   *kye*·res a·*ser al*·go
(esta noche)?   (es·ta *no*·che)

Yes, I'd love to.
Me encantaría.   me en·kan·ta·*ree*·a

No, I'm afraid I can't.
Lo siento, pero no puedo.   lo *syen*·to *pe*·ro no *pwe*·do

I'm busy.
Estoy ocupado/a. m/f   es·*toy* o·koo·*pa*·do/a

Not if you were the last person on Earth!
¡Ni aunque fueras la   nee *own*·ke *fwe*·ras la
última persona en el   *ool*·tee·ma per·*so*·na en el
mundo!   *moon*·do

pick-up lines

Would you like a drink?
¿Puedo ofrecerte una copa?   *pwe*·do o·fre·*ser*·te *oo*·na *ko*·pa

What star sign are you?
¿Cuál es tu signo del   kwal es too *seeg*·no del
horóscopo?   o·*ros*·ko·po

Shall we get some fresh air?
¿Vamos a tomar el aire?   *va*·mos a to·*mar* el *ai*·re

Do you study or do you work?
¿Estudias o trabajas?   es·*too*·dyas o tra·*ba*·khas

Do you have a light?
¿Tienes fuego?   *tye*·nes *fwe*·go

You have (a) beautiful …	*Tíenes …*	*tye*·nes …
body	*un cuerpo precioso*	oon *kwer*·po pre·*syo*·so
eyes	*unos ojos preciosos*	*oo*·nos o·khos pre·*syo*·sos
hands	*unas manos preciosas*	*oo*·nas *ma*·nos pre·*syo*·sas
laugh	*una risa preciosa*	*oo*·na *ree*·sa pre·*syo*·sa
personality	*una personalidad preciosa*	*oo*·na per·so·na·lee·*da* pre·*syo*·sa

local talk

What a babe. (referring to a woman)
>*Qué hembra.* — ke *em*·bra
>*Qué mamacita.* **(Per)** — ke ma·ma·*see*·ta
>*Qué mina.* **(Arg)** — ke *mee*·na

He's/She's a hot guy/girl.
>*Está buenísimo/a.* **m/f** — es·*ta* bwe·*nee*·see·mo/a

He/She gets around.
>*Se va a la cama con cualquiera.* — se va a la *ka*·ma kon kwal·*kye*·ra

He's/She's a virgin and proud of it.
>*Es virgen y está orgulloso/a de eso.* **m/f** — es *veer*·khen ee es·*ta* or·goo·*lyo*·so/a de *e*·so

He's a jerk.
>*Él es un cabrón.* **m** — el es oon ka·*bron*

He's …	*Ella es …*	*el*·ya es …
a babe	*un bombón*	oon bom·*bon*
a bitch	*una loca*	*oo*·na *lo*·ka
	(SAm) *una yegua*	*oo*·na ye·gwa

He's/She's …	*Él/Ella es …*	el/*el*·ya es …
hot	*caliente* **m&f**	ka·*lyen*·te
gorgeous	*guapísimo/a* **m/f**	gwa·*pee*·see·mo/a
an idiot	**(SAm)** *conchudo/a* **m/f**	kon·*choo*·do/a

rejections

No, thank you.
No, gracias.   no *gra*·syas

I have a boyfriend/girlfriend.
Tengo novio/a. m/f   *ten*·go no·vyo/a

I'm here with my boyfriend/girlfriend.
Estoy aquí con mi novio/a. m/f   es·toy a·kee kon mee no·vyo/a

Excuse me, I have to go now.
Lo siento, pero me tengo que ir.   lo *syen*·to *pe*·ro me *ten*·go ke eer

Your ego is out of control.
Tu ego está fuera de control.   too *e*·go es·*ta fwe*·ra de kon·*trol*

I'm not interested.
No estoy interesado/a. m/f   no es·toy een·te·re·*sa*·do/a

Hey, I'm not interested in talking to you.
Mira tío/a, es que no me interesa hablar contigo. m/f   *mee*·ra *tee*·o/a es ke no me een·te·*re*·sa a·*blar* kon·*tee*·go

Leave me alone!
Déjame en paz.   *de*·kha·me en pas

Piss off!
¡Andate a la mierda!   an·da·te a la *myer*·da

getting closer

You're very nice.
Eres muy simpático/a. m/f   *e*·res mooy seem·*pa*·tee·ko/a

You're great.
Eres estupendo/a. m/f   *e*·res es·too·*pen*·do/a

You're very attractive.
Eres muy guapo/a. m/f   *e*·res mooy *gwa*·po/a

I'm interested in you.
  Me fascinas mucho. me fa·*see*·nas *moo*·cho

I like you very much.
  Me gustas mucho. me *goos*·tas *moo*·cho

Do you like me too?
  ¿Me tienes algo de me tye·nes *al*·go de
  cariño también? ka·*ree*·nyo tam·*byen*

Can I kiss you?
  ¿Te puedo besar? te *pwe*·do be·*sar*

Will you take me home?
  ¿Me acompañas a casa? me a·kom·*pa*·nyas a *ka*·sa

Do you want to come inside for a while?
  ¿Quieres entrar a tomar algo *kye*·res en·*trar* a to·*mar* al·go

---

false friend

To say you like something you use the expression *me gusta* me *goos*·ta (lit: me it-pleases). Beware of using this expression about people though, as to say *me gustas* (lit: me you-please) has erotic overtones. So, to say that you enjoy someone's company, a less risqué expression is *me caes bien* me *ka*·es byen which equates to the English 'I like you'.

---

sex

el sexo

I want to make love to you.
  Quiero hacerte el amor. *kye*·ro a·*ser*·te el a·*mor*

Do you have a condom?
  ¿Tienes un condón? *tye*·nes oon kon·*don*

I won't do it without protection.
  No lo haré sin preservativos. no lo a·*re* seen pre·ser·va·*tee*·vos

I think we should stop now.
  Pienso que deberíamos parar. *pyen*·so ke de·be·*ree*·a·mos pa·*rar*

Let's go to bed!
  ¡Vamos a la cama! *va*·mos a la *ka*·ma

Kiss me!	¡Bésame!	be·sa·me
I want you.	Te deseo.	te de·se·o
Take this off.	Sácate esto.	sa·ka·te es·to
Touch me here.	Tócame aquí.	to·ka·me a·kee
Do you like this?	¿Esto te gusta?	es·to te goos·ta
I (don't) like that.	Esto (no) me gusta.	es·to (no) me goos·ta
Please stop!	¡Para!	pa·ra
Please don't stop!	¡No pares!	no pa·res
Oh my god!	¡Ay dios qué rico!	ai dyos ke ree·ko
Oh yeah!	¡Así cariño, así!	a·see ka·ree·nyo a·see
That's great.	¡Eso, eso!	e·so e·so
Easy tiger!	¡Con calma!	kon kal·ma

faster	más rápido	mas ra·pee·do
harder	más fuerte	mas fwer·te
slower	más despacio	mas des·pa·syo
softer	más suave	mas swa·ve

That was amazing.
Eso fue increíble.   e·so fwe een·kre·ee·ble

It's my first time.
Es mi primera vez.   es mee pree·me·ra ves

I can't get it up – sorry.
Lo siento, no puedo levantarla.   lo syen·to no pwe·do le·van·tar·la

Don't worry, I'll do it myself.
No te preocupes, lo hago yo.   no te pre·o·koo·pes lo a·go yo

It helps to have a sense of humour.
Ayuda tener un   a·yoo·da te·ner oon
sentido de humor.   sen·tee·do de oo·mor

Can I …?	¿Puedo …?	pwe·do …
call you	llamarte	lya·mar·te
meet you tomorrow	verte mañana	ver·te ma·nya·na
stay over	quedarme	ke·dar·me

love

I'm in love with you.
Estoy enamorado/a de ti. m/f   es·*toy* e·na·mo·*ra*·do/a de ti

I love you.
Te quiero.   te *kye*·ro

Do you love me?
¿Me quieres?   me *kye*·res

I think we're good together.
Creo que estamos   *kre*·o ke es·*ta*·mos
bien juntos.   byen *khoon*·tos

problems

problemas

Are you seeing someone else?
¿Me estás engañando   me es·*tas* en·ga·*nyan*·do
con alguien?   kon *al*·gyen

He's just a friend.
Es un amigo nada más.   es oon a·*mee*·go *na*·da mas

She's just a friend.
Es una amiga nada más.   es *oo*·na a·*mee*·ga *na*·da mas

I don't think it's working out.
Creo que no está funcionando.   *kre*·o ke no es·*ta* foon·syo·*nan*·do

We'll work it out.
Lo resolveremos.   lo re·sol·ve·*re*·mos

I want to end the relationship.
Quiero que terminemos   *kye*·ro ke ter·mee·*ne*·mos
lo nuestro.   lo *nwes*·tro

I want to stay friends.
Me gustaría que   me goos·ta·*ree*·a ke
quedáramos como amigos.   ke·*da*·ra·mos *ko*·mo a·*mee*·gos

I never want to see you again.
No quiero volver a verte.   no *kye*·ro vol·*ver* a *ver*·te

religion

la religión

What's your religion?
¿Cuál es su/tu religión? pol/inf   kwal es soo/too re·lee·*khyon*

I'm (not) ...	*(No) Soy ...*	(no) soy ...
agnostic	*agnóstico/a* m/f	ag·*nos*·tee·ko/a
an atheist	*ateo/a* m/f	a·*te*·o/a
Buddhist	*budista*	boo·*dees*·ta
Catholic	*católico/a* m/f	ka·to·lee·ko/a
Christian	*cristiano/a* m/f	krees·*tya*·no/a
Hindu	*hindú*	een·*doo*
Jewish	*judío/a* m/f	khoo·*dee*·o/a
Muslim	*musulman/*	moo·sool·*man*/
	musulmana m/f	moo·sool·*ma*·na
practising	*practicante*	prak·tee·*kan*·te
religious	*religioso/a* m/f	re·lee·*khyo*·so/a

I (don't) believe in ...	*(No) Creo en ...*	(no) kre·o en ...
fate	*el destino*	el des·*tee*·no
God	*Dios*	dyos

I'd like to go to (the) ...	*Quisiera ir ...*	kee·*sye*·ra eer ...
church	*a la iglesia*	a la ee·*gle*·sya
mosque	*a la mezquita*	a la mes·*kee*·ta
synagogue	*a la sinagoga*	a la see·na·*go*·ga
temple	*al templo*	al *tem*·plo

indigenous languages

Latin America is a fascinating part of the world for anyone with more than a passing interest in languages. Although Spanish is the most widely spoken language, there are literally hundreds of distinct indigenous languages spoken throughout the Americas. In Central America alone there are some 250 indigenous languages, some of which have several dialects. This amazing linguistic diversity has its origins in migration patterns to the continent that began some 12,000 years ago when Latin America's original inhabitants are believed to have brought a number of languages across the Bering Strait from Asia.

In Latin America today, indigenous languages are spoken by at least 17 million people. Some are limited to small tribal communities in remote areas, while others have millions of speakers spread over large geographical areas. Below are some of the most widely-spoken languages:

Language	Where Spoken	Number of Speakers
Aymara	Bol, Chi, Per	3.5 million
Goajiro	Col, Ven	300,000
Guaraní	Arg, Brazil, Par,	5 million
Garifuna	Gua, Hon, Nic	200,000
Mapudungun	Arg, Chi	400,000
Quechua	Arg, Bol, Chi Col, Ecu, Per	8-10 million

While some languages continue to thrive, much of Latin America's rich linguistic heritage has already been lost. The extinction of a number of languages coincided with European settlement, as introduced diseases and slavery decimated entire tribes. Missionaries often contributed to this decline by prohibiting the use of native languages. It's estimated that as many as 2000 separate languages may have been spoken in South America prior to European settlement. Even today, the rate of language extinction continues apace as traditional lifestyles are eroded by development, and

Spanish eclipses native tongues. Their loss is catastrophic as each of these languages embodies the cultural identity and unique world view of its community of speakers. Today only a few hundred languages are spoken on the South American continent and most of these are endangered.

Latin American Spanish has borrowed many words from indigenous languages to describe some of the wonders of the New World. Many of these words spread into English via Latin American Spanish. Here are some of these borrowed words and the languages they come from:

Latin American Spanish	Indigenous Language	English
aguacate	**ahuacatl (Nahuatl)**	avocado
ananá(s)	**ananas (Quechua)**	pineapple
barbacoa	**barbakoa (Taino)**	barbecue
canoa	**canaoua (Carib)**	canoe
caníbal	**caniba (Arawak)**	cannibal
chicle	**chictli (Nahuatl)**	chewing gum
chile	**chilli (Nahuatl)**	chilli
chocolate	**xocolatl (Aztec)**	chocolate
coca	**kúka (Quechua)**	coca leaf
coyote	**coyotl (Nahuatl)**	coyote
hamaca	**hamaca (Taino)**	hammock
huracán	**hurakán (Taino)**	hurricane
jitomate/tomate	**xitomatl (Nahuatl)**	tomato
llama	**llama (Quechua)**	llama
maíz	**mahiz (Taino)**	maize/corn
papaya	**ababai (Carib)**	paw paw
patata/papa	**batata (Taino)**	potato
poncho	**pantho (Araucanian)**	poncho
quina	**kina (Quechua)**	quinine
tabaco	**tabaco (Taino)**	tobacco

For travellers to the Andes, Lonely Planet also has a Quechua phrasebook.

beliefs & cultural differences

Can I ... here?	¿Puedo ... aquí?	pwe·do ... a·kee
Where can I ...?	¿Dónde puedo ...?	don·de pwe·do ...
attend mass	asistir a la misa	a·sees·teer a la mee·sa
make confession	confesarme	kon·fe·sar·me
(in English)	(en inglés)	(en een·gles)
pray	rezar	re·sar
receive communion	comulgar	ko·mool·gar

cultural differences

las diferencias culturales

Is this a local or national custom?
¿Esto es una costumbre es·to es oo·na kos·toom·bre
local o nacional? lo·kal o na·syo·nal

I'm not used to this.
No estoy acostumbrado/a no es·toy a·kos·toom·bra·do/a
a esto. m/f a es·to

I don't mind watching, but I'd rather not join in.
No me importa mirar, no me eem·por·ta mee·rar
pero prefiero no participar. pe·ro pre·fye·ro no par·tee·see·par

I'll try it.
Lo probaré. lo pro·ba·re

Sorry, I didn't mean to say/do anything wrong.
Lo siento, lo dice/hice lo syen·to lo dee·se/ee·se
sin querer. seen ke·rer

This is (very) ...	Esto es (muy) ...	es·to es (mooy) ...
different	diferente	dee·fe·ren·te
fun	divertido	dee·ver·tee·do
interesting	interesante	een·te·re·san·te

I'm sorry, it's	Lo siento, eso va	lo syen·to e·so va
against my ...	en contra de ...	en kon·tra de ...
beliefs	mis creencias	mees kre·en·syas
religion	mi religión	mee re·lee·khyon

When's the gallery open?
¿A qué hora abre la galería? a ke *o*·ra *a*·bre la ga·le·*ree*·a

When's the museum open?
¿A qué hora abre el museo? a ke *o*·ra *a*·bre el moo·*se*·o

What kind of art are you interested in?
¿Qué tipo de arte le/te ke *tee*·po de *ar*·te le/te
interesa? pol/inf een·te·*re*·sa

What's in the collection?
¿Qué hay en la colección? ke ai en la ko·lek·*syon*

What do you think of …?
¿Qué piensa/piensas de …? pol/inf ke *pyen*·sa/*pyen*·sas de …

It's an exhibition of (pottery).
Hay una exposición de ai *oo*·na ek·spo·see·*syon* de
(alfarería). (al·fa·re·*ree*·a)

I like the works of (Fernando Botero).
Me gusta la obra de me *goos*·ta la *o*·bra de
(Fernando Botero). (fer·*nan*·do bo·*te*·ro)

It reminds me of (pre-Columbian art).
Me recuerda (el arte me re·*kwer*·da (el *ar*·te
precolombino). pre·ko·lom·*bee*·no)

I'm interested in … art.	*Me interesa el arte …*	me een·te·*re*·sa el *ar*·te …
Aztec	*azteca*	as·*te*·ka
baroque	*barroco*	ba·*ro*·ko
graphic	*gráfico*	*gra*·fee·ko
impressionist	*impresionista*	eem·pre·syo·*nees*·ta
Inca	*inca*	*een*·ka
Mayan	*maya*	*ma*·ya
pre-Columbian	*precolombino*	pre·ko·lom·*bee*·no
Renaissance	*renacentista*	re·na·sen·*tees*·ta

artwork	*material m gráfico*	ma·te·ryal gra·fee·ko
ceramics	*cerámica f*	se·ra·mee·ka
curator	*conservador/*	kon·ser·va·dor/
	conservadora m/f	kon·ser·va·do·ra
design	*diseño m*	dee·se·nyo
etching	*grabado m*	gra·ba·do
exhibition hall	*salón m de*	sa·lon de
	exhibiciones	ek·see·bee·syo·nes
installation	*instalación f*	een·sta·la·syon
opening	*apertura f*	a·per·too·ra
painter	*pintor/pintora m/f*	peen·tor/peen·to·ra
painting (artform)	*pintura f*	peen·too·ra
painting (canvas)	*cuadro m*	kwa·dro
period	*período m*	pe·ree·o·do
permanent	*colección f*	ko·lek·syon
collection	*permanente*	per·ma·nen·te
pottery	*alfarería f*	al·fa·re·ree·a
print	*reproducción f*	re·pro·dook·syon
sculptor	*escultor/*	es·kool·tor/
	escultora m/f	es·kool·to·ra
sculpture	*escultura f*	es·kool·too·ra
statue	*estatua f*	es·ta·twa
studio	*estudio m*	es·too·dyo
style	*estilo m*	es·tee·lo
technique	*técnica f*	tek·nee·ka
weaving	*tejido m*	te·khee·do

social niceities

Latin Americans are generally gregarious and don't easily take offence. At the same time they're very polite, almost to the point of ceremoniousness, in their public behaviour. Before getting to the point of a conversation it's customary to exchange pleasantries. Not to do so, in fact, is the mark of an ill-bred person. When approaching people for information, never do so without first using the appropriate greeting. It's also polite to greet the assembled company when entering a public place such as a shop or cafe.

For greetings and pleasantries, see **meeting people,** page 89.

sporting interests

los intereses deportivos

Do you like (sport)?
¿Te gustan (los deportes)?
te *goos*·tan (los de·*por*·tes)

Yes, very much.
Sí, mucho.
see *moo*·cho

Not really.
En realidad, no mucho.
en re·a·lee·*da* no *moo*·cho

I like watching it.
Me gusta mirar.
me *goos*·ta mee·*rar*

What sport do you play?
¿Qué deporte practicas?
ke de·*por*·te prak·*tee*·kas

I play (tennis).
Practico (el tenis).
prak·*tee*·ko (el *te*·nees)

What sport do you follow?
¿A qué deporte eres aficionado/a? m/f
a ke de·*por*·te e·res a·fee·syo·*na*·do/a

I follow (cycling).
Soy aficionado/a al (ciclismo). m/f
soy a·fee·syo·*na*·do/a al (see·*klees*·mo)

Who's your favourite sportsman?
¿Quién es tu deportista favorito?
kyen es too de·por·*tees*·ta fa·vo·*ree*·to

Who's your favourite sportswoman?
¿Quién es tu deportista favorita?
kyen es too de·por·*tees*·ta fa·vo·*ree*·ta

Who's your favourite team?
¿Cuál es tu equipo favorito?
kwal es too e·*kee*·po fa·vo·*ree*·to

For more sports, see the **dictionary**.

going to a game

Would you like to go to a (football) game?
¿Te gustaría ir a un partido (de fútbol)?
te goos·ta·*ree*·a eer a oon par·*tee*·do (de *foot*·bol)

Who are you supporting?
¿Con qué equipo vas?
kon ke e·*kee*·po vas

Who's playing?
¿Quién juega?
kyen *khwe*·ga

Who's winning?
¿Quién va ganando?
kyen va ga·*nan*·do

How much time is left?
¿Cuánto tiempo queda?
kwan·to tyem·po ke·da

What's the score?
¿Cómo van?
ko·mo van

It's a draw.
Empatados.
em·pa·*ta*·dos

That was a … game!	¡Ese partido fue …!	e·se par·*tee*·do fwe …
bad	malo	*ma*·lo
boring	aburrido	a·boo·*ree*·do
great	fabuloso	fa·boo·*lo*·so
(Arg)	bárbaro	*bar*·ba·ro

sports talk

What a …!	¡Qué …!	ke …
goal	golazo	go·*la*·so
header	cabezazo	ka·be·*sa*·so
hit	tiro	*tee*·ro
kick/shot	chute	*choo*·te
pass	pase	*pa*·se
save	atajada	a·ta·*kha*·da

playing sport

practicar deportes

Do you want to play?
¿Quieres jugar? — kye·res khoo·gar

Can I join in?
¿Puedo jugar? — pwe·do khoo·gar

Yes, that'd be great.
Sí, me encantaría. — see me en·kan·ta·ree·a

Not at the moment, thanks.
Ahora mismo no, gracias. — a·o·ra mees·mo no gra·syas

I have an injury.
Tengo una lesion. — ten·go oo·na le·syon

Where's the best place to jog around here?
¿Cuál es el mejor sitio — kwal es el me·khor see·tyo
para hacer footing por — pa·ra a·ser foo·teen por
aquí cerca? — a·kee ser·ka

Where's the nearest ...?	*¿Dónde está ...?*	don·de es·ta ...
gym	*el gimnasio*	el kheem·na·syo
	más cercano	mas ser·ka·no
swimming pool	*la piscina más*	la pee·see·na mas
	cercana	ser·ka·na
	(Arg) *la pileta más*	la pee·le·ta mas
	cercana	ser·ka·na
tennis court	*la cancha de tenis*	la kan·cha de te·nees
	más cercana	mas ser·ka·na

What's the charge per ...?	*¿Cúanto cobran por ...?*	kwan·to ko·bran por ...
day	*día*	dee·a
game	*partido*	par·tee·do
hour	*hora*	o·ra
visit	*visita*	vee·see·ta

Can I hire a …?	¿Es posible alquilar una …?	es po·see·ble al·kee·lar oo·na …
ball	pelota	pe·lo·ta
bicycle	bicicleta	bee·see·kle·ta
court	cancha	kan·cha
racquet	raqueta	ra·ke·ta

listen for …

too/mee poon·to pa·sa·me·lo	Tu/Mi punto. ¡Pásamelo!	Your/My point. Kick/Pass it to me!
khwe·gas byen	Juegas bien.	You're a good player.
gra·syas por el par·tee·do	Gracias por el partido.	Thanks for the game.

Do I have to be a member to attend?

¿Hay que ser socio/a para entrar? m/f	ai ke ser so·syo/a pa·ra en·trar

Is there a women-only session?

¿Hay alguna sesión sólo para mujeres?	ai al·goo·na se·syon so·lo pa·ra moo·khe·res

Where are the changing rooms?

¿Dónde están los vestuarios?	don·de es·tan los ves·twa·ryos

Can I have a locker?

¿Puedo usar una lócker?	pwe·do oo·sar oo·na lo·ker

cycling

el ciclismo

Where does the race pass through?

¿Por dónde pasa la carrera?	por don·de pa·sa la ka·re·ra

Where does the race finish?

¿Dónde termina la carrera?	don·de ter·mee·na la ka·re·ra

Who's winning?

¿Quién va ganando?	kyen va ga·nan·do

How many kilometres is today's (stage)?
¿Cuántos kilómetros tiene   kwan·tos kee·*lo*·me·tros *tye*·ne
(la etapa) de hoy?   (la e·*ta*·pa) de oy

My favourite cyclist is (Santiago Botero).
Mi ciclista favorito   mee see·*klees*·ta fa·vo·*ree*·to
es (Santiago Botero).   es (san·tee·*a*·go bo·*te*·ro)

For phrases on getting around by bike, see **transport**, page 48.

diving

el buceo

I'd like to …	*Me gustaría …*	me goos·ta·*ree*·a …
explore wrecks	*explorar*	ek·*splo*·rar
	naufragios	now·*fra*·khyos
go scuba diving	*hacer*	a·*ser*
	submarinismo	soob·ma·*ree*·nees·mo
go snorkelling	*bucear con tubo*	boo·se·*ar* kon *too*·bo
	respiratorio	res·pee·ra·*to*·ryo
hire diving gear	*alquilar equipo*	al·kee·*lar* e·*kee*·po
	de buceo	de boo·*se*·o
hire snorkelling	*alquilar equipo*	al·kee·*lar* e·*kee*·po
gear	*de buceo con*	de boo·*se*·o kon
	tubo	*too*·bo
	respiratorio	res·pee·ra·*to*·ryo
learn to dive	*aprender a bucear*	a·pren·*der* a boo·se·*ar*

Where are some good diving sites?
¿Dónde hay buenos lugares   *don*·de ai *bwe*·nos loo·*ga*·res
para bucear?   *pa*·ra boo·se·*ar*

Are there jellyfish?
¿Hay medusas?   ai me·*doo*·sas

Where can we hire (flippers)?
¿Dónde se puede alquilar   *don*·de se *pwe*·de al·kee·*lar*
(aletas)?   (a·*le*·tas)

dive	bucear	boo·se·ar
diving boat	barca f de buceo	bar·ka de boo·se·o
diving course	curso m de buceo	koor·so de boo·se·o
diving equipment	equipo m de buceo	e·kee·po de boo·se·o
flippers	aletas f pl	a·le·tas
mask	máscara f	mas·ka·ra
snorkel	tubo m	too·bo
	respiratorio	res·pee·ra·to·ryo
wetsuit	traje m	tra·khe
	isotérmico	ee·so·ter·mee·ko

¡Olé!

Although some locals consider it a cruel and uncivilized activity, bullfighting is still popular in many Latin American countries. Here's some terminology that you may come across in connection with this controversial form of entertainment:

capote m	ka·po·te	bullfighter's cloak
corrida f	ko·ree·da	bullfight
espada f	es·pa·da	sword
plaza f de toros	pla·sa de to·ros	bullring
torero m	to·re·ro	bullfighter
toro m bravo	to·ro bra·vo	fighting bull
traje m de luces	tra·khe de loo·ses	bullfighter's highly decorated suit (lit: suit of lights)

extreme sports

los deportes extremos

Are you sure this is safe?
¿De verdad que esto es seguro? de ver·da ke es·to es se·goo·ro

Is the equipment secure?
¿Está seguro el equipo? es·ta se·goo·ro el e·kee·po

This is insane!
Esto es una locura! es·to es oo·na lo·koo·ra

abseiling	*rappel* m	ra·*pel*
bungy-jumping	*banyi* m	*ban*·yee
canoeing	*piragüismo*	pee·ra·*gwees*·mo
canyoning	*canyoning* m	ka·nyo·*neen*
caving	*espeleología* f	es·pe·lyo·lo·*khee*·a
game fishing	*pesca* f *deportiva*	*pes*·ka de·por·*tee*·va
hiking	*excursionismo* m	ek·skoor·syo·*nees*·mo
kayaking	*kayakismo* m	ka·ya·*kees*·mo
mountain biking	*ciclismo* m *de* *montaña*	see·*klees*·mo de mon·*ta*·nya
mountaineering	*alpinismo* m	al·pee·*nees*·mo
paragliding	*parapente* m	pa·ra·*pen*·te
parasailing	*esquí* m *acuático con paracaídas*	es·*kee* a·*kwa*·tee·ko kon pa·ra·ka·*ee*·das
rock-climbing	*escalada* f *de roca*	es·ka·*la*·da de *ro*·ka
skydiving	*paracaidismo* m	pa·ra·kai·*dees*·mo
trekking	*trekking* m	*tre*·keen
white-water rafting	*descenso* m *en aguas bravas*	de·*sen*·so en *a*·gwas *bra*·vas

For words and phrases you might need while hiking, trekking or mountaineering, see **outdoors**, page 135 and **camping**, page 60.

horse riding

la equitación

Is there a horse-riding school around here?
 ¿Hay alguna escuela de equitación por aquí?
 ai al·*goo*·na es·*kwe*·la de e·kee·ta·*syon* por a·*kee*

Are there rides available?
 ¿Es posible dar un paseo a caballo?
 es po·*see*·ble dar oon pa·*se*·o a ka·*ba*·lyo

How long is the ride?
 ¿Cuánto dura el paseo?
 kwan·to *doo*·ra el pa·*se*·o

skiing

el esquí

What are the skiing conditions like at (Bariloche)?
¿Cuáles son las condiciones de las pistas de esquí en (Bariloche)?
kwa·les son las kon·dee·syo·nes de las pees·tas de es·kee en (ba·ree·lo·che)

Is it possible to go cross-country skiing at (Portillo)?
¿Es posible hacer esquí de fondo en (Portillo)?
es po·see·ble a·ser es·kee de fon·do en (por·tee·lyo)

I'd like to hire (ski equipment).
Quisiera alquilar (equipo de esquí).
kee·sye·ra al·kee·lar (e·kee·po de es·kee)

How much is a pass for these slopes?
¿Cuánto cuesta el forfait para estas pistas?
kwan·to kwes·ta el for·fet pa·ra es·tas pees·tas

What level is that slope?
¿De qué nivel es esa pista?
de ke nee·vel es e·sa pees·ta

Can I take lessons?
¿Puedo tomar clases?
pwe·do to·mar kla·ses

soccer

el fútbol

Who plays for (River Plate)?
¿Quién juega para el (River Plate)?
kyen khwe·ga pa·ra el (ree·ver pla·te)

Which team is at the top of the league?
¿Qué equipo está en primera posición en la tabla de clasificaciones?
ke e·kee·po es·ta en pree·me·ra po·see·syon en la ta·bla de kla·see·fee·ka·syo·nes

He's a great (player).
Es un (jugador) bárbaro.
es oon (khoo·ga·dor) bar·ba·ro

He played brilliantly in the match against (Brazil).

Jugó fenomenal en el   khoo·*go* fe·no·me·*nal* en el
partido contra (Brasil).   par·*tee*·do *kon*·tra (bra·*seel*)

What a terrible team!

¡Qué equipo más malo!   ke e·*kee*·po mas *ma*·lo

ball	*balón* m	ba·*lon*
coach	*entrenador/*	en·tre·na·*dor/*
	entrenadora m/f	en·tre·na·*do*·ra
corner kick	*córner* m	*kor*·ner
cup	*copa* f	*ko*·pa
defensive player	*jugador/*	khoo·ga·*dor/*
	jugadora m/f	khoo·ga·*dor*·a
	de defensa	de de·*fen*·sa
expulsion	*expulsión* f	ek·spool·*syon*
foul	*faul* m	fowl
free kick	*tiro* m *libre*	*tee*·ro *lee*·bre
goal	*gol* m	gol
goalkeeper	*portero/a* m/f	por·*te*·ro/a
(Arg)	*arquero/a* m/f	ar·*ke*·ro/a
goal-scorer	*goleador/*	go·le·a·*dor/*
	goleadora m/f	go·le·a·*do*·ra
kickoff	*saque* m	*sa*·ke
league	*liga* f	*lee*·ga
offside	*offside*	*of*·sai
penalty (kick)	*penalty* m	pe·nal·*tee*
(Arg, CAm)	*penal* m	pe·*nal*
player	*jugador/*	khoo·ga·*dor/*
	jugadora m/f	khoo·ga·*do*·ra
red card	*tarjeta* f *roja*	tar·*khe*·ta *ro*·kha
score (a goal)	*marcar*	mar·*kar*
striker	*delantero/a* m/f	de·lan·*te*·ro/a
supporters	*hinchas* f pl	*een*·chas
(Arg)	*hinchadas* f pl	een·*cha*·das
throw-in	*saque* m *de banda*	*sa*·ke de *ban*·da
warning	*amonestación* f	a·mo·ne·sta·*syon*
yellow card	*tarjeta* f *amarilla*	tar·*khe*·ta a·ma·*ree*·lya

tennis

Would you like to play tennis?
¿Quieres jugar al tenis?   kye·res khoo·*gar* al te·nees

Can we play at night?
¿Se puede jugar de noche?   se pwe·de khoo·*gar* de no·che

Game, set, match.
Juego, set y partido.   khwe·go set ee par·*tee*·do

ace	*ace* m	*a*·se
advantage	*ventaja* f	ven·*ta*·kha
fault	*falta* f	*fal*·ta
play doubles (against)	*jugar dobles (contra)*	khoo·*gar* do·bles (kon·tra)
serve	*saque* m	*sa*·ke
set	*set* m	set

gringo lingo

One word you're bound to become well acquainted with in Latin America is *gringo* (or its feminine form *gringa*). In English usage it's a pejorative word meaning roughly 'English-speaking visitor to Latin America' but in Latin American Spanish the term has subtler nuances.

It can be a neutral term meaning simply 'foreign' (as an adjective) or 'foreigner', so if you're addressed, or referred to in this way, it's more than likely that there's no malice intended. *Gringo* is intended as pejorative only in certain contexts or when it's married with an unflattering descriptive word such as *pinche* ('goddam') or said in an unfriendly tone of voice. You'd no doubt pick up on the cues which might signal such intent. It's probably best to take the term with a grain of salt.

But who exactly is a *gringo*? The term can be used to refer to North Americans but, also, in a broader sense to visitors of European heritage. Blonde or fair-haired people are sometimes called *gringos* perhaps because their physical appearance marks them out as obviously foreign. The word is thought to have originated from the Spanish word *griego* meaning 'Greek'.

hiking & mountaineering

el excursionismo & el alpinismo

Where can I …?	¿Dónde se puede …?	don·de se pwe·de …
buy supplies	comprar víveres	kom·prar vee·ve·res
find someone	encontrar a	en·kon·trar a
who knows this area	alguien que conozca el área	al·gyen ke ko·nos·ka el a·re·a
get a map	obtener un mapa	ob·te·ner oon ma·pa
hire hiking gear	alquilar equipo para ir de excursión	al·kee·lar e·kee·po pa·ra eer de ek·skoor·syon
hire mountain-eering gear	alquilar equipo de alpinismo	al·kee·lar e·kee·po de al·pee·nees·mo

Where can I find out about hiking trails?
¿Dónde hay información sobre caminos rurales de la zona?
don·de ai een·for·ma·syon so·bre ka·mee·nos roo·ra·les de la so·na

How long is the trail?
¿Cómo es de largo el camino?
ko·mo es de lar·go el ka·mee·no

How high is the climb?
¿A qué altura se escala?
a ke al·too·ra se es·ka·la

Is the path open (all year)?
¿Está la ruta abierta (todo el año)?
es·ta la roo·ta a·byer·ta (to·do el a·nyo)

Is it safe?
¿Es seguro?
es se·goo·ro

Is there a hut there?
¿Hay una cabaña allí?
ai oo·na ka·ba·nya a·lyee

When does it get dark?
¿A qué hora oscurece?
a ke o·ra os·koo·re·se

Do we need a guide?
¿Se necesita un guía?   se ne·se·*see*·ta oon *gee*·a

Are there guided treks?
¿Se organizan   se or·ga·*nee*·san
excursiones guiadas?   ek·skoor·*syo*·nes gee·*a*·das

Are there guided climbs?
¿Se organizan escaladas   se or·ga·*nee*·san es·ka·*la*·das
guiadas?   gee·*a*·das

Do we need	¿Se necesita	se ne·se·*see*·ta
to take …?	llevar …?	lye·*var* …
bedding	algo en que	*al*·go en ke
	dormir	dor·*meer*
food	comida	ko·*mee*·da
water	agua	*a*·gwa
Is the track …?	¿Es … el sendero?	es … el sen·*de*·ro
(well-)marked	(bien) marcado	(byen) mar·*ka*·do
scenic	pintoresco	peen·to·*res*·ko
Which is the	¿Cuál es el camino	kwal es el ka·*mee*·no
… route?	más …?	mas …
easiest	fácil	*fa*·seel
shortest	corto	*kor*·to
Where's …?	¿Dónde hay …?	*don*·de ai …
a camping site	un lugar de	oon loo·*gar* de
	cámping	*kam*·peen
the nearest	el pueblo	el *pwe*·blo
village	más cercano	mas ser·*ka*·no
Where are the …	¿Dónde hay …?	*don*·de ai …
showers	duchas	*doo*·chas
toilets	baños	*ba*·nyos

Where have you come from?
¿De dónde vienes? · de *don*·de *vye*·nes

How long did it take?
¿Cuánto has tardado? · kwan·to as tar·*da*·do

Does this path go to (Huayna Picchu)?
¿Este camino va a · *es*·te ka·*mee*·no va a
(Huayna Picchu)? · (*wai*·na *pee*·choo)

Can we go through here?
¿Se puede pasar por aquí? · se *pwe*·de pa·*sar* por a·*kee*

Is the water OK to drink?
¿Se puede beber el agua? · se *pwe*·de be·*ber* el *a*·gwa

Where are we on this map?
¿Dónde estamos aquí · *don*·de es·*ta*·mos a·*kee*
en el mapa? · en el *ma*·pa

I'm lost.
Estoy perdido/a. m/f · es·*toy* per·*dee*·do/a

altitude	altura f	al·*too*·ra
binoculars	prismáticos m pl	prees·*ma*·tee·kos
cliff	acantilado m	a·kan·tee·*la*·do
crampon	crampón m	kram·*pon*
glacier	glaciar m	gla·*syar*
gloves	guantes m pl	gwan·tes
harness	arnés m	ar·*nes*
hiking boots	botas f pl de montaña	bo·tas de mon·*ta*·nya
ice	hielo m	*ye*·lo
ice-climbing	subir de hielo	soo·*beer* de *ye*·lo
mountain	montaña f	mon·*ta*·nya
mountain hut	refugio m de montaña	re·foo·*khyo* de mon·*ta*·nya
pass	paso m	*pa*·so
peak	cumbre f	*koom*·bre
pick	piqueta f	pee·*ke*·ta
steep	escarpado/a m/f	es·kar·*pa*·do/a
scale (climb)	trepar	tre·*par*

at the beach

en la playa

Where's the ... beach?	¿Dónde está la playa ...?	don·de es·ta la pla·ya ...
nearest	más cercana	mas ser·ka·na
nicest	más bonita	mas bo·nee·ta
nudist	nudista	noo·dees·ta

Are there any ...?	¿Hay ...?	ai ...
reefs	arrecifes	a·re·see·fes
rips	corrientes	ko·ryen·tes
water hazards	peligros en el agua	pe·lee·gros en el a·gwa

Is it safe to ... here?	¿Es seguro ... aquí?	es se·goo·ro ... a·kee
dive	bucear	boo·se·ar
swim	nadar	na·dar

What time is ... tide?	¿A qué hora es la marea ...?	a ke o·ra es la ma·re·a ...
high	alta	al·ta
low	baja	ba·kha

listen for ...

kwee·da·do kon la ko·ryen·te Cuidado con la corriente.	Be careful of the undertow.
es pe·lee·gro·so ¡Es peligroso!	It's dangerous!
e·res mo·de·lo ¿Eres modelo?	Are you a model?

weather

el tiempo

What's the weather like?
  ¿Qué tiempo hace?   ke *tyem*·po *a*·se

(Today) It's raining.
  (Hoy) Llueve.   (oy) *lywe*·ve

(Tomorrow) It will rain.
  (Mañana) Lloverá.   (ma·*nya*·na) lyo·ve·*ra*

(Today) It's snowing.
  (Hoy) Nieva.   (oy) *nye*·va

(Tomorrow) It will snow.
  (Mañana) Nevará.   (ma·*nya*·na) ne·va·*ra*

Today it's …	*Hoy hace …*	oy *a*·se …
Will it be … tomorrow?	*¿Mañana hará …?*	ma·*nya*·na a·*ra* …
cold	*frío*	*free*·o
freezing	*un frío que pela*	oon *free*·o ke *pe*·la
hot	*calor*	ka·*lor*
sunny	*sol*	sol
warm	*calor*	ka·*lor*
windy	*viento*	*vyen*·to

Where can I buy a/an …?	*¿Dónde puedo comprar …?*	*don*·de *pwe*·do kom·*prar* …
rain jacket	*un impermeable*	oon eem·per·me·*a*·ble
sunblock	*crema solar*	*kre*·ma so·*lar*
umbrella	*un paraguas*	oon pa·*ra*·gwas

dry season	*época* f *seca*	*e*·po·ka *se*·ka
rainy season	*época* f *de lluvias*	*e*·po·ka de *lyoo*·vyas
snow	*nieve* f	*nye*·ve
storm	*tormenta* f	tor·*men*·ta
sun	*sol* m	sol

flora & fauna

		flora & fauna
What ... is that?	¿Qué ... es ése/ésa? m/f	ke ... es e·se/e·sa
animal	animal m	a·nee·mal
flower	flor f	flor
plant	planta f	plan·ta
tree	árbol m	ar·bol
Is it ...?	¿Es ...?	es ...
common	común	ko·moon
dangerous	peligroso/a m/f	pe·lee·gro·so/a
poisonous	venenoso/a m/f	ve·ne·no·so/a
protected	protegido/a m/f	pro·te·khee·do/a

What's it used for?
¿Para qué se usa? — pa·ra ke se oo·sa

Can you eat it?
¿Se puede comerlo? — se pwe·de ko·mer·lo

Is it endangered?
¿Está en peligro de extinción? — es·ta en pe·lee·gro de ek·steen·syon

key language

lenguage clave

breakfast	*desayuno* m	de·sa·*yoo*·no
lunch	*comida* f	ko·*mee*·da
dinner	*cena* f	*se*·na
drink	*beber*	be·*ber*
eat	*comer*	ko·*mer*
snack	*tentempié* m	ten·tem·*pye*

wining & dining

You'll find there's no shortage of eateries where you can snack on the run or dine out at in Latin America. Here are some of the typical establishments you may come across:

bar bar
many offer cheap light meals

chifa *chee*·fa
term for Chinese restaurant in Chile, Bolivia and Peru

churrasquería choo·ras·ke·*ree*·a
restaurant serving mainly barbecued meat

fuente de soda *fwen*·te de *so*·da
cafe-style establishment serving snacks in addition to ice creams and soft drinks (lit: fountain of soda)

lonchería lon·che·*ree*·a
cheap snack bar/diner

parrillada pa·ree·*lya*·da
Argentinian steakhouse – a carnivore's delight!

restaurante chino res·tow·*ran*·te *chee*·no
popular and cheap Chinese restaurants serving bowls of *tallarines* (noodles) with chopped meat

finding a place to eat

Can you recommend a ...?	¿Puede recomendar ...?	pwe·de re·ko·men·dar ...
cafe	una cafetería	oo·na ka·fe·te·ree·a
restaurant	un restaurante	oon res·tow·ran·te

Where would you go for ...?	¿Adónde se va para ...?	a·don·de se va pa·ra ...
a business lunch	una comida de negocios	oo·na ko·mee·da de ne·go·syos
a celebration	festejar	fes·te·khar
a cheap meal	comer una comida barata	ko·mer oo·na ko·mee·da ba·ra·ta
local specialities	comer comida típica	ko·mer ko·mee·da tee·pee·ka

I'd like to reserve a table for ...	Quisiera reservar una mesa para ...	kee·sye·ra re·ser·var oo·na me·sa pa·ra ...
(two) people	(dos) personas	(dos) per·so·nas
(eight) o'clock	las (ocho)	las (o·cho)

I'd like ..., please.	Quisiera ..., por favor.	kee·sye·ra ... por fa·vor
a table for (five)	una mesa para (cinco)	oo·na me·sa pa·ra (seen·ko)
the menu	el menú	el me·noo
the drink list	la lista de bebidas	la lees·ta de be·bee·das
the (non-) smoking section	(no) fumadores	(no) foo·ma·do·res

Do you have …?	¿Tienen …?	tye·nen …
children's meals	comidas para niños	ko·mee·das pa·ra nee·nyos
a menu in English	un menú en inglés	oon me·noo en een·gles

Are you still serving food?
¿Siguen sirviendo comida?   see·gen seer·vyen·do ko·mee·da

How long is the wait?
¿Cuánto hay que esperar?   kwan·to ai ke es·pe·rar

listen for …

a·kee tye·ne
    Aquí tiene.   Here you go!

don·de le goos·ta·ree·a sen·tar·se
    ¿Dónde le gustaría   Where would
    sentarse?   you like to sit?

e·mos se·ra·do
    Hemos cerrado.   We're closed.

en ke le pwe·do ser·veer
    ¿En qué le puedo servir?   What can I get for you?

es·ta·mos lye·nos
    Estamos llenos.   We're fully booked.

ke a·pro·ve·che
    ¡Que aproveche!   Enjoy your meal.

ko·mo lo kye·re pre·pa·ra·do
    ¿Cómo lo quiere   How would you like
    preparado?   that cooked?

no te·ne·mos me·sas
    No tenemos mesas.   We have no tables.

re·ko·myen·do …
    Recomiendo …   I suggest the …

eating out

143

at the restaurant

I'd like the menu, please.
Quisiera el menú, por favor.
kee·*sye*·ra el me·*noo* por fa·*vor*

Is it self-serve?
¿Es de autoservicio?
es de ow·to·ser·*vee*·syo

What would you recommend?
¿Qué me recomienda?
ke me re·ko·*myen*·da

I'll have what they're having.
Tomaré lo mismo que ellos.
to·ma·*re* lo *mees*·mo ke *e*·lyos

I'd like a local speciality.
Quisiera un plato típico.
kee·*sye*·ra oon *pla*·to *tee*·pee·ko

What's in that dish?
¿De qué es ese plato?
de ke es *e*·se *pla*·to

Does it take long to prepare?
¿Se tarda mucho en prepararlo?
se *tar*·da *moo*·cho en pre·pa·*rar*·lo

Is service included in the bill?
¿La cuenta incluye el servicio?
la *kwen*·ta een·*kloo*·ye el ser·*vee*·syo

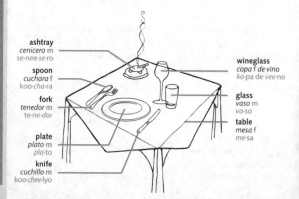

ashtray
cenicero m
se·nee·*se*·ro

spoon
cuchara f
koo·*cha*·ra

fork
tenedor m
te·ne·*dor*

plate
plato m
pla·to

knife
cuchillo m
koo·*chee*·lyo

wineglass
copa f *de vino*
ko·pa de *vee*·no

glass
vaso m
va·so

table
mesa f
me·sa

FOOD

144

Are these complimentary?
    ¿Éstos son gratis?   es·tos son *gra*·tees

Is there (any tomato sauce)?
    ¿Hay (salsa de tomate)?   ai (*sal*·sa de to·*ma*·te)

Please bring …	*Por favor nos*	por fa·*vor* nos
	trae …	*tra*·e …
the bill	*la cuenta*	la *kwen*·ta
a cloth	*un trapo*	oon *tra*·po
a glass	*un vaso*	oon *va*·so
a serviette	*una servilleta*	oo·na ser·vee·*lye*·ta
a wineglass	*una copa*	oo·na *ko*·pa
	de vino	de vee·*no*

---

look for ...

abrebocas	a·bre·*bo*·kas	appetisers
sopas	*so*·pas	soups
de entrada	de en·*tra*·da	starters
ensaladas	en·sa·*la*·das	salads
comidas ligeras	ko·*mee*·das lee·*khe*·ras	light meals
segundos platos	se·*goon*·dos *pla*·tos	main courses
postres	*pos*·tres	desserts
bebidas	be·*bee*·das	drinks
aperitivos	a·pe·ree·*tee*·vos	aperitifs
licores	lee·*ko*·res	spirits
cervezas	ser·*ve*·sas	beers
gaseosas	ga·se·o·sas	soft drinks
vinos blancos	vee·nos *blan*·kos	white wines
vinos de la casa	vee·nos de la *ka*·sa	house wines
vinos del lugar	vee·nos del loo·*gar*	local wines
vinos espumosos	vee·nos es·poo·*mo*·sos	sparkling wines
vinos rosados	vee·nos ro·*sa*·dos	roses
vinos tintos	vee·nos *teen*·tos	red wines
vinos dulces	vee·nos *dool*·ses	dessert wine
digestivos	dee·khes·*tee*·vos	digestifs

For more words you might see on a menu, see the **culinary reader**, page 159.

eating out

talking food

That was delicious!
¡Estaba buenísimo!   es·*ta*·ba bwe·*nee*·see·mo

My compliments to the chef.
Felicitaciones al   fe·lee·see·ta·*syo*·nes al
cocinero.   ko·see·*ne*·ro

I'm full.
Estoy satisfecho/a. m/f   es·*toy* sa·tees·*fe*·cho/a

I love …	*Me encanta …*	me en·*kan*·ta …
this dish	*este plato*	*es*·te *pla*·to
the local	*la comida*	la ko·*mee*·da
cuisine	*típica de*	*tee*·pee·ka de
	la zona	la *so*·na

lunch lingo

The main meal of the day in Latin America is lunch, known as
el almuerzo or *la comida*. Many restaurants in Latin America
provide a set menu for lunch, usually consisting of soup, a
main course and a drink. This cheap and popular option
goes under the following guises:

In Argentina, Central America and Chile:
almuerzo m *completo* or   al·*mwer*·so kom·*ple*·to
comida f *corrida*   ko·*mee*·da ko·*ree*·da

In Colombia:
almuerzo m *corriente*   al·*mwer*·so ko·*ryen*·te

In Costa Rica:
casado m   ka·*sa*·do

In Peru:
menú m   me·*noo*

This is …	Esto está …	es·to es·ta …
(too) cold	*(demasiado) frío*	(de·ma·*sya*·do) *free*·o
(too) hot	*(demasiado)*	(de·ma·*sya*·do)
	caliente	ka·*lyen*·te
burnt	*quemado*	ke·*ma*·do
(too) spicy	*(demasiado)*	(de·ma·*sya*·do)
	picante	pee·*kan*·te
superb	*exquisito*	ek·skee·*see*·to

breakfast

el desayuno

What's a typical (Chilean) breakfast?
¿Cómo es un típico   ko·mo es oon *tee*·pee·ko
desayuno (chileno)?   de·sa·*yoo*·no (chee·*le*·no)

bacon	*tocino* m	to·*see*·no
bread	*pan* m	pan
beans	*frijoles* m pl	free·*kho*·les
butter	*mantequilla* f	man·te·*kee*·lya
	(SAm) *manteca* f	man·*te*·ka
cereal	*cereales* m pl	se·re·*a*·les
cheese	*queso* m	*ke*·so
corn tamales	*humitas* f pl	oo·*mee*·tas
croissants	*medialunas* f pl	me·dya·*loo*·nas
eggs	*huevos* m pl	*we*·vos
jam	*mermelada* f	mer·me·*la*·da
omelette	*tortilla* f	tor·*tee*·lya
milk	*leche* f	*le*·che
muesli	*muesli* m	*moo*·es·lee
toast	*tostadas* f pl	tos·*ta*·das

See **self-catering**, page 153, and the **culinary reader**, page 159 for other breakfast items.

eating out

147

methods of preparation

I'd like it …	Lo quisiera …	lo kee·*sye*·ra …
I don't want it …	No lo quiero …	no lo *kye*·ro …
boiled	hervido	er·*vee*·do
deep-fried	frito en	*free*·to en
	aceite	a·*say*·te
	abundante	a·boon·*dan*·te
fried	frito	*free*·to
grilled	a la parilla	a la pa·*ree*·lya
medium	no muy hecho	no mooy e·cho
rare	vuelta y vuelta	*vwel*·ta ee *vwel*·ta
re-heated	recalentado	re·ka·len·*ta*·do
steamed	al vapor	al va·*por*
well-done	muy hecho	mooy e·cho
with the	con el aliño	kon el a·*ree*·nyo
dressing on	aparte	a·*par*·te
the side		
without (chilli)	sin (chile)	seen (*chee*·le)

in the bar

Excuse me!
¡Oiga!   oy·ga

I'm next.
¡Ahora voy yo!   a·*o*·ra voy yo

I'll have (a glass of red wine).
Para mí, (una copa de   *pa*·ra mee (*oo*·na *ko*·pa de
vino tinto).   *vee*·no *teen*·to)

Same again, please.
Otra de lo mismo.   *o*·tra de lo *mees*·mo

No ice, thanks.
  Sin hielo, gracias.   seen *ye*·lo *gra*·syas

I'd like it straight, please.
  Solo, por favor.   *so*·lo por fa·*vor*

I'll buy you a drink.
  Te invito a una copa.   te een·*vee*·to a *oo*·na *ko*·pa

What would you like?
  ¿Qué quieres tomar?   ke *kye*·res to·*mar*

It's my round.
  Es mi ronda.   es mee *ron*·da

You can get the next one.
  La próxima la pagas tú.   la *prok*·see·ma la *pa*·gas too

Do you serve meals here?
  ¿Sirven comidas aquí?   *seer*·ven ko·*mee*·das a·*kee*

nonalcoholic drinks

bebidas no alcohólicas

Latin Americans drink prodigious quantities of sweet, fizzy drinks. The general term for soft drink is *gaseosa* but in Chile they are *bebidas*, in Panama *refrescos* or *sodas* and in Ecuador *colas*.

soft drink	*gaseosa* f	ga·se·*o*·sa
(orange) juice	*jugo* m *(de naranja)*	*khoo*·go (de na·*ran*·kha)
(fruit) milkshake	*licuado* m *(de frutas)*	lee·*kwa*·do (de *froo*·tas)
(cup of) tea	*(taza de) té*	(*ta*·sa de) te
(cup of) coffee	*(taza de) café*	(*ta*·sa de) ka·*fe*
... **with milk**	... *con leche*	... kon *le*·che
... **without sugar**	... *sin azúcar*	... seen a·*soo*·kar
... **water**	*agua* f ...	*a*·gwa ...
boiled	*hervida*	er·*vee*·da
sparkling mineral	*mineral con gas*	mee·ne·*ral* kon gas
still mineral	*mineral sin gas*	mee·ne·*ral* seen gas

Visitors to Latin America who are expecting out-of-this-world coffee might be surprised to learn that the best beans are shipped overseas to earn export dollars. It's still a popular drink though and here's some vocabulary to help you order what you want:

black coffee		*un café negro*	oon ka·*fe* ne·gro
	(Col)	*un café tinto*	oon ka·*fe teen*·to
instant coffee		*un nescafé*	oon nes·ka·*fe*
milk coffee		*un café con leche*	oon ka·*fe* kon *le*·che
	(Col)	*un perico*	oon pe·*ree*·ko
small cup of		*un cafecito*	oon ka·fe·*see*·to
coffee	**(Arg)**	*un café chico*	oon ka·*fe chee*·ko
coffee with		*un café con leche*	oon ka·*fe* kon *le*·che
milk	**(Arg)**	*un cortado*	oon kor·*ta*·do

alcoholic drinks

bebidas alcohólicas

beer	*cerveza* f	ser·*ve*·sa
brandy	*coñac* m	ko·*nyak*
champagne	*champán* m	cham·*pan*
cocktail	*combinado* m	kom·bee·*na*·do
draught beer	*cerveza* f *de baril*	ser·*ve*·sa de ba·*reel*
wine	*vino* m	*vee*·no
a shot of ...	*un trago de ...*	oon *tra*·go de ...
gin	*ginebra*	khee·*ne*·bra
pisco	*pisco*	*pees*·ko
(grape brandy)		
rum	*ron*	ron
tequila	*tequila*	te·*kee*·la
vodka	*vodka*	*vod*·ka
whisky	*güisqui*	*gwees*·kee

a bottle/glass	una botella/copa	oo·na bo·te·lya/ko·pa
of ... wine	de vino ...	de vee·no ...
dessert	dulce	dool·se
red	tinto	teen·to
rose	rosado	ro·sa·do
sparkling	espumoso	es·poo·mo·so
white	blanco	blan·ko
a ... of beer	... de cerveza	... de ser·ve·sa
glass	un vaso	oon va·so
pint	una pinta	oo·na peen·ta
small bottle	un botellín	oon bo·te·lyeen
large bottle	una litrona	oo·na lee·tro·na
jug	una jarra	oo·na kha·ra
(SAm) un chop		oon chop

one too many?

¿una de más?

Cheers!
¡Salud!
sa·loo

Thanks, but I don't feel like it.
Lo siento, pero no me apetece.
lo syen·to pe·ro no me a·pe·te·se

I don't drink alcohol.
No bebo alcohol.
no be·bo al·kol

I'm tired, I'd better go home.
Estoy cansado/a, mejor me voy a casa. m/f
es·toy kan·sa·do/a me·khor me voy a ka·sa

Where's the toilet?
¿Dónde está el baño?
don·de es·ta el ba·nyo

This is hitting the spot.
Me lo estoy pasando muy bien.
me lo es·toy pa·san·do mooy byen

I'm feeling drunk.
Esto me está subiendo mucho.
es·to me es·ta soo·byen·do moo·cho

The most common term for 'toilets' in Latin America is *baños* but *servicios sanitarios* or just *servicios* is a frequent alternative. When nature calls, make sure you avoid embarrassing incursions into the wrong territory by correctly interpreting the following nomenclature:

Men's toilets:

Caballeros	ka·ba·*lye*·ros	(lit: 'knights' but equivalent to 'gentlemen')
Hombres	*om*·bres	(lit: men)
Varones	va·*ro*·nes	(lit: men)

Women's toilets:

Damas	*da*·mas	(lit: ladies)
Señoras	se·*nyo*·ras	(lit: women)

I feel fantastic!
¡Me siento fenomenal!   me *syen*·to fe·no·me·*nal*

I really, really love you.
Te quiero muchísimo.   te *kye*·ro moo·*chee*·see·mo

I think I've had one too many.
Creo que he tomado   *kre*·o ke e to·*ma*·do
una de más.   *oo*·na de mas

Can you call a taxi for me?
¿Me puedes pedir un taxi?   me *pwe*·des pe·*deer* oon *tak*·see

I don't think you should drive.
No creo que deberías   no *kre*·o ke de·be·*ree*·as
conducir.   kon·doo·*seer*

I'm pissed.
Estoy borracho/a. m/f   es·toy bo·*ra*·cho/a

I feel ill.
Me siento mal.   me *syen*·to mal

I think you've had enough.
Me parece que has tomado   me pa·*re*·se ke as to·*ma*·do
bastante.   bas·*tan*·te

key language

cooked	*cocido/a* m/f	ko·*see*·do/a
dried	*seco/a* m/f	*se*·ko/a
fresh	*fresco/a* m/f	*fres*·ko/a
frozen	*congelado/a* m/f	kon·khe·*la*·do/a
powdered	*en polvo*	en *pol*·vo
raw	*crudo/a* m/f	*kroo*·do/a
vacuum-packed	*envasado/a* m/f	en·va·*sa*·do/a
	al vacío	al va·*see*·o

shop talk

carnicería	kar·nee·se·*ree*·a	butcher
fiambrería	fyam·bre·*ree*·a	delicatessen
frutería	froo·te·*ree*·a	fruit shop
heladería	he·la·de·*ree*·a	ice-cream parlour
lechería	le·che·*ree*·a	dairy shop
mercado	mer·*ka*·do	market
panadería	pa·na·de·*ree*·a	baker
pastelería	pas·te·le·*ree*·a	cake shop
pescadería	pes·ka·de·*ree*·a	fish shop
pollería	po·lye·*ree*·a	poultry shop
supermercado	soo·per·mer·*ka*·do	supermarket
tabaquero	ta·ba·*ke*·ro	tobacconist
verdulería	ver·doo·le·*ree*·a	greengrocer

buying food

How much?
¿Cuánto? — kwan·to

How much is (a kilo of cheese)?
¿Cuánto vale (un kilo de queso)? — kwan·to va·le (oon kee·lo de ke·so)

What's the local speciality?
¿Cuál es la especialidad de la zona? — kwal es la es·pe·sya·lee·da de la so·na

What's that?
¿Qué es eso? — ke es e·so

What's that called?
¿Cómo se llama eso? — ko·mo se lya·ma e·so

Can I taste it?
¿Puedo probarlo/a? m/f — pwe·do pro·bar·lo/a

Can I have a bag, please?
¿Me da una bolsa, por favor? — me da oo·na bol·sa por fa·vor

look for ...

apropiado/a m/f *para cocinar en microondas*	a·pro·prya·do/a pa·ra ko·see·nar en mee·kro·on·das	microwaveable
consúmase dentro de (cuatro) días de abierto	kon·soo·ma·se den·tro de (kwa·tro) dee·as de a·byer·to	consume within (four) days of opening
consúmase antes del ...	kon·soo·ma·se an·tes del ...	use by ...
manténgase en el refrigerador	man·ten·ga·se en el re·free·khe·ra·dor	keep refrigerated

Where can I find the ... section?	¿Dónde está la sección de ...?	don·de es·ta la sek·syon de ...
dairy	productos lácteos	pro·dook·tos lak·te·os
frozen goods	productos congelados	pro·dook·tos kon·khe·la·dos
fruit and vegetable	frutas y verduras	froo·tas ee ver·doo·ras
meat	carne	kar·ne
poultry	aves	a·ves

I'd like ...	Déme ...	de·me ...
(200) grams	(doscientos) gramos	(do·syen·tos) gra·mos
a bottle	una botella	oo·na bo·te·lya
a dozen	una docena	oo·na do·se·na
a jar	una jarra	oo·na kha·ra
a kilo	un kilo	oon kee·lo
(two) kilos	(dos) kilos	(dos) kee·los
a packet	un paquete	oon pa·ke·te
a piece	un trozo	oon tro·so
(three) pieces	(tres) trozos	(tres) tro·sos
a slice	una loncha	oo·na lon·cha
(six) slices	(seis) lonchas	(says) lon·chas
a tin	una lata	oo·na la·ta
some ...	unos/unas ...	oo·nos/oo·nas ...
that one	ése/ésa m/f	e·se/e·sa
this one	esto/esta m/f	es·to/es·ta
Enough.	Ya.	ya
A bit more.	Un poco más.	oon po·ko mas
Less.	Menos.	me·nos

Do you have ...?	¿Tiene ...?	tye·ne ...
anything cheaper	algo más barato	al·go mas ba·ra·to
other kinds	otros tipos	ot·ros tee·pos

listen for ...

al·go mas
¿Algo más? **Anything else?**

en ke le/la pwe·do ser·veer
¿En qué le/la puedo servir? m/f **Can I help you?**

e·so es (oo·na chee·ree·mo·ya)
Eso es (una chirimoya). **That's (a custard apple).**

ke kee·sye·ra
¿Qué quisiera? **What would you like?**

no ke·da mas
No queda más. **There's none left.**

no ten·go
No tengo. **I don't have any.**

cooking utensils

utensilios de cocina

Could I please borrow (a bottle opener)?
¿Me puede prestar
(un abrebotellas)?
me pwe·de pres·tar
(oon a·bre·bo·te·lyas)

Where's (a can opener)?
¿Dónde hay (un abrelatas)? don·de ai (oon a·bre·la·tas)

For more cooking implements, see the **dictionary**.

ordering food

pedir comida

Is there a ... restaurant near here?	*¿Hay un restaurante ... por aquí?*	ai oon res·tow·*ran*·te ... por a·*kee*
halal	*halal*	a·*lal*
kosher	*kosher*	ko·sher
vegetarian	*vegetariano*	ve·khe·ta·*rya*·no

I'm vegan.
Soy vegetariano/a soy ve·khe·ta·*rya*·no/a
estricto/a. m/f es·*treek*·to/a

Do you have (vegetarian) food?
¿Tienen comida *tye*·nen ko·*mee*·da
(vegetariana)? (ve·khe·ta·*rya*·na)

I don't eat (red meat).
No como (carne roja). no *ko*·mo (*kar*·ne *ro*·kha)

Is it cooked in/with (butter)?
¿Está cocinado en/con es·*ta* ko·see·*na*·do en/kon
(mantequilla)? (man·te·*kee*·lya)

Is this ...?	*¿Esto es ...?*	*es*·to es ...
cholesterol-free	*sin colesterol*	seen ko·les·te·*rol*
decaffeinated	*sin cafeína*	seen ka·fe·*ee*·na
free of animal produce	*sin productos de animales*	seen pro·*dook*·tos de a·nee·*ma*·les
free-range	*de corral*	de ko·*ral*
genetically modified	*transgénico/a* m/f	trans·*khe*·nee·ko/a
gluten-free	*sin gluten*	seen *gloo*·ten
low-fat	*bajo/a* m/f *en grasas*	ba·kho/a en *gra*·sas
low in sugar	*bajo/a* m/f *en azúcar*	ba·kho/a en a·*soo*·kar
organic	*orgánico/a* m/f	or·*ga*·nee·ko/a
salt-free	*sin sal*	seen sal

Could you	¿Me puede	me *pwe*·de
prepare a meal	preparar una	pre·pa·*rar* oo·na
without …?	comida sin …?	ko·*mee*·da seen …
butter	mantequilla	man·te·*kee*·lya
eggs	huevos	*we*·vos
fish	pescado	pes·*ka*·do
meat/fish	caldo de carne/	*kal*·do de *kar*·ne/
stock	pescado	pes·*ka*·do
pork	cerdo	*ser*·do
poultry	aves	*a*·ves
red meat	carne roja	*kar*·ne ro·kha

listen for …

le pre·goon·ta·*re* al ko·see·ne·ro
Le preguntaré al cocinero.   **I'll check with the cook.**

to·do *lye*·va (kar·ne)
Todo lleva (carne).   **It all has (meat) in it.**

pwe·de ko·*mer* …
¿Puede comer …?   **Can you eat …?**

special diets & allergies

dietas especiales & alergias

I'm on a special diet.
Estoy a dieta especial.   es·*toy* a *dye*·ta es·pe·*syal*

I'm allergic to …	Soy alérgico/a … m/f	soy a·*ler*·khe·ko/a …
dairy produce	a los productos lácteos	a los pro·*dook*·tos *lak*·te·os
eggs	a los huevos	a los *we*·vos
fish	al pescado	al pes·*ka*·do
gelatin	a la gelatina	a la khe·la·*tee*·na
gluten	al gluten	al *gloo*·ten
honey	a la miel	a la myel
MSG	al glutamato monosódico	al gloo·ta·*ma*·to mo·no·*so*·dee·ko
nuts	a las nueces	a las *nwe*·ses
peanuts	al maní	al ma·*nee*
seafood	al marisco	al ma·*rees*·ko

A

a la plancha a la *plan*·cha grilled
al vapor ⓜ al va·*por* steamed
a punto a *poon*·to medium (steak)
aceite ⓜ a·*say*·te oil
aceitunas ⓕ pl a·say·*too*·nas olives
— **alinadas (Cub)** a·lee·*na*·das olives marinated in cummin, hot pepper, lemon, garlic & vinegar
— **rellenas** re·*lye*·nas stuffed olives
achicoria ⓕ a·chee·ko·*rya* chicory · endive
achuras ⓕ pl a·*choo*·ras offal
adobo ⓜ a·*do*·bo paste of garlic, oregano, paprika, peppercorn, salt, olive, lime juice & vinegar for seasoning meat
agua ⓕ a·gwa water
— **de canilla** de ka·*nee*·lya tap water
— **de jamaica (CAm)** de kha·*mai*·ka sweet, red, iced tea made from hibiscus flowers
— **de la llave** de la *lya*·ve tap water
— **del tubo** del *too*·bo tap water
— **de vertiente** de ver·*tyen*·te spring water
— **de panel (Col)** de pa·*nel* unrefined sugar melted in hot water
— **mineral** mee·ne·*ral* mineral water
aguacate ⓜ a·gwa·*ka*·te avocado
— **salsa (Cub)** *sal*·sa avocado sauce containing tomato, capsicum, olive, tomato & white rum
aguardiente ⓜ **(Col)** a·gwar·*dyen*·te spirit flavoured with anise
ahumado/a ⓜ/ⓕ a·oo·*ma*·do/a smoked
ají ⓜ a·*khee* red chilli · chilli sauce

ajiaco ⓜ a·*khya*·ko spicy potato stew · in Colombia, soup with chicken & three varieties of potato, served with corn & capers
ajili-mójili ⓜ **(Pue)** a·khee·lee·*mo*·khee·lee tangy garlic sauce
ajillo, al a·*khee*·lyo, al in garlic
ajo ⓜ a·kho garlic
ajoporro ⓜ a·kho·*po*·ro leek
al horno al *or*·no baked
albahaca ⓕ al·*ba*·ka basil
albóndigas ⓕ pl al·*bon*·dee·gas meatballs
alcachofa ⓕ al·ka·*cho*·fa artichoke
alcaparra ⓕ al·ka·*pa*·ra caper
alcaucil ⓜ **(SAm)** al·*kow*·seel artichoke
alcohol ⓜ al·*kol* alcohol
aliado ⓜ **(Chi)** a·*lya*·do sandwich with cold ham & cheese
alita ⓕ a·*lee*·ta wing (bird or poultry)
allioli ⓜ a·*lyo*·lee garlic sauce
almejas ⓕ pl al·*me*·khas clams
almendra ⓕ al·*men*·dra almond
almuerzo ⓜ al·*mwer*·so lunch
alubias ⓕ pl a·*loo*·byas kidney beans
amarillos ⓜ pl **(Pue)** a·ma·*ree*·lyos fried ripe plantains coated with cinnamon, sugar & wine sauce
ananá(s) ⓜ a·na·*na*(s) pineapple
anca ⓜ *an*·ka haunch
anchoas ⓕ pl an·*cho*·as anchovies
anguila ⓜ an·*gee*·la eel
anís ⓜ a·*nees* anise · aniseed
anticucho ⓜ **(Chi, Per, Bol)** an·tee·*koo*·cho kebab
apio ⓜ *a*·pyo celery
arenque ⓜ a·*ren*·ke herring

arepa ① **(Ven)** a-re-pa *small toasted or fried maize pancake sometimes stuffed*

areperas ① **(Ven)** a-re-pe-ras *snack bars selling* **arepas**

arreglados ⓜ pl **(Cos)** a-re-gla-dos *savoury filled puff pastries*

arrollado ⓜ a-ro-lya-do *rolled pork*

arroz ⓜ a-ros *rice*
 — **con habichuelas (Pue)** kon a-bee-chwe-las *main course of rice & beans*
 — **con leche** kon le-che *rice pudding*
 — **con pollo** kon po-lyo *dish of rice & chicken*

arveja ① **(Ecu)** ar-ve-kha *pea stew*
 — **seca** se-ka *split pea*

arvejas ① pl ar-ve-khas *peas*

asado ⓜ **(SAm)** a-sa-do *mixed grill*
 — **al espiedo** al es-pye-do *spit roast*

asado/a ⓜ/① a-sa-do/a *roasted*
 — **al horno** al or-no *oven roasted*

asopao ⓜ **de pollo (Pue)** a-so-pa-o de po-lyo *chicken stew with* **adobo** *seasoning*

atún ⓜ a-toon *tuna*
 — **con ron (Cub)** kon ron *tuna with a rum sauce*

auyama ⓜ **(Col, Ven)** ow-ya-ma *pumpkin*

ave ⓜ a-ve *fowl • poultry*

avellana ① a-ve-lya-na *hazelnut*

azafran ⓜ a-sa-fran *saffron*

azucar ⓜ a-soo-kar *sugar*

B

bacalao ⓜ ba-ka-la-o *(salted) cod*

baho ⓜ **(Nic)** ba-o *stew of beef, various types of plantains & yuca*

baleadas ① pl **(Hon)** ba-le-a-das *white flour tortillas filled with refried beans, cream & crumbled cheese*

banana ① **(Arg, Peru)** ba-na-na *banana*

banano ⓜ **(CAm,Col)** ba-na-no *banana*

bandeja ① **(Col)** ban-de-kha *main course*
 — **paisa (Col)** pai-sa *traditional dish consisting of ground beef, sausage, red beans, rice, green banana, egg, salt pork & avocado*

baracoa ⓜ **special (Cub)** ba-ra-ko-a spe-syal *cocktail of rum, coconut cream, grapefruit juice & limejuice*

Barros Jarpa ⓜ **(Chi)** ba-ros khar-pa *sandwich with cold ham & melted cheese – named after a Chilean painter*

Barros Luco ⓜ **(Chi)** ba-ros loo-ko *steak sandwich with melted cheese – named after a Chilean president*

batata ① ba-ta-ta *sweet potato*

bebida ① be-bee-da *drink (beverage)*

beicon ⓜ **con queso** bay-kon kon ke-so *cold bacon with cheese*

berberechos ⓜ pl ber-be-re-chos *cockles*

berenjena ① be-ren-khe-na *eggplant • aubergine*

berro ⓜ be-ro *watercress*

besugo ⓜ be-soo-go *bream*

betarraga ① **(Chi, Bol)** ba-ta-ra-ga *beetroot*

bien asado/a ⓜ/① byen a-sa-do/a *well-done*

bien hecho/a ⓜ/① byen e-cho/a *well-done*

bife ⓜ **(Arg, Par, Uru)** bee-fe *steak*
 — **a caballo** a ka-ba-lyo *steak served with two eggs & chips*
 — **asado** a-sa-do *roast beef*
 — **de chorizo** de cho-ree-so *rump steak*
 — **de costilla** de kos-tee-lya *T-bone steak – also called* **chuleta**
 — **de lomo** ⓜ de lo-mo *tenderloin*

bistec ⓜ bees-tek *steak*
 — **con patatas** kon pa-ta-tas *steak & chips*

blanco ⓜ blan-ko *white (wine)*

bocadillo ⓜ **(Cub)** bo·ka·*dee*·lyo
sandwich filled with ham or cheese

bocaditos ⓜ pl **(Cub)** bo·ka·*dee*·tos
substantial snack dishes

bocas ⓕ pl **(Cos, Pan)** bo·kas *savoury
side dishes served at bars*

bollos ⓜ pl bo·lyos *bread rolls*

boniatillo ⓜ **(Cub)** bo·nya·*tee*·lyo
*dessert made from sweet potato, sugar,
cinnamon, lime, egg yolks & sherry*

boniato ⓜ **(Arg)** bo·*nya*·to
sweet potato

bori-bori ⓜ **(Par)** bo·ree·bo·ree
chicken soup with corn meal balls

botella ⓕ bo·te·lya *bottle*

breva ⓕ *bre*·va *fig*

brócoli ⓜ *bro*·ko·lee *broccoli*

budín ⓜ boo·*deen* *pudding*

buey ⓜ bway *ox*

C

caballa ⓕ ka·*ba*·lya *mackerel*

cabeza ⓕ ka·*be*·sa *head*

cabra ⓕ *ka*·bra *goat*

cacao ⓜ ka·*ka*·o *cocoa*

cachapa ⓕ **(Ven)** ka·*cha*·pa *large
round corn pancake often served
with cheese ham or both*

cachito ⓜ **(Ven)** ka·*chee*·to
*a type of hot croissant filled with
chopped ham*

café ⓜ ka·*fe* *coffee*
　— **doble** *do*·ble *long black coffee*
　— **marrón** (Ven) ma·*ron* *coffee
consisting of half coffee & half milk*
　— **negro** *ne*·gro *black coffee*
　— **tinto** (Col) *teen*·to *black coffee*
　— **chico** (Arg) *chee*·ko *small cup of
coffee*
　— **solo** ⓜ *so*·lo *black coffee*

cafecito ⓜ ka·fe·*see*·to *small cup of
coffee*

cajeta ⓕ **(Cos)** ka·*khe*·ta *similar to
dulce de leche*

calabacín ⓜ **(Cub)** ka·la·ba·*seen* *zucchini ·
courgette*

calabaza ⓕ ka·la·*ba*·sa *pumpkin ·
gourd · marrow*

calamares ⓜ pl ka·la·*ma*·res *calamari ·
squid*

caldereta ⓕ kal·de·*re*·ta *stew*

caldillo ⓜ **cubano (Cub)** kal·*dee*·lyo
koo·*ba*·no *hotpot made with steak,
onions, potatoes, potatoes, hot
pepper, garlic, brown sugar & cumin*

caldo ⓜ *kal*·do *broth · stock*
　— **de gallina** de ga·*lyee*·na
chicken soup
　— **de patas (Ecu)** de *pa*·tas
soup made of boiled cattle hooves

caliente ka·*lyen*·te *hot*

callampas ⓕ **(Chi)** ka·*lyam*·pas
mushrooms

camarón ⓜ ka·ma·*ron*
shrimp · small prawn

cambur ⓜ **(Ven)** kam·*boor* *banana*

camomila ⓕ ka·mo·*mee*·la
camomile tea

camote ⓜ ka·*mo*·te *sweet potato*

caña ⓕ ka·*nya* *cane alcohol ·
aguardiente*
　— **de azúcar** de a·*soo*·kar *sugar cane*

canela ⓕ ka·*ne*·la *cinnamon*

canelones ⓜ pl ka·ne·*lo*·nes
cannelloni

cangrejo ⓜ kan·*gre*·kho *crab*
　— **de río** de *ree*·o *crayfish*

cañita ⓕ **(Pue)** ka·*nyee*·ta *homemade,
illegal rum*

capitàn ⓜ **(Chi)** ka·pee·*tan* *vermouth*

capón (SAm) ⓜ ka·*pon* *mutton*

carabinero ⓜ ka·ra·bee·*ne*·ro
large prawn

caracol ⓜ ka·ra·*kol* *snail*

carbonada ⓕ **(Arg)** kar·bo·*na*·da
*beef stew of rice, potatoes, maize,
squash, apples & peaches*

carimañola ⓕ **(Pan)** ka·ree·ma·*nyo*·la
*deep-fried roll filled with meat, made
from ground & boiled* **yuca**

carne ⓕ *kar*·ne *meat*
— **de caballo** de ka·*ba*·lyo *horsemeat*
— **de vaca** de *va*·ka *beef*
— **fría** *free*·a *cold meat*
— **mechada (Pue)** me·*cha*·da
roast beef
— **molida** mo·*lee*·da *minced meat*
carnicería ⓕ kar·nee·se·*ree*·a
butcher's shop
carpa ⓕ *kar*·pa *carp*
casado ⓜ **(Cos)** ka·*sa*·do *platter of
rice, black beans, plantain, meat or
fish, cabbage, an egg or avocado*
— **vegetariano (Cos)**
ve·khe·ta·*rya*·no *vegetarian version
of casado*
casamiento ⓜ **(Sal)** ka·sa·*myen*·to
rice & beans mixed together
castaña ⓕ kas·*ta*·nya *chestnut*
— **de Pará** de pa·*ra* *brazil nut*
cave ⓜ **(Hon)** *ka*·ve
a type of coffee liqueur
caza ⓕ *ka*·sa *game (meat)*
— **de temporada** de tem·po·*ra*·da
game in season
cazuela ⓕ ka·*swe*·la *casserole •
fish stew (Arg)*
— **de mariscos (Chi)** de ma·*rees*·kos
shellfish soup
cebada ⓕ se·*ba*·da *barley*
cebolla ⓕ se·*bo*·lya *onion*
cerdo ⓜ *ser*·do *pig • pork*
cereales ⓜ pl se·re·*a*·les *cereal*
cereza ⓕ se·*re*·sa *cherry*
cerveza ⓕ ser·*ve*·sa *beer*
— **de barril** de ba·*reel*
draught beer • beer on tap
— **de malta** de *mal*·ta *dark beer*
— **lager** *la*·ger *lager beer*
— **negra** *ne*·gra *stout*
ceviche ⓜ se·*vee*·che *raw fish
marinated in lemon juice, chilli or
onions or both*
chacarero ⓜ **(Chi)** cha·ka·*re*·ro
beefsteak with tomato & vegetables

chairo ⓜ **(Bol)** *chai*·ro *mutton or beef
soup served with chuños, fresh
potato & dried maize*
chajchu ⓜ **(Bol)** *chakh*·choo *beef with
freeze-dried potatoes, hard-boiled
egg, cheese & hot red pepper sauce*
chalote ⓜ cha·*lo*·te *spring onion •
shallot*
champán ⓜ cham·*pan* *champagne*
champiñones ⓜ pl cham·pee·*nyo*·nes
mushrooms
— **al ajillo** al a·*khee*·lyo
garlic mushrooms
chapalele ⓜ **(Chi)** cha·pa·*le*·le *boiled
potato & flour bread*
chaque ⓜ **(Bol)** *cha*·ke *similar to
chupe but much thicker & with more
grain*
charque ⓜ **(Bol)** *char*·ke *dried beef,
llama or other red meat*
— **kan** kan *charque served with
mashed hominy*
chauchas ⓕ pl *chow*·chas *string beans*
chicha ⓕ **(Per, Bol)** *chee*·cha *maize
beer associated with ceremonial &
ritual occasions in Peru*
chicharrón ⓜ chee·cha·*ron* *fried pork fat*
chifa ⓕ **(Bol, CAm, Per)** *chee*·fa
chinese restaurant
chilcano ⓜ **(Chi, Per)** cheel·*ka*·no
*ginger ale – may be served with **pisco***
chile ⓜ *chee*·le *pimento, (small red
pepper)*
chimichurri ⓜ **(Arg, Uru)**
chee·mee·*choo*·ree *strong olive oil,
parsley & garlic barbecue sauce*
chinchulines ⓜ pl cheen·choo·*lee*·nes
*small intestines – a common **asado**
dish*
chipa ⓕ **de almidón (Par)** *chee*·pa
de al·mee·*don* *like **chipa guazú** but
made with manioc flour rather than
corn meal*
chipa ⓕ **guazú (Par)** *chee*·pa gwa·*soo*
*dish resembling a cheese souffle
containing corn meal*

chipirón ⓜ chee·pee·*ron* small squid

chirimoya ⓕ chee·ree·*mo*·ya custard apple

chispa tren ⓕ (Cub) *chees*·pa tren 'train sparks' – Cuban firewater

chivito ⓜ (Uru) chee·*vee*·to tasty & filling steak sandwich with a variety of additions including cheese, lettuce, tomato & bacon
— **al plato** al *pla*·to steak served with a fried egg, potato salad, green salad & french fries

chivo ⓜ *chee*·vo kid • baby goat

choclo ⓜ *cho*·klo maize • corn on the cob

choco ⓜ *cho*·ko cuttlefish

chocolate ⓜ cho·ko·*la*·te chocolate
— **caliente** ka·*lyen*·te hot chocolate drink
— **santafereño (Col)** san·ta·fe·re·*nyo* cup of hot chocolate accompanied by a piece of cheese & bread

chola ⓕ (Bol) *cho*·la bread roll filled with meat, onion, tomato & escabeche

chop ⓜ chop draught beer

choripán ⓜ (Arg) cho·ree·*pan* spicy sausage sandwich

chorizo ⓜ cho·*ree*·so spicy pork sausage
— **al horno** al *or*·no spicy baked sausage

chorlito ⓜ chor·*lee*·to plover (small game bird)

chuleta ⓕ choo·*le*·ta chop • cutlet • T-bone steak (Arg)
— **de puerco** de *pwer*·ko pork chop

chuños ⓜ pl (Bol) *choo*·nyos freeze-dried potatoes made by leaving potatoes out in the winter cold

chupe ⓜ *choo*·pe stew • soup • in Bolivia, a vegetable, meat & grain soup with a clear broth flavoured with *ají*, tomato, cumin or onion
— **de camarones (Per)** de ka·ma·*ro*·nes prawn soup
— **de cóngrio (Chi)** de *kon*·gryo conger eel stew
— **de locos (Chi)** de *lo*·kos abalone stew

churrasco ⓜ choo·*ras*·ko rib steak • in Ecuador, a hearty dish of rice, fried beef, fried eggs, vegetables, fried potatoes, a slice of avocado, tomato & rice

ciruela ⓕ see·*rwe*·la plum
— **seca** *se*·ka prune

ckocko ⓕ (Bol) *ko*·ko spicy chicken cooked in wine or **chicha** & served with maize, olives, raisins & aromatic condiments

clericó ⓜ (Uru) kle·ree·*ko* usually a mixture of white wine, fruit juice, a liqueur, fruit salad, ice & a carbonated soft drink or cider

cocina ⓕ ko·*see*·na kitchen • cuisine

cocinado/a ⓜ/ⓕ ko·see·*na*·do/a cooked

cocinar ko·see·*nar* to cook

cocinero/a ⓜ/ⓕ ko·see·*ne*·ro/a chef

coco ⓜ *ko*·ko coconut

codorniz ⓕ ko·dor·*nees* quail

coles ⓜ pl **de Bruselas** *ko*·les de broo·*se*·las Brussels sprouts

coliflor ⓕ ko·lee·*flor* cauliflower

combinado ⓜ kom·bee·*na*·do cocktail

completo ⓜ (Chi) kom·*ple*·to a hot dog with the lot

con gas ⓜ&ⓕ kon gas fizzy

con leche ⓜ kon *le*·che with milk

coñac ⓜ ko·*nyak* brandy

conejo ⓜ ko·*ne*·kho rabbit

confitería ⓕ kon·fee·te·*ree*·a sweet shop • candy store

confites ⓜ pl **(Bol)** kon·*fee*·tes *festive candies consisting of coloured sugar syrup, nuts, aniseed, fruits, biscuit or coconut*

copa ⓕ *ko*·pa *glass*

corazón ⓜ ko·ra·*son heart*

cordero ⓜ kor·*de*·ro *lamb*

cortado ⓜ **(Arg)** kor·*ta*·do *coffee with a little milk*

costilla ⓕ kos·*tee*·lya *loin · spare rib*
— **de cerdo** de *ser*·do *pork chop*

costillar ⓜ **de cordero** kos·tee·*lyar* de kor·*de*·ro *rack of lamb*

crema ⓕ *kre*·ma *cream*
— **batida** ba·*tee*·da *whipped cream*

croquetas (Cub) ⓕ pl kro·*ke*·tas *popular fried ham or chicken croquettes*

crudo/a ⓜ/ⓕ *kroo*·do/a *raw*

crustáceos ⓜ pl kroos·*ta*·se·os *shellfish*

cuadril ⓜ kwa·*dreel rump steak*

cubierto ⓜ koo·*byer*·to *cover charge*

cubo ⓜ **de hielo** koo·bo de ye·lo *ice cube*

cucharita ⓕ koo·cha·*ree*·ta *teaspoon*

cuenta ⓕ *kwen*·ta *bill · check*

curanto ⓜ **(Chi)** koo·*ran*·to *hearty stew of fish, shellfish, chicken, pork, lamb, beef & potato*

curtido ⓜ **(Sal)** koor·*tee*·do *mixture of pickled beets, cabbage & carrots served with* **pupusas**

cuy ⓜ kooy *grilled or roasted guinea pig*

D

damasco ⓜ da·*mas*·ko *apricot*

dátil ⓜ *da*·teel *date*

descafeinado/a ⓜ/ⓕ des·ka·fay·*na*·do/a *decaffeinated*

desnatado/a ⓜ/ⓕ des·na·*ta*·do/a *low-fat*

digestivo ⓜ dee·khes·*tee*·vo *digestif*

dorado/a ⓜ/ⓕ do·*ra*·do/a *browned*

dulce ⓜ **de leche (Arg)** *dool*·se de *le*·che *caramelised condensed milk · a filling in sweet pastries*

dulce *dool*·se *sweet*

dulces ⓜ pl *dool*·ses *confectionery · sweets*

E

(de) elaboración ⓕ **propia**
(de) e·la·bo·ra·*syon* pro·pya *made on the premises*

elote ⓜ **(CAm)** e·*lo*·te *corn · corn on the cob*

empanada ⓕ em·pa·*na*·da *stuffed meat & vegetable turnover*

empanadilla ⓕ **(Pue)**
em·pa·na·*dee*·lya *pocket of plantain or* **yuca** *dough stuffed with meat*

empanadillas ⓕ pl **de jueyes (Pue)**
em·pa·na·*dee*·lyas de *khwe*·yes *highly seasoned land crab meat baked into an* **empanadilla** *of cassava paste*

empana (Cub) ⓕ em·*pa*·na *meat or vegetable pattie*

en escabeche ⓜ **(Pue)** en es·ka·*be*·che *way of preparing seafood by frying then chilling & pickling it*

en rodajas en ro·*da*·khas *sliced*

enchilladas ⓕ pl **(Hon)**
en·chee·*lya*·das *crisp fried tortilla topped with spicy meat, salad & crumbled cheese*

endulzado/a ⓜ/ⓕ en·dool·*sa*·do/a *sweetened*

eneldo ⓜ e·*nel*·do *dill*

ensalada ⓕ en·sa·*la*·da *salad · in El Salvador, a mixed fruit juice served with fruit salad floating on top*
— **mixta** *meeks*·ta *mixed salad*
— **rusa** *roo*·sa *vegetable salad with mayonnaise*
— **verde** *ver*·de *green salad*

entremeses ⓕ pl en·tre·*me*·ses *hors-d'oeuvres*

erizos ⓜ pl **(Chi)** e·*ree*·sos *sea urchins*

escabeche ⓜ **(Bol)** es·ka·*be*·che *vegetables, onion & peppers preserved in vinegar*

espagueti ⓜ es·pa·*ge*·tee *spaghetti*

espárragos ⓜ pl es·*pa*·ra·gos *asparagus*

especialidad ⓕ es·pe·sya·lee·*da speciality*
— **de la casa** de la *ka*·sa *speciality of the house*
— **del día** del *dee*·a *speciality of the day*

espinacas ⓕ pl es·pee·*na*·kas *spinach*

espumoso/a ⓜ/ⓕ es·poo·*mo*·so/a *sparkling*

estofado ⓜ es·to·*fa*·do *stew*

estofado/a ⓜ/ⓕ es·to·*fa*·do/a *braised*

estragón ⓜ es·tra·*gon tarragon*

F

faba ⓜ *fa*·ba *type of dried bean*

facturas ⓕ pl **(Arg)** fak·*too*·ras *buns, cakes*

faisán ⓜ fai·*san pheasant*

falso conejo ⓜ **(Bol)** *fal*·so ko·*ne*·kho *'false rabbit' – greasy, glutinous meat-based dish*

fideos ⓜ pl fee·*de*·os *noodles*

filete ⓜ fee·*le*·te *fillet of meat or fish*
— **de bife** de *bee*·fe *beef fillet*

flan ⓜ flan *egg custard • creme caramel*

frambuesa ⓕ fram·*bwe*·sa *raspberry*

fresa ⓕ *fre*·sa *strawberry*

fresco/a ⓜ/ⓕ *fres*·ko/a *fresh*

frescos ⓜ pl **(Hon)** *fres*·kos *fruit drinks blended with water & sugar*

fricasés ⓜ **(Bol)** free·ka·*ses pork or chicken stew with maize grits*

frijol ⓜ free·*khol bean*
— **blanco** *blan*·ko *large butter bean*

frijoles ⓜ pl free·*kho*·les *beans*
— **con arroz (Gua)** kon *a*·ros *beans & rice*

frío/a ⓜ/ⓕ *free*·o/a *cold*

fritada ⓕ free·*ta*·da *scraps of fried or roast pork*

fritanga ⓕ free·*tan*·ga *hotpot or stew •* in Bolivia, spicy hot pork with mint & hominy

frito/a ⓜ/ⓕ *free*·to/a *fried*
— **a la sartén** a la sar·*ten pan-fried*

fruta ⓕ *froo*·ta *fruit*

frutilla ⓕ froo·*tee*·lya *strawberry*

fuerte *fwer*·te *strong*

G

galleta ⓕ ga·*lye*·ta *biscuit • cookie*

gallina ⓕ ga·*lyee*·na *chicken*

gallito ⓜ ga·*lyee*·to *cockerel*

gallo ⓜ *ga*·yo *rooster*

gallo ⓜ **pinto (Cos, Nic, Pan)** *ga*·lyo peen·to *lightly spiced mixture of rice & black beans traditionally served for breakfast, sometimes with **natilla** or fried eggs*

gallos ⓜ pl **(Cos)** *ga*·lyos *tortilla sandwiches containing meat, beans or cheese*

gambas ⓕ pl **rebozadas** *gam*·bas rebo·*sa*·das *batter-fried scampi (large prawns)*

ganso ⓜ *gan*·so *goose*

garbanzo ⓜ gar·*ban*·so *chickpea • garbanzo*

gaseoso/a ⓜ/ⓕ ga·se·o·*so*/a *fizzy*

gazpacho ⓜ ga·*spa*·cho *cold tomato & vegetable soup*

ginebra ⓕ **bols (Arg)** khee·*ne*·bra bols *alcoholic drink similar to gin*

girasol ⓜ khee·ra·*sol sunflower*

glaseado/a ⓜ/ⓕ gla·se·a·*do*/a *glazed • iced*

gol ⓜ **(Chi)** gol *translucent alcoholic mixture of butter, sugar & milk*

granada ⓕ gra·*na*·da *pomegranate*

grande *gran*·de *large • big*

grasa ⓕ *gra*·sa *grease • fat*

gratinado/a ⓜ/ⓕ gra·tee·*na*·do/a *au gratin*

grosella ① gro·se·lya *redcurrant*
— **espinosa** es·pee·no·sa *gooseberry*
— **negra** ne·gra *blackcurrant*

guífiti ⑩ **(Hon)** gi·fee·tee *mix of aguardiente with aromatic & marine plants – a Garífuna specialty*

guinda ① **(Per)** geen·da *sweet cherry brandy*

guindado ⑩ **(Chi)** geen·da·do *fermented alcoholic drink made from a cherry-like fruit, brandy, cinnamon & cloves*

guindilla ① geen·dee·lya *hot chilli*

guisantes ⑩ pl gee·san·tes *peas*

guiso ⑩ **(Cos)** gee·so *stew*

güisqui ⑩ gwees·kee *whisky*

H

haba ① a·ba *broad bean • Lima bean*

hallaca ① **(Ven)** a·lya·ka *chopped pork, beef or chicken or both with vegetables & olives, all folded in a maize dough, wrapped in banana leaves & steamed*

hamburguesa ① am·boor·ge·sa *hamburger*

harina ① a·ree·na *flour*

hecho/a ⑩/① e·cho/a *made • prepared*

heladería ① e·la·de·ree·a *ice-cream parlour*

helado/a ⑩/① e·la·do/a *chilled • iced*

helado ⑩ e·la·do *ice cream*

hervido/a ⑩/① er·vee·do/a *boiled*
— **a fuego lento** a fwe·go len·to *simmered*

hervir er·veer *boil*

hierba ① yer·ba *herb*

hierbabuena ① yer·ba·bwe·na *mint*

hígado ⑩ ee·ga·do *liver*

higo ⑩ ee·go *fig*

hocico ⑩ o·see·ko *snout*

hongo ⑩ on·go *button mushroom*

horchata ① **(Cos)** or·cha·ta *rice-based drink flavoured with cinnamon*
— **de cebada (Sal)** de se·ba·da *sweet barley-based beverage spiced with cinnamon*

hormiga ① **culona (Col)** or·mee·ga koo·lo·na *large fried ants – unique to Santander*

horneado/a ⑩/① or·ne·a·do/a *baked*

hornear or·ne·ar *bake*

horno ⑩ or·no *oven*

horno, al or·no, al *oven baked*

hortalizas ① pl or·ta·lee·sas *vegetables*

hueso ⑩ we·so *bone*

huevos ⑩ pl we·vos *eggs*
— **cocidos** ko·see·dos *boiled eggs*
— **de paslama** de pas·la·ma *turtle eggs – a popular dish in Nicaragua though ecologically suspect*
— **duros** doo·ros *hard-boiled eggs*
— **estrellados** es·tre·lya·dos *fried eggs*
— **fritos** free·tos *fried eggs*
— **pericos** pe·ree·kos *scrambled eggs with fried onions*
— **revueltos** re·vwel·tos *scrambled eggs*

humitas ① pl **(Bol)** oo·mee·tas *corn tamales filled with spiced beef, vegetables & potatoes*
— **en chala (Chi)** en cha·la *popular & tasty snack of steamed tamales wrapped in corn husks*

húngaros ⑩ pl **(Uru)** oon·ga·ros *spicy sausages on a hot dog roll*

I

infusión ⑩ een·foo·syon *herbal tea*

J

jabalí ⑩ kha·ba·lee *wild boar*

jamón ⑩ kha·mon *ham*
— **dulce** dool·se *boiled ham*
— **serrano** se·ra·no *cured ham*

jengibre ⑩ khen·khee·bre *ginger*

jochi ⓜ *kho·chee* agouti (a rodent prized for its meat)

jolque ⓜ **(Bol)** *khol·ke* kidney soup

jueyes ⓜ pl **(Pue)** *khwe·yes* land crabs – an island staple

jugo ⓜ *khoo·go* juice
— **exprimido** ⓜ *ek·spree·mee·do* freshly-squeezed juice

jugoso/a ⓜ/ⓕ *khoo·go·so/a* succulent

K

kala purkha ⓕ **(Bol)** *ka·la poor·ka* soup made from maize cooked in a ceramic dish by adding a steaming chunk of heavy pumice

kosher *ko·sher* kosher

kuchen ⓜ **(Chi)** *koo·chen* pastries filled with local fruit baked by Chileans of German descent

L

lager *la·ger* light-coloured or pale beer • lager

langosta ⓕ *lan·gos·ta* spiny lobster

langostino ⓜ *lan·gos·tee·no* prawn • lobster

lawa ⓕ **(Bol)** *la·wa* soup made from a broth thickened with corn starch or wheat flour

leche ⓕ *le·che* milk
— **desnatada** *des·na·ta·da* skimmed milk

lechón ⓜ *le·chon* suckling pig – a speciality of Cochabamba in Bolivia & found elsewhere as a fiesta dish

lechona ⓕ **(Col)** *le·cho·na* pig carcass stuffed with its own meat, rice & dried peas, then baked in an oven

lechuga ⓕ *le·choo·ga* lettuce

legumbre ⓕ *le·goom·bre* pulse

lengua ⓕ *len·gwa* tongue

lenguado ⓜ *len·gwa·do* lemon sole • dab

lenteja ⓕ *len·te·kha* lentil • in Ecuador, a lentil stew

lentejas ⓕ pl *len·te·khas* lentils

licuados ⓜ pl *lee·kwa·dos* milk-blended fruit drinks

lima ⓕ *lee·ma* lime

limón ⓜ *lee·mon* lemon

limonadas ⓕ pl *lee·mo·na·das* lemonade made with lime or lemon juice, water & sugar

lista ⓕ **de vinos** *lees·ta de vee·nos* wine list

llajhua ⓕ **(Bol)** *lya·khwa* hot salsa made from tomatoes & hot pepper pods

llano/a ⓜ/ⓕ *lya·no/a* plain

llapingachos ⓜ pl **(Ecu)** *lya·peen·ga·chos* fried mashed-potato-&-cheese pancakes often served with fritada

llaucha ⓕ pl **paceña (Bol)** *lyow·cha pa·se·nya* doughy cheese bread

locotos ⓜ pl **(Bol)** *lo·ko·tos* small hot pepper pods

locro ⓜ *lo·kro* in Argentina & Paraguay, a maize stew • in Ecuador, potato soup with corn & avocado or cheese topping

lomo ⓜ *lo·mo* loin
— **a lo pobre (Chi)** *a lo po·bre* enormous slab of beef topped with two fried eggs & served with french fries
— **con pimientos** *kon pee·myen·tos* pork sausage with peppers
— **de cerdo** *de ser·do* pork loin • sausage
— **saltado (Per)** *sal·ta·do* chopped steak fried with onions, tomatoes, potatoes & served with rice

longaniza ⓕ *lon·ga·nee·sa* dark pork sausage

M

macarrones ⓜ pl *ma·ka·ro·nes* macaroni

maíz ⓜ *ma·ees* corn • maize • sweet corn

mallorca ⓕ **(Pue)** *ma·lyor·ka* sweet pastry covered with powdered sugar

malta ① **(Pue)** *mal·ta* nonalcoholic, vitamin-fortified malt beverage

mandarina ① *man·da·ree·na* tangerine

mango ⓜ *man·go* mango

maní ⓜ *ma·nee* peanut

mantequilla ① *man·te·kee·lya* butter

manzana ① *man·sa·na* apple

maracuyá ① *ma·ra·koo·ya* passionfruit

marinado/a ⓜ/① *ma·ree·na·do/a* marinated

mariscos ⓜ pl *ma·rees·kos* seafood · shellfish

masaco ⓜ **(Bol)** *ma·sa·ko* llama charque served with mashed plantain or yuca

matambre relleno (Arg) ⓜ *ma·ta·am·bre re·lye·no* stuffed & rolled flank steak, baked or eaten cold as an appetiser

mate ⓜ *ma·te* tea prepared from **yerba mate** – the most popular hot beverage in Argentina, Paraguay & Uruguay
— **de coca (Bol, Per)** de *ko·ka* coca-leaf tea

mavi ⓜ **(Pue)** *ma·vee* a root-beer-like drink made from the bark of the ironwood tree

mayonesa ① *ma·yo·ne·sa* mayonnaise

mazamorro ⓜ *ma·sa·mo·ro* in Costa Rica, a pudding made from corn starch · in Paraguay, corn mush

mazapán ⓜ *ma·sa·pan* marzipan · almond paste

mazorca ① *ma·sor·ka* corn on the cob

mbaipy heé ⓜ **(Par)** *mba·ee·pee e·e* dessert of corn, milk & molasses

mbaipy soó ⓜ **(Par)** *mba·ee·pee so·o* hot maize pudding with meat chunks

mbeyú ⓜ **(Par)** *mbe·yoo* grilled manioc pancake

medialunas ① pl *me·dya·loo·nas* 'half moons' – small croissants which are a popular breakfast food in Argentinian cafes

mediana ① *me·dya·na* bottle (third of a litre)

medianoche ⓜ **(Pue)** *me·dya·no·che* ham, pork & cheese sandwich

medio y medio (Uru) *me·dyo ee me·dyo* mixture of sparkling wine & white wine

mejilla ① *me·khee·lya* cheek

mejillones ⓜ pl *me·khee·lyo·nes* mussels
— **al vapor** al va·por steamed mussels

melocotón ⓜ *me·lo·ko·ton* peach

melón ⓜ *me·lon* melon

membrillo ⓜ *mem·bree·lyo* quince

menta ① *men·ta* mint

menú ⓜ *me·noo* menu

menudencias ① pl **(SAm)** *me·noo·den·syas* giblets

menudo de pollo ⓜ *me·noo·do de po·lyo* gizzard · poultry entrails

mercado ⓜ *mer·ka·do* market

merengadas ① pl **(Ven)** *me·ren·ga·das* milkshake containing juice

merluza ① pl *mer·loo·sa* hake – in Argentina, it's served batter-fried with mashed potatoes
— **a la plancha** ① a la *plan·cha* grilled hake

mermelada ① *mer·me·la·da* jam

miel ① *myel* honey

migas ① pl *mee·gas* fried bread-crumb dish

milhojas ① pl **(Pue)** *meel o·khas* 'a thousand leaves' – layers of thin pastry filled with almond & honey paste

milanesa ① *mee·la·ne·sa* schnitzel

milcao ⓜ **(Chi)** *meel·kow* potato bread

mojama ① *mo·kha·ma* cured tuna

mojo isleño (Pue) ⓜ *mo·kho ees·le·nyo* piquant sauce of vinegar, tomato sauce, olive oil, onions, capers, pimentos, olives, bay leaves & garlic – often served with fried fish

molleja ① *mo·lye·kha* sweetbread

mondongo ⓜ **(Ven)** mon·*don*·go *seasoned tripe cooked in bouillon with maize, potatoes & other vegetables*

montado ⓜ mon·*ta*·do *tiny sandwich served as an appetiser*

mora ① *mo*·ra *blackberry*

morcilla ① mor·*see*·lya *blood sausage – a common* **asado** *dish*

moros y cristianos ⓜ pl **(Cub)** *mo*·ros ee krees·*tya*·nos *'Moors & Christians' – dish of black beans & rice*

mostaza ① mos·*ta*·sa *mustard*

mosto ⓜ **(Par)** *mos*·to *sugar-cane juice*

mote ⓜ **con huesillo (Chi)** *mo*·te kon we·*see*·lyo *peach nectar with barley kernels*

muchacho ⓜ **(Ven)** moo·*cha*·cho *'boy' – roast loin of beef served in sauce*

muslo ⓜ *moos*·lo *thigh*

muy hecho/a ⓜ&① mooy *e*·cho/a *well-done*

N

nabo ⓜ *na*·bo *turnip*

nacatamales ⓜ pl **(Nic)** na·ka·ta·*ma*·les *cornmeal, meat, vegetables & herbs wrapped in banana leaves*

naranja ① na·*ran*·kha *orange*

naranjadas ① pl na·ran·*kha*·das *lemonades made with orange juice*

nata ① *na*·ta *cream*

natilla ① **(Cos)** na·*tee*·lya *sour cream*

natillas ① pl na·*tee*·lyas *custard • creamy milk dessert*

nuez ⓜ nwes *nut • walnut*

O

ocas ① pl **(Bol)** *o*·kas *tough, purple, potato-like tubers*

ojo ⓜ **de bife** *o*·kho de *bee*·fe *eye of round steak*

olímpicos ⓜ pl **(Uru)** o·*leem*·pee·kos *club sandwiches*

oporto ⓜ o·*por*·to *port*

orejón ⓜ o·re·*khon* *dried apricot*

orgánico/a ⓜ or·*ga*·nee·ko/a *organic*

ostión ⓜ os·*tyon* *scallop*

ostiones ⓜ pl **(Cub)** os·*tyo*·nes *drink or appetiser containing mussels or oysters, rum, lime juice, salt & pepper*

ostras ① pl *os*·tras *oysters*

oveja ① o·*ve*·kha *ewe*

P

pabellón ⓜ **(Ven)** pa·be·*lyon* *main course consisting of shredded beef, rice, beans & fried plantain – Venezuela's national dish*

pacumutas ① pl **(Bol)** pa·koo·*moo*·tas *enormous chunks of grilled meat accompanied by* **yuca**, *onions & other trimmings*

paila ① **marina (Chi)** *pai*·la ma·*ree*·na *fish & shellfish chowder*

pajarito ⓜ pa·kha·*ree*·to *small bird*

paleta ① pa·*le*·ta *shoulder*

palillo ⓜ pa·*lee*·lyo *toothpick*

palmitos ⓜ pl **(Cos)** pal·*mee*·tos *hearts of palm – usually served in a vinegar dressing*

paloma ① pa·*lo*·ma *pigeon*

palta ① **(SAm)** *pal*·ta *avocado*
— **a la jardinera (Per)** a la khar·dee·*ne*·ra *avocado stuffed with cold vegetables & mayonnaise*
— **a la reina (Per)** a la *ray*·na *avocado stuffed with chicken salad*

pan ⓜ pan *bread*
— **de coco (Hon)** de *ko*·ko *coconut bread*

panapen ⓜ **(Pue)** pa·*na*·pen *breadfruit*

panchos ⓜ pl **(Uru, Arg)** pan·chos *mild sausages on a hot dog roll*

panes ⓜ pl **(Sal)** pa·nes *French breads sliced open & stuffed with chicken or turkey*

papas ① pl *pa·*pas potatoes
— **fritas** *free·*tas chips • French fries
— **rellenas (Bol)** re·*lye·*nas stuffed potatoes – a speciality from the central highlands

papitas ① pl pa·*pee·*tas crisps • potato chips

parrilla ① pa·*ree·*lya grill

parrillada ① pa·*ree·*lya·da mixed grill – huge slabs of grilled meat prepared over hot coals served with spicy sauces & vegetables • steak house – an institution in Argentina

pasa ① *pa·*sa raisin

pasankalla ① **(Bol)** pa·san·*ka·*lya puffed maize with caramel – very sticky & chewy concoction

pasta ① *pas·*ta pasta

pastel ⓜ pas·*tel* pastry • cake • in Puerto Rico, a sweeter version of an empanadilla with a stuffing of raisins, beans, fish or pork
— **de choclo (Chi)** de *cho·*klo maize casserole filled with vegetables, chicken & beef

pastelillos ⓜ pl **(Pue)** pas·te·*lee·*lyos smaller version of a pastel stuffed with meat & cheese

patacones ⓜ pl **(Pan, Cos)** pa·ta·*ko·*nes fried green plantains cut into thin pieces, salted & then pressed & fried

patisería ① pa·tee·se·*ree·*a cake shop

patita ① **de cerdo** pa·*tee·*ta de ser·do pig's trotter

pato ⓜ *pa·*to duck

pavo ⓜ *pa·*vo turkey

pebre ⓜ **(Chi)** *pe·*bre tasty condiment made from chopped tomatoes, onion, garlic, chilli peppers, coriander & parsley

pechuga ① pe·*choo·*ga breast meat

pedido ⓜ pe·*dee·*do order

pejibaye ⓜ **(Cos)** pe·khee·*ba·*ye starchy palm fruit also eaten as a salad

pepinillo ⓜ pe·pee·*nee·*lyo gherkin

pepino ⓜ pe·*pee·*no cucumber

pera ① *pe·*ra pear

perca ① *per·*ka perch

perdiz ① per·*dees* partridge

perejil ⓜ pe·re·*kheel* parsley

perico ⓜ **(Col)** pe·*ree·*ko small milk coffee

pescadería ① pes·ka·de·*ree·*a fish shop

pescadilla ① pes·ka·*dee·*lya whiting

pescado ⓜ pes·*ka·*do fish
— **de agua dulce** de *a·*gwa *dool·*se freshwater fish
— **de mar** ⓜ de mar saltwater fish

pescaíto ⓜ pes·ka·*ee·*to tiny fried fish

pez ⓜ **espada** pes es·*pa·*da swordfish

picada ① **(Arg)** pee·*ka·*da snack

picadillo ⓜ pee·ka·*dee·*lyo minced meat • in Cuba, ground beef hash with capsicum, raisins, ham, spices, olives & rice

picante pee·*kan·*te spicy

pierna ① *pyer·*na leg

pil pil ⓜ peel peel often spicy garlic sauce

pimentón ⓜ pee·men·*ton* paprika

pimienta ① pee·*myen·*ta pepper

pimiento ⓜ pee·*myen·*to capsicum • bell pepper

piña ① *pee·*nya pineapple

pinchita ① **(Pue)** peen·*chee·*ta homemade, illegal rum

pincho ⓜ *peen·*cho kebab

piñón ⓜ pee·*nyon* pine nut

pintado ⓜ **(Col)** peen·*ta·*do small milk coffee

piononos ⓜ pl **(Pue)** pyo·*no·*nos deep-fried cones made from plantains stuffed with cheese (or meat) & coated with egg batter

pipas ① pl **(Cos)** *pee·*pas green coconuts with a straw to drink the milk

pique ⓜ **a lo macho (Bol)** *pee·*ke a lo *ma·*cho chunked grilled beef & sausage served with french fries, lettuce, tomatoes, onions, capsicum & locotos

pisco ⓜ **(Chi, Per)** pees·ko grape brandy – often served as a **pisco sauer** with egg white, lemon juice & powdered sugar

pistacho ⓜ pees·ta·cho pistachio

plancha ⓕ plan·cha grill

plátano ⓜ pla·ta·no banana · plantain

— **maduro (Pan)** ma·doo·ro slices of ripe plantains baked or broiled with butter, brown sugar & cinnamon

platija ⓕ pla·tee·kha flounder

plato ⓜ pla·to plate · dish

poché po·che poached

poco hecho/a ⓜ/ⓕ po·ko e·cho/a rare

pollo ⓜ po·lyo chicken

— **a la canasta (Bol)** a la ka·nas·ta 'chicken in a basket' – chicken served with mustard, fries or **yuca** & **ají**

polvo ⓜ pol·vo powder

pomelo ⓜ po·me·lo grapefruit

porotos ⓜ pl po·ro·tos beans

porrón ⓜ **de cerveza** po·ron de ser·ve·sa bottled beer

postre ⓜ pos·tre dessert

potaje ⓜ po·ta·khe stew

primer ⓜ **plato** pree·mer pla·to first course · entree

puchero ⓜ **(Arg)** poo·che·ro casserole with beef, chicken, bacon, sausage, blood sausage, maize, peppers, tomatoes, onions, cabbage, sweet potatoes & squash

puerros ⓜ pl pwe·ros leek

pukacapa ⓕ **(Bol)** poo·ka·ka·pa circular **empanada** filled with cheese, olives, onions & hot pepper sauce

pulpo ⓜ pool·po octopus

— **a la gallega** a la ga·lye·ga octopus in sauce

punto, a poon·to, a medium (steak)

pupusas ⓕ pl **(Sal)** poo·poo·sas cornmeal pastry stuffed with farmer's cheese, refried beans, **chicharrón**, or all three (called **revuelta**)

Q

queque ⓜ ke·ke cake

— **seco** se·ko pound cake

quesillos ⓜ pl **(Nic)** ke·see·lyos soft cheese & onions folded in a **tortilla**

quesito ⓜ **(Pue)** ke·see·to sweet baked shell stuffed with cheese & topped with honey

queso ⓜ ke·so cheese

— **fruta bomba (Cub)** froo·ta bom·ba appetiser of warm papaya & cheese

quinoa ⓜ **(Bol)** kee·no·a nutritious indigenous grain high in protein & used to thicken stews

quinto ⓜ keen·to very small bottle

R

rábano ⓜ ra·ba·no radish

rabo ⓜ ra·bo tail

ración ⓕ ra·syon small tapas plate or dish

rancio/a ⓜ/ⓕ ran·syo/a stale

ranga ⓕ **(Bol)** ran·ga potato soup with chopped liver

rape ⓜ ra·pe monkfish

raspados ⓜ pl **(Pan)** ras·pa·dos cones made of shaved ice topped with fruit syrup & sweetened condensed milk

refresco ⓜ **(Bol)** re·fres·ko fruit-based juice with a dried peach in it

refrescos ⓜ pl re·fres·kos soft drinks

relleno ⓜ re·lye·no stuffing · in Bolivia, a stuffed corn fritter similar to **humitas**

relleno/a ⓜ/ⓕ re·lye·no/a stuffed

remolacha ⓕ re·mo·la·cha beetroot

repollo ⓜ re·po·lyo cabbage

revoltijo ⓜ re·vol·tee·kho scrambled egg

revuelta ⓕ **(Sal)** re·vwel·ta cornmeal pastry stuffed with farmer's cheese, refried beans and fried pork fat

riñón ⓜ ree·nyon kidney

rodaja ① ro·da·kha *slice*

romero ⓜ ro·me·ro *rosemary*

ron ⓜ ron *rum*

rondón ⓜ **(Cos)** ron·don *thick seafood-based soup blended with coconut milk*

ropa ① **vieja** **(Pan)** ro·pa vye·kha *'old clothes' – spicy shredded beef combination served over rice*

rosado ⓜ ro·sa·do *rosé*

rostro ⓜ **asado** **(Bol)** ros·tro a·sa·do *roasted sheep's head*

ruibarbo ⓜ roo·ee·bar·bo *rhubarb*

S

sal ① sal *salt*

salado/a ⓜ/① sa·la·do *salted • salty*

salchichas ① pl sal·chee·chas *sausages similar to hot dogs*

salmón ⓜ sal·mon *salmon*

salpicón ⓜ **(Cub)** sal·pee·kon *salad made from cold meat, potatoes, olives, capers, onion, lettuce, pineapple, capsicum & vinegar*

salsa ① sal·sa *sauce*
— **de carne** de kar·ne *gravy*

salteado/a ⓜ/① sal·te·a·do/a *sauteed*

salteñas ① pl **(Bol)** sal·te·nyas *delicious rugby-ball shaped meat & vegetable pasties that originated in Salta (Argentina)*

salvaje sal·va·khe *wild*

sancocho ⓜ san·ko·cho *In Panama, a spicy chicken & vegetable stew • in Puerto Rico, vegetable soup containing plantains, tomatoes, green pepper, chilli pepper, cilantro leaves, onion & corn kernels • in Venezuela, vegetable stew with meat, fish or chicken*

sandía ① san·dee·a *watermelon*

sangre ① san·gre *blood*

sangría ① san·gree·a *sangria (red wine punch)*

sardina ① sar·dee·na *sardine*

seco ⓜ **(Ecu)** se·ko *'dry' – meat stew served with rice*

seco/a ⓜ/① se·ko/a *dry • dried*

segundo ⓜ **plato** se·goon·do pla·to *main course*

sémola ① se·mo·la *semolina*

sepia ① se·pya *cuttlefish*

servilleta ① ser·vee·lye·ta *serviette • napkin*

sésamo ⓜ se·sa·mo *sesame*

sesos ⓜ pl se·sos *brains*

sidra ① see·dra *cider*

silpancho ⓜ **(Bol)** seel·pan·cho *a thin greasy schnitzel*

sin cubierto ⓜ seen koo·byer·to *no cover charge*

sin gas ⓜ seen gas *still*

sin grasa seen gra·sa *lean*

sobrasada ① so·bra·sa·da *soft pork sausage*

sofrito ⓜ **(Pue)** so·free·to *seasoning consisting of garlic, onions & pepper browned in olive oil then flavoured with annatto seeds*

soja ① so·kha *soya*

solomillo ⓜ so·lo·mee·lyo *sirloin*

sooyo sopy ⓜ **(Par)** soo·yo so·pee *thick soup of ground meat, accompanied by rice or noodles*

sopa ① so·pa *soup*
— **a la criolla** **(Per)** a la kryo·lya *lightly spiced noodle soup with beef, egg, milk & vegetables*
— **de caracol** **(Hon)** de ka·ra·kol *conch soup made with coconut*
— **de mariscos** **(Chi)** de ma·rees·kos *shellfish soup*
— **de mondongo** **(Hon)** de mon·don·go *tripe soup – reputed to be a good hangover remedy*
— **de pescado** de pes·ka·do *fish soup*
— **paraguaya** **(Par)** ① pa·ra·gwa·ya *corn bread with cheese & onion*

sopaipa ① **(Chi)** so·pai·pa *dark-brown unbaked wheat & flour bread*

sopaipillas ① **(Bol)** so·pai·*pee*·lyas *sweet fried breads*

sopón ⓜ **de pescado (Pue)** so·*pon* de pes·*ka*·do *fish soup flavoured with garlic, onions & sherry*

submarino ⓜ **(Arg)** soob·ma·*ree*·no *breakfast beverage consisting of a semisweet chocolate bar dissolved in steamed milk*

suflé ⓜ soo·*fle* *souffle*

T

tajadas ① pl **(Nic, Pan, Ven)** ta·*kha*·das *sliced plantains served as a base for grilled meat & cabbage salad*

tajaditas ① pl **(Hon)** ta·kha·*dee*·tas *crispy, fried banana chips*

tallarines ⓜ pl ta·lya·*ree*·nes *noodles mixed with pork, chicken, beef or vegetables sold at chifas*

tamales ⓜ pl ta·*ma*·les *cornmeal dough filled with spiced beef, vegetables & potatoes & wrapped in a maize husk & fried, grilled or baked · in Colombia, chopped pork with rice & vegetables folded in a maize dough, wrapped in banana leaves & steamed*

— **asados (Cos)** a·*sa*·dos *sweet cornmeal cakes*

tarta ① *tar*·ta *cake*

tasajo ⓜ **(Pan)** ta·*sa*·kho *dried meat cooked with vegetables*

tatú ⓜ ta·*too* *armadillo*

tawa-tawas ⓜ **(Bol)** ta·wa·*ta*·was *type of donut*

té ⓜ te *tea*

— **con leche** kon *le*·che *tea with milk*

— **con limón** kon lee·*mon* *tea with lemon*

— **de menta** de *men*·ta *mint tea*

— **sin leche** seen *le*·che *black tea*

tembleque ⓜ **(Pue)** tem·*ble*·ke *pudding-like concoction of coconut milk & cinnamon*

tereré ⓜ **(Par)** te·re·*re* *ice-cold mate*

ternera ① ter·*ne*·ra *veal*

thimpu ⓜ **(Bol)** teem·poo *spicy lamb & vegetable stew*

tibio/a ⓜ/① *tee*·bee·o/a *warm*

timochenko ⓜ **(Hon)** tee·mo·*chen*·ko **aguardiente** *mixed with aromatic plants of the region*

tinto ⓜ *teen*·to *red (wine) · in Colombia, a small cup of black coffee*

tira ① **de asado** *tee*·ra de a·*sa*·do *a narrow strip of rib roast*

tocino ⓜ to·*see*·no *bacon*

— **ahumado** a·oo·*ma*·do *smoked bacon*

— **con queso** kon *ke*·so *cold bacon with cheese*

tojorí ⓜ **(Bol)** to·kho·*ree* *oatmeal-like concoction of mashed corn, cinnamon & sugar*

tomatada ① **de cordero (Bol)** to·ma·*ta*·da de kor·*de*·ro *lamb stew with tomato sauce*

tomate ⓜ to·*ma*·te *tomato*

torta ① *tor*·ta *tart · cake · flan*

tortilla ① tor·*tee*·lya *omelette*

— **de maíz (Pan, Ecu)** de ma·*ees* *thick, fried cornmeal tortilla*

tortillas ① pl **con quesillo (Hon)** tor·*tee*·lyas kon ke·*see*·lyo *two crisp fried tortillas with melted white cheese between them*

tortuga ① tor·*too*·ga *turtle*

tostada ① tos·*ta*·da *toast*

tostones ⓜ pl **(Pue)** tos·*to*·nes *fried green plantains*

trigo ⓜ *tree*·go *wheat*

tripa ① *tree*·pa *tripe*

— **gorda** *gor*·da *large intestine – a common asado dish*

tripas ① pl *tree*·pas *offal*

trozo ⓜ *tro*·so *slice · piece*

trucha ① *troo*·cha *trout*

trufa ① *troo*·fa *truffle*

tubo ⓜ *too·bo* tall glass (quarter of a litre)

tucumana ⓕ **(Bol)** *too·koo·ma·na* tasty, heavily spiced puff-pastry shell packed with egg, potatoes, chicken & onions

tuétano ⓜ *twe·ta·no* bone marrow

turrón ⓜ *too·ron* almond nougat

U

ubre ⓕ *oo·bre* udder

uva ⓕ *oo·va* grape

V

vaca ⓕ *va·ka* beef

vacío ⓜ *va·see·o* flank steak – textured & chewy, but tasty

vainilla ⓕ *vay·nee·lya* vanilla

vapor ⓜ *va·por* steam

vapor, al *va·por, al* steamed

vaso ⓜ *va·so* glass

vegetal ⓜ *ve·khe·tal* vegetable

vegetariano/a ⓜ/ⓕ *ve·khe·ta·rya·no/a* vegetarian

venado ⓜ *ve·na·do* venison

venera ⓕ *ve·ne·ra* scallop

verduras ⓕ pl *ver·doo·ras* green vegetables

vigorón ⓜ **(Nic)** *vee·go·ron* cassava steamed & topped with fried pork rind & cabbage salad, usually served on a banana leaf

vinagre ⓜ *vee·na·gre* vinegar

vino ⓜ *vee·no* wine

— **de la casa** de la *ka·sa* house wine

— **espumoso** *es·poo·mo·so* sparkling wine

— **muy seco** mooy *se·ko* very dry wine

— **seco** *se·ko* dry wine

W

wafle ⓜ *wa·fle* waffle

witu ⓜ **(Bol)** *gwee·to* beef stew with pureed tomatoes

Y

yaguarlocro ⓜ **(Ecu)** *ya·gwar·lo·kro* potato soup with chunks of barely congealed blood sausage floating in it

yerba ⓕ **mate** dried chopped leaf of Ilex Paraguayensis which is made into a tea in Argentina, Uruguay & Paraguay

yogur ⓜ *yo·goor* yogurt

yuca ⓕ *yoo·ka* cassava – a common staple in Latin American cuisine

Z

zanahoria ⓕ *sa·na·o·rya* carrot

zapallo ⓜ **(SAm)** *sa·pa·lyo* pumpkin

zarzuela ⓕ **de marisco** *sar·swe·la de ma·rees·ko* seafood stew

emergencies

emergencias

Help!	¡Socorro!	so·*ko*·ro
Stop!	¡Pare!	*pa*·re
Go away!	¡Váyase!	*va*·ya·se
Thief!	¡Ladrón!	la·*dron*
Fire!	¡Fuego!	*fwe*·go
Watch out!	¡Cuidado!	kwee·*da*·do

Call the police!
¡Llame a la policía! — *lya*·me a la po·lee·*see*·a

Call a doctor!
¡Llame a un médico! — *lya*·me a oon *me*·dee·ko

Call an ambulance!
¡Llame a una ambulancia! — *lya*·me a *oo*·na am·boo·*lan*·sya

It's an emergency.
Es una emergencia. — es *oo*·na e·mer·*khen*·sya

Could you help me, please?
¿Me puede ayudar, por favor? — me *pwe*·de a·yoo·*dar* por fa·*vor*

I have to use the telephone.
Necesito usar el teléfono. — ne·se·*see*·to oo·*sar* el te·*le*·fo·no

I'm lost.
Estoy perdido/a. m/f — es·toy per·*dee*·do/a

Where are the toilets?
¿Dónde están los baños? — *don*·de es·*tan* los *ba*·nyos

signs

Comisaría de Policía	ko·me·sa·*ree*·a de po·lee·*see*·a	Police Station
Policía	po·lee·*see*·a	Police
Urgencias	oor·*khen*·syas	Casualty

Is it safe …?	¿Es seguro …?	es se·*goo*·ro …
at night	*por la noche*	por la *no*·che
for foreigners	*para los*	*pa*·ra los
	extranjeros	ek·stran·*khe*·ros
for gay	*para viajeros*	*pa*·ra vya·*khe*·ros
travellers	*gay*	gay
for women	*para viajeras*	*pa*·ra vya·*khe*·ras
travellers		

police

la policía

As police in Latin America can wield considerable power, it's best to adopt a respectful and deferential attitude when dealing with them.

Where's the police station?
¿Dónde está la comisaría?   don·de es·*ta* la ko·mee·sa·*ree*·a

I want to report an offence.
Quiero denunciar un   *kye*·ro de·noon·*syar* oon
delito.   de·*lee*·to

(My bag) was stolen.
(Mi bolso) fue robado.   (mee *bol*·so) fwe ro·*ba*·do

I've lost (my wallet).
He perdido (mi cartera).   e per·*dee*·do (mee kar·*te*·ra)

I've been robbed.
Me han robado.   me an ro·*ba*·do

He's/She's been assaulted.
Le/La han asaltado. m/f   le/la an a·sal·*ta*·do

I've been raped.
He sido violado/a. m/f   e *see*·do vyo·*la*·do/a

He's/She's been raped.
Ha sido violado/a. m/f   a see·do vyo·la·do/a

He/She tried to ... me. *Él/Ella intentó ...* el/e·lya een·ten·to ...

assault	*asaltarme*	a·sal·tar·me
rape	*violarme*	vyo·lar·me
rob	*robarme*	ro·bar·me

I want to contact my embassy/consulate.
Quiero ponerme en contacto con mi embajada/ consulado.
kye·ro po·ner·me en kon·tak·to kon mee em·ba·kha·da/ kon·soo·la·do

Can I call someone?
¿Puedo llamar a alguien?
pwe·do lya·mar a al·gyen

Can I call a lawyer?
¿Puedo llamar a un abogado?
pwe·do lya·mar a oon a·bo·ga·do

I need a lawyer who speaks English.
Necesito un abogado que hable inglés.
ne·se·see·to oon a·bo·ga·do ke a·ble een·gles

Can I pay an on-the-spot fine?
¿Puedo pagar una multa al contado?
pwe·do pa·gar oo·na mool·ta al kon·ta·do

This drug is for personal use.
Esta droga es para uso personal.
es·ta dro·ga es pa·ra oo·so per·so·nal

I have a prescription for this drug.
Tengo receta para este medicamento.
ten·go re·se·ta pa·ra es·te me·dee·ka·men·to

What am I accused of?
¿De qué me acusan?
de ke me a·koo·san

I apologise.
Lo siento.
lo syen·to

I didn't realise I was doing anything wrong.
No sabía que estaba   no sa·*bee*·a ke es·*ta*·ba
haciendo algo mal.   a·*syen*·do *al*·go mal

I'm innocent.
Soy inocente.   soy ee·no·*sen*·te

I (don't) understand.
(No) Entiendo.   (no) en·*tyen*·do

the police may say ...

You'll be charged with ...	*Será acusado/a de ...* m/f	se·*ra* a·koo·*sa*·do/a de ...
He'll/She'll be charged with ...	*Él/Ella será acusado/a de ...* m/f	el/e·lya se·*ra* a·koo·*sa*·do/a de ...
anti-government activities	*actividades contra el gobierno*	ak·tee·vee·*da*·des *kon*·tra el go·*byer*·no
assault	*asalto*	a·*sal*·to
disturbing the peace	*alterar el orden público*	al·te·*rar* el *or*·den *poo*·blee·ko
murder	*homicidio*	o·mee·*see*·dyo
overstaying your visa	*quedarse más tiempo de lo que permite el visado*	ke·*dar*·se mas *tyem*·po de lo ke per·*mee*·te el vee·*sa*·do
possession (of illegal substances)	*posesión (de sustancias ilegales)*	po·se·*syon* (de soos·*tan*·syas ee·le·*ga*·les)
rape	*violación*	vyo·la·*syon*
shoplifting	*ratería*	ra·te·*ree*·a
speeding	*exceso de velocidad*	ek·*se*·so de ve·lo·*see*·da
theft	*robo*	*ro*·bo

doctor

el médico

Where's the nearest …?	¿Dónde está … más cercano/a? m/f	don·de es·ta … mas ser·ka·no/a
(night) chemist	la farmacia f (de guardia)	la far·ma·sya (de gwar·dya)
(Col)	la droguería f (de guardia)	la dro·ge·ree·a (de gwar·dya)
dentist	el dentista m	el den·tees·ta
doctor	el/la médico/a m/f	el/la me·dee·ko/a
hospital	el hospital m	el os·pee·tal
medical centre	el consultorio m	el kon·sool·to·ryo
optometrist	el oculista m	el o·koo·lees·ta

I need a doctor (who speaks English).
Necesito un médico (que hable inglés).
ne·se·see·to oon me·dee·ko (ke a·ble een·gles)

Could I see a female doctor?
¿Puede examinarme una médica?
pwe·de ek·sa·mee·nar·me oo·na me·dee·ka

Can the doctor come here?
¿Puede visitarme el médico?
pwe·de vee·see·tar·me el me·dee·ko

Can I see someone who practises (acupunture)?
¿Puedo ver a alguien que practique (la acupuntura)?
pwe·do ver a al·gyen ke prak·tee·ke (la a·koo·poon·too·ra)

I've been vaccinated against ...	Estoy vacunado/a contra ... m/f	es·toy va·koo·na·do/a kon·tra ...
He's/She's been vaccinated against ...	Está vacunado/a contra ... m/f	es·ta va·koo·na·do/a kon·tra ...
(yellow) fever	la fiebre (amarilla)	la fye·bre (a·ma·ree·lya)
hepatitis A/B/C	la hepatitis A/B/C	la e·pa·tee·tees a/be/se
tetanus	el tétano	el te·ta·no
typhoid	la tifus	la tee·foos

I need new glasses.
Necesito anteojos nuevos.   ne·se·see·to an·te·o·khos nwe·vos

I need new contact lenses.
Necesito lentes de   ne·se·see·to len·tes de
contacto nuevas.   kon·tak·to nwe·vas

I've run out of my medication.
Se me terminaron los   se me ter·mee·na·ron los
medicamentos.   me·dee·ka·men·tos

Can I have a receipt for my insurance?
¿Puede darme un recibo   pwe·de dar·me oon re·see·bo
para mi seguro médico?   pa·ra mee se·goo·ro me·dee·ko

Please use a new syringe.
Por favor, use una   por fa·vor oo·se oo·na
jeringa nueva.   khe·reen·ga nwe·va

I have my own syringe.
Tengo mi propia jeringa.   ten·go mee pro·pya khe·reen·ga

I don't want a blood transfusion.
No quiero que me hagan   no kye·ro ke me a·gan
una transfusión de sangre.   oo·na trans·foo·syon de san·gre

I don't use Western medicine.
No uso la medicina   no oo·so la me·dee·see·na
occidental.   ok·see·den·tal

What's the problem?
¿Qué le pasa?　　　　　　ke le *pa*·sa

Where does it hurt?
¿Dónde le/la duele? m/f　　*don*·de le/la *dwe*·le

Do you have a temperature?
¿Tiene fiebre?　　　　　　*tye*·ne *fye*·bre

How long have you been like this?
¿Desde cuándo se siente así?　*des*·de *kwan*·do se *syen*·te a·*see*

Have you had this before?
¿Ha tenido esto antes?　　a te·*nee*·do *es*·to *an*·tes

Are you sexually active?
¿Es usted sexualmente　　es oos·*te* sek·swal·*men*·te
activo/a? m/f　　　　　　ak·*tee*·vo/a

Have you had unprotected sex?
¿Ha tenido relaciones　　a te·*nee*·do re·la·*syo*·nes
sexuales sin protección?　sek·*swa*·les seen pro·tek·*syon*

Are you allergic to anything?
¿Tiene usted alergias?　　*tye*·ne oos·*te* a·*ler*·khyas

Are you on medication?
¿Se encuentra bajo　　　se en·*kwen*·tra *ba*·kho
medicación?　　　　　　me·dee·ka·*syon*

Do you ...?	*¿Usted ...?*	oos·*te* ...
drink	*bebe*	be·be
smoke	*fuma*	*foo*·ma
take drugs	*toma drogas*	*to*·ma *dro*·gas

How long are you travelling for?
¿Por cuánto tiempo está　por *kwan*·to *tyem*·po es·*ta*
viajando?　　　　　　　vya·*khan*·do

You need to be admitted to hospital.
Necesita ingresar al　　ne·se·*see*·ta een·gre·*sar* al
hospital.　　　　　　　os·pee·*tal*

You should return home for treatment.
Debería regresar a casa　de·be·*ree*·a re·gre·*sar* a *ka*·sa
para obtener tratamiento.　*pa*·ra ob·te·*ner* tra·ta·*myen*·to

symptoms & conditions

I'm sick.
Estoy enfermo/a. m/f
es·*toy* en·*fer*·mo/a

My friend is sick.
Mi amigo está enfermo. m
mee a·*mee*·go es·*ta* en·*fer*·mo
Mi amiga está enferma. f
mee a·*mee*·ga es·*ta* en·*fer*·ma

It hurts here.
Me duele aquí.
me *dwe*·le a·*kee*

I've been injured.
He sido herido.
e *see*·do e·*ree*·do

I've been vomiting.
He estado vomitando.
e es·*ta*·do vo·mee·*tan*·do

I'm dehydrated.
Estoy deshidratado/a. m/f
es·*toy* des·ee·dra·*ta*·do/a

I can't sleep.
No puedo dormir.
no *pwe*·do dor·*meer*

I feel ...	*Tengo ...*	*ten*·go ...
hot and cold	*escalofríos*	es·ka·lo·*free*·os
breathless	*falta de*	*fal*·ta de
	aliento	a·*lyen*·to

I feel ...	*Me siento ...*	me *syen*·to ...
anxious	*ansioso/a* m/f	an·*syo*·so/a
better	*mejor*	me·*khor*
depressed	*deprimido/a* m/f	de·pree·*mee*·do/a
dizzy	*mareado/a* m/f	ma·re·*a*·do/a
nauseous	*con nauseas*	kon *now*·se·as
shivery	*destemplado/a* m/f	des·tem·*pla*·do/a
strange	*raro/a* m/f	*ra*·ro/a
weak	*débil*	*de*·beel
worse	*peor*	pe·*or*

I have (a) ...	Tengo ...	ten·go ...
altitude sickness	soroche	so·ro·che
cough	tos	tos
fever	fiebre	fye·bre
headache	dolor de cabeza	do·lor de ka·be·sa
migraine	migraña	mee·gra·nya

I'm ...	Soy ...	soy ...
asthmatic	asmático/a m/f	as·ma·tee·ko/a
diabetic	diabético/a m/f	dya·be·tee·ko/a
epileptic	epiléptico/a m/f	e·pee·lep·tee·ko/a

I have a cold.
Estoy resfriado/a. m/f   es·*toy* res·*frya*·do/a
Tengo un resfrío. **(SAm)**   *ten*·go oon res·*free*·o

I have a heart condition.
Sufro del corazón.   *soo*·fro del ko·ra·*son*

I've (recently) had ...
(Hace poco) He tenido ...   (*a*·se *po*·ko) e te·*nee*·do ...

He's/She's (recently) had ...
(Hace poco) Ha tenido ...   (*a*·se *po*·ko) a te·*nee*·do ...

I'm on medication for ...
Estoy bajo medicación   es·*toy* ba·kho me·dee·ka·*syon*
para ...   *pa*·ra ...

He's/She's on medication for ...
Está bajo medicación   es·*ta* ba·kho me·dee·ka·*syon*
para ...   *pa*·ra ...

This is my usual medicine.
Éste es mi medicamento   *es*·te es mee me·dee·ka·*men*·to
habitual.   a·bee·*twal*

I think it's the medication I'm on.
Me parece que son los   me pa·*re*·se ke son los
medicamentos que estoy   me·dee·ka·*men*·tos ke es·*toy*
tomando.   to·*man*·do

For more symptoms and conditions, see the **dictionary**.

women's health

I think I'm pregnant.
Creo que estoy embarazada. kre·o ke es·toy em·ba·ra·sa·da

I'm pregnant.
Estoy embarazada. es·toy em·ba·ra·sa·da

I'm on the Pill.
Tomo la píldora. to·mo la peel·do·ra

I haven't had my period for (five) days/weeks.
Hace (cinco) días/semanas a·se (seen·ko) dee·as/se·ma·nas
que no me viene la regla. ke no me vye·ne la re·gla

I've noticed a lump here.
Me he fijado que tengo un me e fee·kha·do ke ten·go oon
bulto aquí. bool·to a·kee

the doctor may say ...

Are you sexually active?
¿Es usted sexualmente es oos·te sek·swal·men·te
activa? ak·tee·va

Are you using contraception?
¿Usa anticonceptivos? oo·sa an·tee·kon·sep·tee·vos

Are you menstruating?
¿Tiene la menstruación? tye·ne la mens·trwa·syon

Are you pregnant?
¿Está embarazada? es·ta em·ba·ra·sa·da

When did you last have your period?
¿Cuándo le vino la regla kwan·do le vee·no la re·gla
por última vez? por ool·tee·ma ves

You're pregnant.
Está embarazada. es·ta em·ba·ra·sa·da

I need ...	*Quisiera ...*	kee·*sye*·ra ...
contraception	*usar algún*	oo·*sar* al·*goon*
	método	*me*·to·do
	anticonceptivo	an·tee·kon·sep·*tee*·vo
the morning-	*tomar la píldora*	to·*mar* la *peel*·do·ra
after pill	*del día siguiente*	del *dee*·a see·*gyen*·te
a pregnancy test	*una prueba de*	*oo*·na *prwe*·ba de
	embarazo	em·ba·*ra*·so

For more terms which relate to women's health, see the **dictionary**.

allergies

alergias

I'm allergic to ...	*Soy alérgico/a* ... m/f	soy a·*ler*·khee·ko/a ...
He's/She's allergic to ...	*Es alérgico/a* ... m/f	es a·*ler*·khee·ko/a ...
antibiotics	*a los antibióticos*	a los an·tee·*byo*·tee·kos
anti-inflammatories	*a los anti-inflamatorios*	a los an·tee·een·fla·ma·*to*·ryos
aspirin	*a la aspirina*	a la as·pee·*ree*·na
bees	*a las abejas*	a las a·*be*·khas
codeine	*a la codeina*	a la ko·de·*ee*·na
penicillin	*a la penicilina*	a la pe·nee·see·*lee*·na
pollen	*al polen*	al po·*len*

I have hay fever.
Tengo alergia al polen.   ten·go a·*ler*·khya al po·*len*

I have a skin allergy.
Tengo una alergia en la piel.   ten·go *oo*·na a·*ler*·khya en la pyel

For food-related allergies, see **vegetarian & special meals**, page 158.

parts of the body

My (knee) hurts.
Me duele (la rodilla).
me *dwe*·le (la ro·*dee*·lya)

I can't move (my ankle).
No puedo mover (el tobillo).
no *pwe*·do mo·*ver* (el to·*bee*·lyo)

I have a cramp (in my foot).
Tengo calambres (en el pie).
ten·go ka·*lam*·bres (en el pye)

(My arm) is swollen.
Se me hinchó (el brazo).
se me een·*cho* (el *bra*·so)

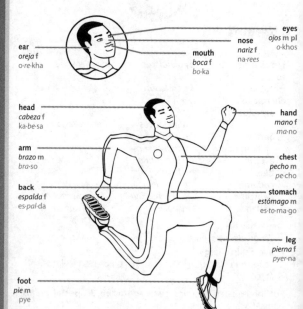

eyes
ojos m pl
o·khos

nose
nariz f
na·*rees*

ear
oreja f
o·*re*·kha

mouth
boca f
bo·ka

head
cabeza f
ka·*be*·sa

hand
mano f
ma·no

arm
brazo m
bra·so

chest
pecho m
pe·cho

back
espalda f
es·*pal*·da

stomach
estómago m
es·*to*·ma·go

leg
pierna f
pyer·na

foot
pie m
pye

chemist

la farmacia

I need something for (diarrhoea).
Necesito algo para   ne·se·*see*·to al·go *pa*·ra
(diarrea).   (dee·a·*re*·a)

Do I need a prescription for (antihistamines)?
¿Necesito receta para   ne·se·*see*·to re·*se*·ta *pa*·ra
(antihistamínicos)?   (an·tee·ees·ta·*mee*·nee·kos)

I have a prescription.
Tengo receta médica.   *ten*·go re·*se*·ta *me*·dee·ka

How many times a day?
¿Cuántas veces al día? *kwan*·tas *ve*·ses al *dee*·a

Will it make me drowsy?
¿Me producirá   me pro·doo·see·*ra*
somnolencia?   som·no·*len*·sya

health

187

dentist

I have a broken tooth.
Se me ha roto un diente. — se me a *ro*·to oon *dyen*·te

I have a cavity.
Tengo una caries. — ten·go oo·na *ka*·ryes

I have a toothache.
Me duele una muela. — me *dwe*·le *oo*·na *mwe*·la

I've lost a filling.
Se me ha caído un empaste. — se me a ka·*ee*·do oon em·*pas*·te

I need a filling.
Necesito un empaste. — ne·se·*see*·to oon em·*pas*·te

My dentures are broken.
Se me han roto los dientes postizos. — se me an *ro*·to los *dyen*·tes pos·*tee*·sos

My gums hurt.
Me duelen las encías. — me *dwe*·len las en·*see*·as

I don't want it extracted.
No quiero que me lo arranque. — no *kye*·ro ke me lo a·*ran*·ke

I need an anaesthetic.
Necesito anestesia. — ne·se·*see*·to a·nes·*te*·sya

Ouch!
¡Ay! — ai

listen for ...

a·bra
Abra. — **Open wide.**

en·*khwa*·ge
Enjuague. — **Rinse.**

es·to le/la *pwe*·de do·*ler* oon *po*·ko
Esto le/la puede doler un poco. m/f — **This might hurt a little.**

es·to no le/la do·*le*·ra
Esto no le/la dolerá. m/f — **This won't hurt a bit.**

mwer·da *es*·to
Muerda esto. — **Bite down on this.**

Nouns in the dictionary have their gender indicated by ⓜ or ⓕ. If it's a plural noun, you'll also see pl. When a word that could be either a noun or a verb has no gender indicated, it's a verb.

A

(be) able *poder* po·*der*
aboard *a bordo* a *bor*·do
abortion *aborto* ⓜ a·*bor*·to
about *sobre* so·bre
above *arriba* a·*ree*·ba
abroad *en el extranjero* en el ek·stran·*khe*·ro
accept *aceptar* a·sep·*tar*
accident *accidente* ⓜ ak·see·*den*·te
accommodation *alojamiento* ⓜ a·lo·kha·*myen*·to
across *a través* a tra·*ves*
activist *activista* ⓜ&ⓕ ak·tee·*vees*·ta
acupuncture *acupuntura* ⓕ a·koo·poon·*too*·ra
adaptor *adaptador* ⓜ a·dap·ta·*dor*
addicted *adicto/a* ⓜ/ⓕ a·*deek*·to/a
address *dirección* ⓕ dee·rek·*syon*
administration *administración* ⓕ ad·mee·nees·tra·*syon*
admission price *precio* ⓜ *de entrada* *pre*·syo de en·*tra*·da
admit (accept) *admitir* ad·mee·*teer*
admit (acknowledge) *reconocer* re·ko·no·*ser*
admit (allow to enter) *dejar entrar* de·*khar* en·*trar*
adult *adulto/a* ⓜ/ⓕ a·*dool*·to/a
advertisement *anuncio* ⓜ a·*noon*·syo
advice *consejo* ⓜ kon·*se*·kho
advise *aconsejar* a·kon·se·*khar*
aerobics *aeróbic* ⓜ a·e·ro·beek
Africa *África* ⓕ *a*·free·ka
after *después de* des·*pwes* de

aftershave *loción* ⓕ *para después del afeitado* lo·*syon* pa·ra des·*pwes* del a·fay·*ta*·do
again *otra vez* o·tra ves
age *edad* ⓕ e·*da*
aggressive *agresivo/a* ⓜ/ⓕ a·gre·*see*·vo/a
agree *estar de acuerdo* es·*tar* de a·*kwer*·do
agriculture *agricultura* ⓕ a·gree·kool·*too*·ra
AIDS *SIDA* ⓜ *see*·da
air *aire* ⓜ *ai*·re
airmail *correo* ⓜ *aéreo* ko·re·o a·e·re·o
(by) airmail *por vía aérea* por *vee*·a a·*e*·re·a
air-conditioned *con aire acondicionado* kon *ai*·re a·kon·dee·syo·*na*·do
airline *aerolínea* ⓕ a·e·ro·*lee*·ne·a
airport *aeropuerto* ⓜ a·e·ro·*pwer*·to
airport tax *tasa* ⓕ *del aeropuerto* *ta*·sa del a·e·ro·*pwer*·to
aisle (plane, train) *pasillo* ⓜ pa·*see*·lyo
alarm clock *despertador* ⓜ des·per·ta·*dor*
alcohol *alcohol* ⓜ al·*kol*
all (singular) *todo/a* ⓜ/ⓕ sg *to*·do/a
all (plural) *todos/as* ⓜ/ⓕ pl *to*·dos/as
allergy *alergia* ⓕ a·*ler*·khya
allow *permitir* per·mee·*teer*
almond *almendra* ⓕ al·*men*·dra
almost *casi* *ka*·see
alone *solo/a* ⓜ/ⓕ *so*·lo/a
already *ya* ya
also *también* tam·*byen*

altar *altar* ⓜ al·tar
altitude *altura* ⓕ al·too·ra
altitude sickness *soroche* ⓜ so·ro·che
always *siempre* syem·pre
amateur *amateur* ⓜ&ⓕ a·ma·toor
ambassador *embajador/ embajadora* ⓜ/ⓕ em·ba·kha·dor/ em·ba·kha·do·ra
ambulance *ambulancia* ⓕ am·boo·lan·sya
America *América* ⓕ a·me·ree·ka
among *entre* en·tre
amount *cantidad* kan·tee·da
anarchist *anarquista* ⓜ&ⓕ a·nar·kees·ta
ancient *antiguo/a* ⓜ/ⓕ an·tee·gwo/a
and *y* ee
angry *enojado/a* ⓜ/ⓕ e·no·kha·do/a
animal *animal* ⓜ a·nee·mal
animal rights *derechos* ⓜ pl *de animales* de·re·chos de a·nee·ma·les
ankle *tobillo* ⓜ to·bee·lyo
annoyed *fastidiado/a* ⓜ/ⓕ fas·tee·dya·do/a
answer *respuesta* ⓕ res·pwes·ta
answering machine *contestador* ⓜ *automático* kon·tes·ta·dor ow·to·ma·tee·ko
ant *hormiga* ⓕ or·mee·ga
antibiotics *antibióticos* ⓜ pl an·tee·byo·tee·kos
antihistamines *antihistaminicos* ⓜ pl an·tee·ees·ta·mee·nee·kos
antimalarial tablets *pastillas* ⓕ pl *antipalúdicas* pas·tee·lyas an·tee·pa·loo·dee·kas
antinuclear *antinuclear* an·tee·noo·kle·ar
antique *antigüedad* ⓕ an·tee·gwe·da
antiseptic *antiséptico* an·tee·sep·tee·ko
any (singular) *alguno/a* ⓜ/ⓕ sg al·goo·no/a
any (plural) *algunos/as* ⓜ/ⓕ pl al·goo·nos/as
appendix *apéndice* ⓜ a·pen·dee·se
apple *manzana* ⓕ man·sa·na
appointment *cita* ⓕ see·ta

apricot ⓜ *damasco* da·mas·ko
archaeological *arqueológico/a* ⓜ/ⓕ ar·ke·o·lo·khee·ko/a
architect *arquitecto/a* ⓜ/ⓕ ar·kee·tek·to/a
architecture *arquitectura* ⓕ ar·kee·tek·too·ra
Argentina *Argentina* ⓕ ar·khen·tee·na
argue *discutir* dees·koo·teer
arm *brazo* ⓜ bra·so
armadillo *armadillo* ⓜ ar·ma·dee·lyo
army *ejercito* ⓜ e·kher·see·to
arrest *detener* de·te·ner
arrivals *llegadas* ⓕ pl lye·ga·das
arrive *llegar* lye·gar
art *arte* ⓜ ar·te
art gallery *museo* ⓜ *de arte* moo·se·o de ar·te
artist *artista* ⓜ&ⓕ ar·tees·ta
ashtray *cenicero* ⓜ se·nee·se·ro
Asia ⓕ *Asia* a·sya
ask (a question) *preguntar* pre·goon·tar
ask (for something) *pedir* pe·deer
aspirin *aspirina* ⓕ as·pee·ree·na
ass (bum) *culo* ⓜ koo·lo
asthma *asma* ⓜ as·ma
athletics *atletismo* ⓜ at·le·tees·mo
atmosphere *atmósfera* ⓕ at·mos·fe·ra
aubergine *berenjena* ⓕ be·ren·khe·na
aunt *tía* ⓕ tee·a
Australia *Australia* ⓕ ows·tra·lya
automatic *automático/a* ⓜ/ⓕ ow·to·ma·tee·ko/a
automatic teller machine *cajero* ⓜ *automático* ka·khe·ro ow·to·ma·tee·ko
autumn *otoño* ⓜ o·to·nyo
avenue *avenida* ⓕ a·ve·nee·da
avocado *palta* ⓕ pal·ta

B

B&W (film) *blanco y negro* blan·ko ee ne·gro
baby *bebé* ⓜ&ⓕ be·be
baby food *comida* ⓕ *de bebé* ko·mee·da de be·be
baby powder *talco* ⓜ tal·ko

babysitter *babysitter* ⓜ&ⓕ
be·bee·*see*·ter
back (body) *espalda* ⓕ es·*pal*·da
backpack *mochila* ⓕ mo·*chee*·la
bacon *tocino* ⓜ to·*see*·no
bad *malo/a* ⓜ/ⓕ *ma*·lo/a
bag (general) *bolso* ⓜ *bol*·so
bag (shopping) *bolsa* ⓕ *(de compras)*
bol·sa (de kom·*pras*)
baggage *equipaje* ⓜ e·kee·*pa*·khe
baggage allowance *límite* ⓜ *de*
equipaje *lee*·mee·te de e·kee·*pa*·khe
baggage claim *recogida* ⓕ *de*
equipajes re·ko·*khee*·da de
e·kee·*pa*·khes
bakery *panadería* ⓕ pa·na·de·*ree*·a
balance (account) *saldo* ⓜ *sal*·do
balcony *balcón* ⓜ bal·*kon*
ball *pelota* ⓕ pe·*lo*·ta
ballet *ballet* ⓜ ba·*le*
ballpoint pen *bolígrafo* ⓜ bo·*lee*·gra·fo
banana (CAm) *plátano* ⓜ *pla*·ta·no
banana (SAm) *banana* ⓕ ba·*na*·na
banana (Ven) *cambur* ⓜ kam·*boor*
band (music) *grupo* ⓜ *groo*·po
bandage *vendaje* ⓜ ven·*da*·khe
Band-Aids *curitas* ⓕ pl koo·*ree*·tas
bank (money) *banco* ⓜ *ban*·ko
bank account *cuenta* ⓕ *bancaria*
kwen·ta ban·*ka*·rya
banknotes *billetes* ⓜ pl *de banco*
bee·*lye*·tes de *ban*·ko
baptism *bautizo* ⓜ bow·*tee*·so
bar *bar* ⓜ bar
barber *barbero* ⓜ bar·*be*·ro
baseball *béisbol* ⓜ *bays*·bol
basket *canasta* ⓕ ka·*nas*·ta
basketball *basquetbol* ⓜ *bas*·ket·bol
bath *baño* ⓜ *ba*·nyo
bath tub *bañera* ⓕ ba·*nye*·ra
bathing suit *traje* ⓜ *de baño* ·
malla ⓕ *de baño* *tra*·khe de *ba*·nyo ·
ma·lya de *ba*·nyo
bathroom *baño* ⓜ *ba*·nyo
battery (car) *batería* ⓕ ba·te·*ree*·a
battery (general) *pila* ⓕ *pee*·la
be *ser · estar* ser · es·*tar*

beach *playa* ⓕ *pla*·ya
beans *frijoles* ⓜ pl free·*kho*·les
beautician *esteticista* ⓜ&ⓕ
es·te·tee·*sees*·ta
beautiful *bello/a* ⓜ/ⓕ *be*·lyo/a
beauty salon *salón* ⓜ *de belleza*
sa·*lon* de be·*lye*·sa
because *porque* por·*ke*
bed *cama* ⓕ *ka*·ma
bedding *ropa* ⓕ *de cama* *ro*·pa de
ka·ma
bedroom *habitación* ⓕ a·bee·ta·*syon*
bee *abeja* ⓕ a·*be*·kha
beef *carne* ⓕ *de vaca* *kar*·ne de *va*·ka
beer *cerveza* ⓕ ser·*ve*·sa
beetroot *remolacha* ⓕ re·mo·*la*·cha
before *antes* *an*·tes
beggar *mendigo/a* ⓜ/ⓕ men·*dee*·go/a
begin *comenzar* ko·men·*sar*
behind *detrás de* de·*tras* de
bell pepper *pimiento* ⓜ pee·*myen*·to
below *abajo* a·*ba*·kho
Belize *Belice* ⓕ be·*lee*·se
best *mejor* me·*khor*
bet *apuesta* ⓕ a·*pwes*·ta
better *mejor* me·*khor*
between *entre* *en*·tre
bible *biblia* ⓕ *bee*·blya
bicycle *bicicleta* ⓕ bee·see·*kle*·ta
big *grande* *gran*·de
bike *bici* ⓕ *bee*·see
bike chain *cadena* ⓕ *de bici* ka·*de*·na
de *bee*·see
bike path *camino* ⓜ *de bici* ka·*mee*·no
de *bee*·see
bill (account) *cuenta* ⓕ *kwen*·ta
biodegradable *biodegradable*
byo·de·gra·*da*·ble
biography *biografía* ⓕ byo·gra·*fee*·a
bird *pájaro* ⓜ *pa*·kha·ro
birth certificate *partida* ⓕ
de nacimiento par·*tee*·da de
na·see·*myen*·to
birthday *cumpleaños* ⓜ
koom·ple·*a*·nyos
biscuit *galleta* ⓕ ga·*lye*·ta
bite (dog) *mordedura* ⓕ mor·de·*doo*·ra

bite (insect) *picadura* ⓕ pee·ka·*doo*·ra
black *negro/a* ⓜ/ⓕ *ne*·gro/a
blanket *frazada* ⓕ fra·*sa*·da
blind *ciego/a* ⓜ/ⓕ *sye*·go/a
blister *ampolla* ⓕ am·*po*·lya
blocked *atascado/a* ⓜ/ⓕ a·*tas*·ka·do/a
blood *sangre* ⓕ *san*·gre
blood group *grupo* ⓜ *sanguíneo*
groo·po san·*gee*·ne·o
blood pressure *presión* ⓕ *arterial*
pre·*syon* ar·te·*ryal*
blood test *análisis* ⓜ *de sangre*
a·*na*·lee·sees de *san*·gre
blue *azul* a·*sool*
board (plane, ship) *embarcarse*
em·bar·*kar*·se
boarding house *pensión* ⓕ pen·*syon*
boarding pass *tarjeta* ⓕ *de embarque*
tar·*khe*·ta de em·*bar*·ke
boat *barco* ⓜ *bar*·ko
body *cuerpo* ⓜ *kwer*·po
Bolivia *Bolivia* ⓕ bo·*lee*·vya
bomb *bomba* ⓕ *bom*·ba
bone *hueso* ⓜ *we*·so
book *libro* ⓜ *lee*·bro
book (reserve) *reservar* re·ser·*var*
booked out *lleno/a* ⓜ/ⓕ *lye*·no/a
bookshop *librería* ⓕ lee·bre·*ree*·a
boots *botas* ⓕ pl *bo*·tas
border (frontier) *frontera* ⓕ fron·*te*·ra
borders (photography) *marcos* ⓜ pl
mar·kos
(be) bored (estar) *aburrido/a* ⓜ/ⓕ
(es·*tar*) a·boo·*ree*·do/a
boring *aburrido/a* ⓜ/ⓕ a·boo·*ree*·do/a
borrow *pedir* pe·*deer*
botanic garden *jardín* ⓜ *botánico*
khar·*deen* bo·ta·nee·ko
both *ambos* ⓜ/ⓕ pl *am*·bos
bottle *botella* ⓕ bo·*te*·lya
bottle opener *abrebotellas* ⓜ
a·bre·bo·te·lyas
(at the) bottom (al) *fondo* (de)
(al) *fon*·do (de)
bowl *bol* ⓜ bol
box *caja* ⓕ *ka*·kha
boxing *boxeo* ⓜ bok·*se*·o

boy *chico* ⓜ *chee*·ko
boyfriend *novio* ⓜ *no*·vyo
bra *corpiño* ⓜ kor·*pee*·nyo
Braille *Braille* ⓜ bray·e·le
brake *freno* ⓜ pl *fre*·no
brandy *coñac* ko·*nyak*
brave *valiente* va·*lyen*·te
Brazil *Brasil* ⓜ bra·*seel*
bread *pan* ⓜ pan
  rye bread *pan* ⓜ *de centeno*
  pan de sen·*te*·no
  sourdough bread *pan* ⓜ *de*
  masa fermentada pan de *ma*·sa
  fer·men·*ta*·da
  white bread *pan* ⓜ *blanco*
  pan *blan*·ko
  wholemeal bread *pan* ⓜ *integral*
  pan een·te·*gral*
bread rolls *bollos* ⓜ pl *bo*·lyos
break *romper* rom·*per*
break down *descomponerse*
des·kom·po·*ner*·se
breakfast *desayuno* ⓜ de·sa·*yoo*·no
breast (poultry) *pechuga* ⓕ pe·*choo*·ga
breasts *senos* ⓜ *se*·nos
breathe *respirar* res·pee·*rar*
bribe (CAm) *mordida* ⓕ mor·*dee*·da
bribe (SAm) *coima* ⓕ *koy*·ma
bribe *coimear* koy·me·*ar*
bridge *puente* ⓜ *pwen*·te
briefcase *maletín* ⓜ ma·le·*teen*
brilliant *brillante* bree·*lyan*·te
bring *traer* tra·*er*
broken *roto/a* ⓜ/ⓕ *ro*·to/a
broken down (machine)
averiado/a ⓜ/ⓕ a·ve·*rya*·do/a
bronchitis *bronquitis* ⓜ bron·*kee*·tees
brother *hermano* ⓜ er·*ma*·no
brown *marrón* ma·*ron*
bruise *moretón* ⓜ mo·re·*ton*
Brussels sprouts *coles* ⓕ pl *de*
Bruselas ko·les de broo·se·las
bucket *balde* ⓜ *bal*·de
budget *presupuesto* ⓜ pre·soo·*pwes*·to
Buddhist *budista* ⓜ&ⓕ boo·*dees*·ta
buffet (meal) *buffet* ⓜ *boo*·fet
bug *bicho* ⓜ *bee*·cho

build *construir* kons·troo·*eer*
building *edificio* ⓜ e·dee·*fee*·syo
bulb *bombillo* ⓜ bom·*bee*·lyo
bulb (Ecu, Per) *foco* ⓜ *fo*·ko
bull *toro* ⓜ *to*·ro
bullfight *corrida* ① ko·*ree*·da
bullring *plaza* ① *de toros pla*·sa de *to*·ros
bum (ass) *culo* ⓜ *koo*·lo
burn *quemadura* ① ke·ma·*doo*·ra
burn *quemar* ke·*mar*
bus (city) *autobús* ⓜ ow·to·*boos*
bus (intercity) *ómnibus* ⓜ *om*·nee·boos
bus station (city) *estación* ① *de
    autobuses* es·ta·*syon* de ow·to·*boo*·ses
bus station (intercity) *estación* ①
    de ómnibuses es·ta·*syon* de
    om·nee·boo·ses
bus stop (city) *parada* ① *de autobús*
    pa·*ra*·da de ow·to·*boos*
bus stop (intercity) *parada* ① *de
    ómnibus* pa·*ra*·da de *om*·nee·boos
business *negocio* ⓜ ne·*go*·syo
business class *clase* ① *preferente*
    kla·se pre·fe·*ren*·te
business person *comerciante* ⓜ&①
    ko·mer·*syan*·te
busker *artista callejero/a* ⓜ/①
    ar·*tees*·ta ka·lye·*khe*·ro/a
busy *ocupado/a* ⓜ/① o·koo·*pa*·do/a
but *pero* *pe*·ro
butcher's shop *carnicería* ①
    kar·nee·se·*ree*·a
butter *mantequilla* ① man·te·*kee*·lya
butterfly *mariposa* ① ma·ree·*po*·sa
button *botón* ⓜ bo·*ton*
buy *comprar* kom·*prar*
buzzard *gallinazo* ⓜ ga·lyee·*na*·so

C

cabbage *repollo* ⓜ re·*po*·lyo
cable *cable* ⓜ *ka*·ble
cable car *teleférico* ⓜ te·le·*fe*·ree·ko
cactus *cactus* ⓜ *kak*·toos
cafe *cafetería* ① ka·fe·te·*ree*·a
cake *torta* ① *tor*·ta
cake shop *pastelería* ① pas·te·le·*ree*·a

calculator *calculadora* ①
    kal·koo·la·*do*·ra
calendar *calendario* ⓜ ka·len·*da*·ryo
call *llamar* lya·*mar*
camera *cámara* ① *(fotográfica)*
    ka·ma·ra (fo·to·*gra*·fee·ka)
camera shop *tienda* ① *de fotografía*
    tyen·da de fo·to·gra·*fee*·a
camp *acampar* a·*kam*·par
campsite *cámping* ⓜ *kam*·peen
camping store *tienda* ① *de
    provisiones de cámping* *tyen*·da de
    pro·vee·*syo*·nes de *kam*·peen
can (tin) *lata* ① *la*·ta
can (be able) *poder* po·*der*
can opener *abrelatas* ① a·bre·*la*·tas
Canada *Canadá* ⓜ ka·na·*da*
cancel *cancelar* kan·se·*lar*
cancer *cáncer* ⓜ *kan*·ser
candle *vela* ① *ve*·la
candy *dulces* ⓜ pl *dool*·ses
cantaloupe *cantalupo* ⓜ kan·ta·*loo*·po
capsicum *pimiento* ⓜ pee·*myen*·to
car *carro* ⓜ *ka*·ro
car hire *alquiler* ① *de carro* al·kee·*ler*
    de *ka*·ro
car owner's title *papeles* ⓜ pl *del
    auto* pa·*pe*·les del *ow*·to
car park *parking* ⓜ *par*·keen
car registration *matrícula* ①
    ma·*tree*·koo·la
caravan *caravana* ① ka·ra·*va*·na
cards *cartas* ① pl *kar*·tas
care (about something) *preocuparse
    por* pre·o·koo·*par*·se por
care (for someone) *cuidar de*
    kwee·*dar* de
caring *bondadoso/a* ⓜ/①
    bon·da·*do*·so/a
carriage (train) *vagón* ⓜ va·*gon*
carpenter *carpintero* ⓜ kar·peen·*te*·ro
carrot *zanahoria* ① sa·na·o·rya
carry *llevar* lye·*var*
carton *cartón* ⓜ kar·*ton*
cash *dinero* ⓜ *en efectivo* dee·*ne*·ro en
    e·fek·*tee*·vo
cash (a cheque) *cobrar (un cheque)*
    ko·*brar* (oon *che*·ke)

cash register *caja* ① *registradora* ka·kha re·khees·tra·do·ra

cashew *castaña* ① *de cajú* kas·ta·nya de ka·khoo

cashier *cajero/a* ⑩/① ka·khe·ro/a

casino *casino* ⑩ ka·see·no

cassette *casete* ① ka·set

castle *castillo* ⑩ kas·tee·lyo

casual work *trabajo* ⑩ *eventual* tra·ba·kho e·ven·twal

cat *gato/a* ⑩/① ga·to/a

cathedral *catedral* ① ka·te·dral

Catholic *católico/a* ⑩/① ka·to·lee·ko/a

cauliflower *coliflor* ko·lee·flor

cave *cueva* ① kwe·va

cavity (tooth) *caries* ① ka·ryes

CD *cómpact* ⑩ kom·pak

celebration *celebración* ① se·le·bra·syon

cell phone *teléfono* ⑩ *móvil* te·le·fo·no mo·veel

cemetery *cementerio* ⑩ se·men·te·ryo

cent *centavo* ⑩ sen·ta·vo

centimetre *centímetro* ⑩ sen·tee·me·tro

Central America *Centroamérica* ① sen·tro·a·me·ree·ka

Central American *centroamericano/a* ⑩/① sen·tro·a·me·ree·ka·no/a

central heating *calefacción* ① *central* ka·le·fak·syon sen·tral

centre *centro* ⑩ sen·tro

ceramic *cerámica* ① se·ra·mee·ka

cereal *cereales* se·re·a·les

certificate *certificado* ⑩ ser·tee·fee·ka·do

chain *cadena* ① ka·de·na

chair *silla* ① see·lya

chance *oportunidad* ① o·por·too·nee·da

change (money) *cambio* ⑩ kam·byo

change *cambiar* kam·byar

changing room *vestuario* ⑩ ves·twa·ryo

charming *encantador/encantadora* ⑩/① en·kan·ta·dor/en·kan·ta·do·ra

chat up *tratar de ligar* tra·tar de lee·gar

cheap *barato/a* ⑩/① ba·ra·to/a

cheat *tramposo/a* ⑩/① tram·po·so/a

check (bill) *cuenta* ① kwen·ta

check *revisar* re·vee·sar

check-in (airport) *facturación* ① fak·too·ra·syon

check-in (baggage) *facturación* ① *de equipaje* fak·too·ra·syon de e·kee·pa·khe

check-in (hotel) *registrar* re·khees·trar

checkpoint *control* ⑩ kon·trol

cheese *queso* ⑩ ke·so

chef *cocinero/a* ⑩/① ko·see·ne·ro/a

chemist (shop) *farmacia* ① far·ma·sya

chemist (person) *farmacéutico/a* ⑩/① far·ma·see·oo·tee·ko/a

cheque *cheque* ⑩ che·ke

chess *ajedrez* ⑩ a·khe·dres

chest *pecho* ⑩ pe·cho

chewing gum *chicle* ⑩ chee·kle

chicken *pollo* ⑩ po·lyo

chickpeas *garbanzos* ⑩ pl gar·ban·sos

child *niño/a* ⑩/① nee·nyo/a

child's car seat *asiento* ⑩ *de seguridad para bebés* a·syen·to de se·goo·ree·da pa·ra be·bes

childminding service *guardería* ① gwar·de·ree·a

Chile *Chile* ① chee·le

chilli *ají* ⑩ a·khee

chilli sauce *salsa* ① *de ají* sal·sa de a·khee

chocolate *chocolate* ⑩ cho·ko·la·te

cholera *cólera* ① ko·le·ra

choose *escoger* es·ko·kher

chopping board *tabla* ① *de cortar* ta·bla de kor·tar

Christian *cristiano/a* ⑩/① krees·tya·no/a

Christmas *Navidad* ① na·vee·da

Christmas Eve *Nochebuena* ① no·che·bwe·na

church *iglesia* ① ee·gle·sya

cider *sidra* ① see·dra

cigar *cigarro* ⑩ see·ga·ro

cigarette *cigarillo* ⑩ see·ga·ree·lyo

cigarette lighter *mechero* ⑩ me·che·ro

cigarette paper *papel* ⑩ *de fumar* pa·pel de foo·mar

cinema *cine* ⑩ see·ne

circus *circo* ⑩ seer·ko

citizenship *ciudadanía* ⓕ
syoo·da·da·*nee*·a

city *ciudad* ⓕ syoo·*da*

city centre *centro* ⓜ *de la ciudad*
sen·tro de la syoo·*da*

civil rights *derechos* ⓜ pl *civiles*
de·*re*·chos see·*vee*·les

classical *clásico/a* ⓜ/ⓕ *kla*·see·ko/a

clean *limpio/a* ⓜ/ⓕ *leem*·pyo/a

cleaning *limpieza* ⓕ leem·*pye*·sa

client *cliente/a* ⓜ/ⓕ *klyen*·te/a

cliff *acantilado* ⓜ a·kan·tee·*la*·do

climb *subir* soo·*beer*

cloak *capote* ⓜ ka·*po*·te

cloakroom *guardarropa* ⓜ
gwar·da·*ro*·pa

clock *reloj* ⓜ re·*lokh*

close (nearby) *cerca ser*·ka

close (shut) *cerrar* se·*rar*

closed *cerrado/a* ⓜ/ⓕ se·*ra*·do/a

clothes line *cuerda* ⓕ *para tender la*
ropa kwer·da *pa*·ra ten·*der* la *ro*·pa

clothing *ropa* ⓕ *ro*·pa

clothing store *tienda* ⓕ *de ropa*
tyen·da de *ro*·pa

cloud *nube* ⓕ *noo*·be

cloudy *nublado/a* ⓜ/ⓕ noo·*bla*·do/a

clutch *embrague* ⓜ em·*bra*·ge

coach (sport) *entrenador/entrenadora*
ⓜ/ⓕ en·tre·na·*dor*/en·tre·na·*do*·ra

coast *costa* ⓕ *kos*·ta

coat *saco* ⓜ *sa*·ko

coke (drug) *coca* ⓕ *ko*·ka

cocaine *cocaína* ⓕ ko·ka·*ee*·na

coca plant *coca* ⓕ *ko*·ka

cockroach *cucaracha* ⓕ koo·ka·*ra*·cha

cocoa *cacao* ⓜ ka·*kow*

coconut *coco* ⓜ *ko*·ko

coconut palm *palma* ⓕ *de coco*
pal·ma de *ko*·ko

codeine *codeína* ⓕ ko·de·*ee*·na

coffee *café* ⓜ ka·*fe*

coins *monedas* ⓕ pl mo·*ne*·das

coke (drug) *coca* ⓕ *ko*·ka

cold *frío/a* ⓜ/ⓕ *free*·o/a

(have a) cold *(tener) resfrío* (te·*ner*)
res·*free*·o

colleague *colega* ⓜ&ⓕ ko·*le*·ga

collect call *llamada* ⓕ *a cobro revertido*
lya·*ma*·da a *ko*·bro re·ver·*tee*·do

college (hall of residence)
residencia ⓕ *de estudiantes*
re·see·*den*·sya de es·too·*dyan*·tes

college (school) *colegio* ⓜ ko·*le*·khyo

college (university) *universidad* ⓕ
oo·nee·ver·see·*da*

Colombia *Colombia* ⓕ ko·*lom*·bya

colour *color* ⓜ ko·*lor*

comb *peine* ⓜ *pay*·ne

come *venir* ve·*neer*

comedy *comedia* ⓕ ko·*me*·dya

comics *cómics* ⓜ pl *ko*·meeks

comfortable *cómodo/a* ⓜ/ⓕ
ko·mo·do/a

communion *comunión* ⓕ ko·moo·*nyon*

communist *comunista* ⓜ&ⓕ
ko·moo·*nees*·ta

companion *compañero/a* ⓜ/ⓕ
kom·pa·*nye*·ro/a

company *compañía* ⓕ kom·pa·*nyee*·a

compass *brújula* ⓕ *broo*·khoo·la

complain *quejarse* ke·*khar*·se

computer *computadora* ⓕ
kom·poo·ta·*do*·ra

computer game *juego* ⓜ *de*
computadora khwe·go de
kom·poo·ta·*do*·ra

concert *concierto* ⓜ kon·*syer*·to

conditioner *acondicionador* ⓜ
a·kon·dee·syo·na·*dor*

condom *condón* ⓜ kon·*don*

condor *cóndor* ⓜ *kon*·dor

confession *confesión* ⓕ kon·fe·*syon*

confirm *confirmar* kon·feer·*mar*

connection *conexión* ⓕ ko·nek·*syon*

conservative *conservador/*
conservadora ⓜ/ⓕ kon·ser·va·*dor*/
kon·ser·va·*do*·ra

constipation *estreñimiento* ⓜ
es·tre·nyee·*myen*·to

consulate *consulado* ⓜ kon·soo·*la*·do

contact lenses *lentes* ⓕ pl *de*
contacto len·tes de kon·*tak*·to

contemporary *contemporáneo/a* ⓜ/ⓕ
kon·tem·po·*ra*·ne·o/a

contraceptive *anticonceptivo* ⓜ
an·tee·kon·sep·*tee*·vo

contract *contrato* ⓜ kon·*tra*·to

convenience store *tienda* ⓕ *de
artículos básicos* tyen·da de
ar·*tee*·koo·los ba·see·kos

convent *convento* ⓜ kon·*ven*·to

cook *cocinero/a* ⓜ/ⓕ ko·see·*ne*·ro/a

cook *cocinar* ko·see·*nar*

cookie *galleta* ⓕ ga·*lye*·ta

corkscrew *sacacorchos* ⓜ sa·ka·*kor*·chos

corn *maíz* ⓜ ma·*ees*

cornflakes *copos* ⓜ pl *de maíz*
ko·pos de ma·*ees*

corner *esquina* ⓕ es·*kee*·na

corrupt *corrupto/a* ⓜ/ⓕ ko·*roop*·to/a

cost *coste* ⓜ *kos*·te

cost *costar* kos·*tar*

Costa Rica *Costa Rica* ⓕ *kos*·ta *ree*·ka

cottage cheese *requesón* ⓜ re·ke·*son*

cotton *algodón* ⓜ al·go·*don*

cotton balls *bolas* ⓕ pl *de algodón*
bo·las de al·go·*don*

cough *tos* ⓕ tos

cough medicine *jarabe* ⓜ kha·*ra*·be

count *contar* kon·*tar*

counter (shop) *mostrador* ⓜ
mos·tra·*dor*

country (nation) *país* ⓜ pa·*ees*

countryside *campo* ⓜ *kam*·po

coupon *cupón* ⓜ koo·*pon*

courgette *calabacín* ⓜ ka·la·ba·*seen*

court (legal) *tribunal* ⓜ tree·boo·*nal*

court (tennis) *cancha* ⓕ *kan*·cha

cousin *primo/a* ⓜ/ⓕ *pree*·mo/a

cover charge (restaurant) *precio* ⓜ
del cubierto pre·syo del koo·*byer*·to

cover charge (venue) *precio* ⓜ *de
entrada* pre·syo de en·*tra*·da

cow *vaca* ⓕ *va*·ka

craft market *mercado* ⓜ *de artesanía*
mer·*ka*·do de ar·te·sa·*nee*·a

craft *artesanía* ⓕ ar·te·sa·*nee*·a

crash (accident) *choque* ⓜ *cho*·ke

crazy *loco/a* ⓜ/ⓕ *lo*·ko/a

cream *crema* ⓕ *kre*·ma

cream cheese *queso* ⓜ *cremoso*
ke·so kre·*mo*·so

creche *guardería* ⓕ gwar·de·*ree*·a

credit card *tarjeta* ⓕ *de crédito*
tar·*khe*·ta de *kre*·dee·to

cricket (sport) *críquet* ⓜ *kree*·ket

crocodile *cocodrilo* ⓜ ko·ko·*dree*·lo

crop *cosecha* ⓕ ko·*se*·cha

crowded *abarrotado/a* ⓜ/ⓕ
a·ba·ro·*ta*·do/a

Cuba *Cuba* ⓕ *koo*·ba

cucumber *pepino* ⓜ pe·*pee*·no

cup *taza* ⓕ *ta*·sa

cupboard *armario* ⓜ ar·*ma*·ryo

currency exchange *cambio* ⓜ
(de dinero) kam·byo (de dee·*ne*·ro)

current *corriente* ⓕ ko·*ryen*·te

current affairs *informativo* ⓜ
een·for·ma·*tee*·vo

curry *curry* ⓜ *koo*·ree

curry powder *curry* ⓜ *en polvo* *koo*·ree
en *pol*·vo

customs *aduana* ⓕ a·*dwa*·na

cut *cortar* kor·*tar*

cutlery *cubiertos* ⓜ pl koo·*byer*·tos

CV *historial* ⓜ *profesional* ees·to·*ryal*
pro·fe·syo·*nal*

cycle *andar en bicicleta* an·*dar* en
bee·see·*kle*·ta

cycling *ciclismo* ⓜ see·*klees*·mo

cyclist *ciclista* ⓜ&ⓕ see·*klees*·ta

cystitis *cistitis* ⓕ sees·*tee*·tees

D

dad *papá* ⓜ pa·*pa*

daily *diariamente* dya·rya·*men*·te

dance *baile* ⓕ *bai*·le

dance *bailar* bai·*lar*

dangerous *peligroso/a* ⓜ/ⓕ
pe·lee·*gro*·so/a

dark *oscuro/a* ⓜ/ⓕ os·*koo*·ro/a

date (appointment) *cita* ⓕ *see*·ta

date (day) *fecha* ⓕ *fe*·cha

date (a person) *salir con* sa·*leer* kon

date of birth *fecha* ① *de nacimiento*
fe·cha de na·see·*myen*·to

daughter *hija* ① ee·kha

dawn *alba* ① *al*·ba

day *día* ⓜ *dee*·a

day after tomorrow *pasado mañana*
pa·*sa*·do ma·*nya*·na

day before yesterday *anteayer*
an·te·a·*yer*

dead *muerto/a* ⓜ/① *mwer*·to/a

deaf *sordo/a* ⓜ/① *sor*·do/a

decide *decidir* de·see·*deer*

deep *profundo/a* ⓜ/① pro·*foon*·do/a

deforestation *deforestación* ①
de·fo·res·ta·*syon*

delay *demora* ① de·*mo*·ra

deliver *entregar* en·tre·*gar*

democracy *democracia* ①
de·mo·kra·*see*·a

demonstration (protest)
manifestación ① ma·nee·fes·ta·*syon*

dengue fever *fiebre* ① *del dengue*
fye·bre del *den*·ge

dental floss *hilo* ⓜ *dental* ee·lo den·*tal*

dentist *dentista* ⓜ&① den·*tees*·ta

deodorant *desodorante* ⓜ
de·so·do·*ran*·te

depart (person) *partir* par·*teer*

depart (plane etc) *salir* sa·*leer*

department store *grande almacén* ⓜ
gran·de al·ma·*sen*

departure (person) *partida* ①
par·*tee*·da

departure (plane etc) *salida* ① sa·*lee*·da

deposit (bank) *depósito* ⓜ de·*po*·see·to

descendant *descendiente* ⓜ
de·sen·*dyen*·te

desert *desierto* ⓜ de·*syer*·to

design *diseño* ⓜ dee·*se*·nyo

destination *destino* ⓜ des·*tee*·no

detail *detalle* ⓜ de·*ta*·lye

detective novel *novela* ① *negra*
no·*ve*·la *ne*·gra

diabetes *diabetes* ① dya·*be*·tes

dial tone *tono* ⓜ *to*·no

diaper *pañal* ⓜ pa·*nyal*

diaphragm *diafragma* ① dya·*frag*·ma

diarrhoea *diarrea* ① dya·*re*·a

diary *agenda* ① a·*khen*·da

dictionary *diccionario* ⓜ
deek·syo·na·ryo

die *morir* mo·*reer*

diet (customary food) *dieta* ① *dye*·ta

diet (slimming) *régimen* ⓜ *re*·khee·men

different *diferente* dee·fe·*ren*·te

difficult *difícil* dee·*fee*·seel

dining car *vagón* ⓜ *restaurante*
va·*gon* res·tow·*ran*·te

digital camera *cámara* ① *digital*
ka·ma·ra dee·khee·*tal*

dinner *cena* ① *se*·na

direct *directo/a* ⓜ/① dee·*rek*·to/a

direct-dial *servicio* ⓜ *telefónico
automático* ⓜ *re·vee·syo*
te·le·fo·nee·ko ow·to·ma·*tee*·ko

director *director/directora* ⓜ/①
dee·rek·*tor*/dee·rek·*to*·ra

dirty *sucio/a* ⓜ/① *soo*·syo/a

disabled *minusválido/a* ⓜ/①
mee·noos·*va*·lee·do/a

disco *discoteca* ① dees·ko·*te*·ka

discount *descuento* ⓜ des·*kwen*·to

discover *descubrir* des·koo·*breer*

discrimination *discriminación* ①
dees·kree·mee·na·*syon*

disease *enfermedad* ① en·fer·mee·*da*

disk *disco* ⓜ *dees*·ko

disposable camera *cámara* ①
descartable ka·ma·ra des·kar·*ta*·ble

diving *submarinismo* ⓜ
soob·ma·ree·*nees*·mo

diving equipment *equipo* ⓜ *de
inmersión* e·*kee*·po de een·mer·*syon*

dizzy *mareado/a* ⓜ/① ma·re·a·do/a

do *hacer* a·*ser*

doctor *médico/a* ⓜ/① *me*·dee·ko/a

dog *perro/a* ⓜ/① *pe*·ro/a

dole *subsidio* ⓜ *de desempleo*
soob·*see*·dyo de des·em·*ple*·o

doll *muñeca* ① moo·*nye*·ka

dollar *dólar* ⓜ *do*·lar

domestic (country) *nacional* na·syo·*nal*

domestic flight *vuelo* ⓜ *doméstico*
vwe·lo do·*mes*·tee·ko

Dominican Republic *República* ① *Dominicana* re·poo·blee·ka do·mee·nee·ka·na
donkey *burro* ⑩ boo·ro
door *puerta* ① pwer·ta
dope *droga* ① dro·ga
double *doble* do·ble
double bed *cama* ① *de matrimonio* ka·ma de ma·tree·mo·nyo
double copies (photos) *dos copias* ① pl dos ko·pyas
double room *habitación* ① *doble* a·bee·ta·syon do·ble
down *hacia abajo* a·see·a a·ba·kho
downhill *cuesta abajo* kwes·ta a·ba·kho
dozen *docena* ① do·se·na
drama *drama* ⑩ dra·ma
draw *dibujar* dee·boo·khar
dream *soñar* so·nyar
dress *vestido* ⑩ ves·tee·do
drink *copa* ① ko·pa
drink *tomar* to·mar
drinkable *potable* po·ta·ble
drive *conducir* kon·doo·seer
drivers licence *carnet* ⑩ kar·net
drug (medicinal) *medicina* ① me·dee·see·na
drug addiction *drogadicción* ① dro·ga·deek·syon
drug dealer *traficante* ⑩ *de drogas* tra·fee·kan·te de dro·gas
drugs (illegal) *drogas* ① pl dro·gas
drums *batería* ① ba·te·ree·a
drunk *borracho/a* ⑩/① bo·ra·cho/a
dry *seco/a* ⑩/① se·ko/a
dry *secar* se·kar
duck *pato* ⑩ pa·to
dummy (pacifier) *chupete* ⑩ choo·pe·te
during *durante* doo·ran·te
DVD *DVD* de oo·ve·da
dysentry *disentería* ① dee·sen·te·ree·a

E

each *cada* ka·da
ear *oreja* ① o·re·kha
early *temprano* tem·pra·no
earn *ganar* ga·nar

earplugs *tapones* ⑩ pl *para los oídos* ta·po·nes pa·ra los o·ee·dos
earrings *aretes* ⑩ pl a·re·tes
Earth *Tierra* ① tye·ra
earthquake *terremoto* ⑩ te·re·mo·to
east *este* ⑩ es·te
Easter *Pascua* ① pas·kwa
easy *fácil* fa·seel
eat *comer* ko·mer
economy class *clase* ① *turística* kla·se too·rees·tee·ka
eczema *eczema* ① ek·se·ma
Ecuador *Ecuador* ⑩ e·kwa·dor
education *educación* ① e·doo·ka·syon
egg *huevo* ⑩ we·vo
eggplant *berenjena* ① be·ren·khe·na
elections *elecciones* ① pl e·lek·syo·nes
electrician *electricista* ⑩&① e·lek·tree·sees·ta
electricity *electricidad* ① e·lek·tree·see·da
elevator *ascensor* ⑩ a·sen·sor
El Salvador *El Salvador* ⑩ el sal·va·dor
embarrassed *avergonzado/a* ⑩/① a·ver·gon·sa·do/a
embassy *embajada* ① em·ba·kha·da
emergency *emergencia* ① e·mer·khen·sya
emotional *emocional* e·mo·syo·nal
employee *empleado/a* ⑩/① em·ple·a·do/a
employer *patrón/patrona* ⑩/① pa·tron/pa·tro·na
empty *vacío/a* ⑩/① va·see·o/a
end *fin* ⑩ feen
end *acabar* a·ka·bar
endangered species *especies* ① pl *en peligro de extinción* es·pe·syes en pe·lee·gro de ek·steen·syon
engagement (marriage) *compromiso* ⑩ kom·pro·mee·so
engine *motor* ⑩ mo·tor
engineer *ingeniero/a* ⑩/① een·khe·nye·ro/a
engineering *ingeniería* ① een·khe·nye·ree·a
England *Inglaterra* ① een·gla·te·ra

English (language) inglés ⓜ een·gles
English inglés/inglésa ⓜ/ⓕ een·gles/
  een·gle·sa
enjoy (oneself) divertirse dee·ver·teer·se
enough suficiente soo·fee·syen·te
enter entrar en·trar
entertainment guide guía ⓕ de
  los espectáculos gee·a de los
  es·pek·ta·koo·los
envelope sobre ⓜ so·bre
environment medio ⓜ ambiente
  me·dyo am·byen·te
epilepsy epilepsia ⓕ e·pee·lep·sya
equality igualdad ⓕ ee·gwal·da
equipment equipo ⓜ e·kee·po
escalator escalera ⓕ mecánica
  es·ka·le·ra me·ka·nee·ka
euro euro ⓜ e·oo·ro
Europe Europa ⓕ e·oo·ro·pa
euthanasia eutanasia ⓕ e·oo·ta·na·sya
evening noche ⓕ no·che
everything todo to·do
example ejemplo ⓜ e·khem·plo
excellent excelente ek·se·len·te
excess baggage exceso ⓜ de
  equipaje ek·se·so de e·kee·pa·khe
exchange cambio ⓜ de dinero
  kam·byo de dee·ne·ro
exchange cambiar kam·byar
exchange rate tipo ⓜ de cambio
  tee·po de kam·byo
excluded no incluido/a ⓜ/ⓕ
  no een·kloo·ee·do/a
exhaust (car) escape ⓜ es·ka·pe
exhibition exposición ⓕ ek·spo·see·syon
exit salida ⓕ sa·lee·da
expensive caro/a ⓜ/ⓕ ka·ro/a
experience experiencia ⓕ
  ek·spe·ryen·sya
exploitation explotación ⓕ
  ek·splo·ta·syon
express expreso/a ⓜ/ⓕ ek·spre·so/a
express mail correo ⓜ urgente ko·re·o
  oor·khen·te
extension (visa) prolongación ⓕ
  pro·lon·ga·syon
eye ojo ⓜ o·kho
eye drops gotas ⓕ pl para los ojos
  go·tas pa·ra los o·khos

F

fabric tela ⓕ te·la
face cara ⓕ ka·ra
factory fábrica ⓕ fa·bree·ka
factory worker obrero/a ⓜ/ⓕ
  o·bre·ro/a
fall (tumble) caída ⓕ ka·ee·da
fall (season) otoño ⓜ o·to·nyo
family familia ⓕ fa·mee·lya
family name apellido ⓜ a·pe·lyee·do
famous conocido/a ⓜ/ⓕ
  ko·no·see·do/a
fan (person) hincha ⓜ&ⓕ een·cha
fan (machine) ventilador ⓜ
  ven·tee·la·dor
fan belt correa ⓕ del ventilador
  ko·re·a del ven·tee·la·dor
fantasy fantasía ⓕ fan·ta·see·a
far lejos le·khos
farm granja ⓕ gran·kha
farmer agricultor/agricultora ⓜ/ⓕ
  a·gree·kool·tor/a·gree·kool·to·ra
fast rápido/a ⓜ/ⓕ ra·pee·do/a
fat gordo/a ⓜ/ⓕ gor·do/a
father padre ⓜ pa·dre
father-in-law suegro ⓜ swe·gro
faucet grifo ⓜ gree·fo
fault (someone's) culpa ⓕ kool·pa
faulty defectuoso/a ⓜ/ⓕ
  de·fek·two·so/a
feel sentir sen·teer
feelings sentimientos ⓜ pl
  sen·tee·myen·tos
fence cerca ⓕ ser·ka
fencing (sport) esgrima ⓕ es·gree·ma
festival festival ⓜ fes·tee·val
fever fiebre ⓕ fye·bre
few pocos/as ⓜ/ⓕ pl po·kos/as
fiance(e) prometido/a ⓜ/ⓕ
  pro·me·tee·do/a
fiction (literature)
  (literatura de) ficción ⓕ
  (lee·te·ra·too·ra de) feek·syon
fig higo ⓜ ee·go
fight pelea ⓕ pe·le·a
film (cinema) film ⓜ feelm

film (roll for camera) *película* ①
pe·*lee*·koo·la

film speed *sensibilidad* ①
sen·see·bee·lee·*da*

filtered *con filtro* kon *feel*·tro

find *encontrar* en·kon·*trar*

fine *multa* ① *mool*·ta

finger *dedo* ⓜ *de*·do

finish *terminar* ter·mee·*nar*

fire *fuego* ⓜ *fwe*·go

firewood *leña* ① *le*·nya

first *primero/a* ⓜ/① pree·*me*·ro/a

first class *primera clase* ① pree·*me*·ra
kla·se

first-aid kit *maletín* ⓜ *de primeros
auxilios* ma·le·*teen* de pree·*me*·ros
ow·*see*·lyos

fish *pez* ⓜ pes

fish (as food) *pescado* ⓜ pes·*ka*·do

fish shop *pescadería* ① pes·ka·de·*ree*·a

fishing *pesca* ① *pes*·ka

flag *bandera* ① ban·*de*·ra

flamingo *flamenco* ① fla·*men*·ko

flash (camera) *flash* flash

flashlight (torch) *linterna* ① leen·*ter*·na

flannel (wash cloth) *toallita* ①
to·a·*lyee*·ta

flat *llano/a* ⓜ/① *lya*·no/a

flea *pulga* ① *pool*·ga

flip-chart *flip chart* ⓜ fleep chart

flood *inundación* ① ee·noon·da·*syon*

floor (ground) *suelo* ⓜ *swe*·lo

floor (storey) *piso* ⓜ *pee*·so

florist *florista* ⓜ&① flo·*rees*·ta

flour *harina* ① a·*ree*·na

flower *flor* ① flor

flu *gripe* ① *gree*·pe

fly *mosca* ① *mos*·ka

fly *volar* vo·*lar*

foggy *brumoso/a* ⓜ/① broo·*mo*·so/a

follow *seguir* se·*geer*

food *comida* ① ko·*mee*·da

food poisoning *intoxicación* ①
alimenticia een·tok·see·ka·*syon*
a·lee·men·*tee*·sya

food supplies *víveres* ⓜ pl *vee*·ve·res

foot *pie* ⓜ pye

football (soccer) *fútbol* ⓜ *foot*·bol

footpath *acera* ① a·*se*·ra

footpath (CAm) *andén* ⓜ an·*den*

footpath (SAm) *vereda* ① ve·*re*·da

foreign *extranjero/a* ⓜ/①
ek·stran·*khe*·ro/a

foreigner *extranjero/a* ⓜ/①
ek·stran·*khe*·ro/a

forest *bosque* ⓜ *bos*·ke

forever *para siempre* pa·ra syem·pre

forget *olvidar* ol·vee·*dar*

forgive *perdonar* per·do·*nar*

fork *tenedor* ⓜ te·ne·*dor*

fortnight *quincena* ① keen·*se*·na

foyer *vestíbulo* ⓜ ves·*tee*·boo·lo

fragile *frágil* fra·*kheel*

France *Francia* ① *fran*·sya

free (gratis) *gratis* *gra*·tees

free (not bound) *libre* *lee*·bre

freeze *congelar* kon·khe·*lar*

fridge *refrigeradora* ①
re·free·khe·ra·*do*·ra

friend *amigo/a* ⓜ/① a·*mee*·go/a

frog *rana* ① *ra*·na

frost *escarcha* ① es·*kar*·cha

frostbite *congelación* ①
kon·khe·la·*syon*

frozen foods *productos* ⓜ pl
congelados pro·*dook*·tos
kon·khe·*la*·dos

fruit *fruta* ① *froo*·ta

fruit picking *recolección* ① *de fruta*
re·ko·lek·*syon* de *froo*·ta

fry *freír* fre·*eer*

frying pan *sartén* ① sar·*ten*

full-time *a tiempo completo* a *tyem*·po
kom·*ple*·to

fun *diversión* ① dee·ver·*syon*

funeral *funeral* ⓜ foo·ne·*ral*

funny *gracioso/a* ⓜ/① gra·syo·so/a

furniture *muebles* ⓜ pl *mwe*·bles

future *futuro* ⓜ foo·*too*·ro

G

game (play) *juego* ⓜ *khwe*·go

game (sport) *partido* ⓜ par·*tee*·do

garage (car repair) *taller* ⓜ ta·*lyer*

garage (car shelter) *garage* ⓜ ga·ra·khe
garden *jardín* ⓜ khar·deen
gardening *jardinería* ⓕ khar·dee·ne·ree·a
garlic *ajo* ⓜ a·kho
gas (for cooking) *gas* ⓜ gas
gas (petrol) *gasolina* ⓕ ga·so·lee·na
gas cartridge *cartucho de gas* ⓜ kar·too·cho de gas
gastroenteritis *gastroenteritis* ⓕ gas·tro·en·te·ree·tees
gate *verja* ⓕ ver·kha
gay *gay* gay
gears *marchas* ⓕ pl mar·chas
general *general* khe·ne·ral
Germany *Alemania* ⓕ a·le·ma·nya
gift *regalo* ⓜ re·ga·lo
gig *actuación* ⓕ ak·twa·syon
ginger *jengibre* ⓜ khen·khee·bre
girl *chica* ⓕ chee·ka
girlfriend *novia* ⓕ no·vya
give *dar* dar
glandular fever *fiebre* ⓕ *glandular* fye·bre glan·doo·lar
glass (drinking) *vaso* ⓜ va·so
glass (material) *vidrio* ⓜ vee·dryo
glasses *anteojos* ⓜ pl an·te·o·khos
glossy *brillante* bree·lyan·te
gloves *guantes* ⓜ pl gwan·tes
go *ir* eer
go out with *salir con* sa·leer kon
goat *cabra* ⓕ ka·bra
god *dios* dyos
goggles *anteojos* ⓜ pl an·te·o·khos
gold *oro* o·ro
golf ball *pelota de golf* pe·lo·ta de golf
golf course *cancha* ⓕ *de golf* kan·cha de golf
good *bueno/a* ⓜ/ⓕ bwe·no/a
government *gobierno* ⓜ go·byer·no
grams *gramos* ⓜ pl gra·mos
grandchild *nieto/a* ⓜ/ⓕ nye·to/a
grandfather *abuelo* ⓜ a·bwe·lo
grandmother *abuela* ⓕ a·bwe·la
grapefruit *pomelo* ⓜ po·me·lo
grapes *uvas* ⓕ pl oo·vas

grass *hierba* ⓕ yer·ba
grave *tumba* ⓕ toom·ba
great *fantástico/a* ⓜ/ⓕ fan·tas·tee·ko/a
green *verde* ver·de
greengrocer *verdulero/a* ⓜ/ⓕ ver·doo·le·ro/a
grey *gris* grees
grocer's *almacén* ⓜ al·ma·sen
groundnut *maní* ⓜ ma·nee
group *grupo* ⓜ groo·po
grow *crecer* kre·ser
Guatemala *Guatemala* ⓕ gwa·te·ma·la
guess *adivinar* a·dee·vee·nar
guide (audio) *guía* ⓕ *audio* gee·a ow·dyo
guide (person) *guía* ⓜ&ⓕ gee·a
guide dog *perro* ⓜ *guía* pe·ro gee·a
guidebook *guía* ⓕ gee·a
guided tour *recorrido* ⓜ *guiado* re·ko·ree·do gee·a·do
guilty *culpable* kool·pa·ble
guinea pig *cuy* ⓜ kooy
guitar *guitarra* ⓕ gee·ta·ra
gum (chewing) *chicle* ⓜ chee·kle
gum (mouth) *encía* ⓕ en·see·a
gymnastics *gimnasia* ⓕ kheem·na·sya
gynaecologist *ginecólogo/a* ⓜ/ⓕ khee·ne·ko·lo·go/a

H

hail *granizo* ⓜ gra·nee·so
hair *pelo* ⓜ pe·lo
haircut *corte* ⓜ *de pelo* kor·te de pe·lo
hairdresser *peluquero/a* ⓜ/ⓕ pe·loo·ke·ro/a
halal *halal* a·lal
half *medio/a* ⓜ/ⓕ me·dyo/a
hallucinate *alucinar* a·loo·see·nar
ham *jamón* ⓜ kha·mon
hammer *martillo* ⓜ mar·tee·lyo
hammock *hamaca* ⓕ a·ma·ka
hand *mano* ⓕ ma·no
handbag *bolso* ⓜ bol·so
handicraft *artesanía* ⓕ ar·te·sa·nee·a
handkerchief *pañuelo* ⓕ pa·nywe·lo
handlebar *manillar* ⓜ ma·nee·lyar

handmade *hecho/a* ⓜ/ⓕ *a mano* e·cho/a a ma·no

handsome *buen mozo/a* ⓜ/ⓕ bwen mo·so/a

happy *feliz* fe·lees

harassment *acoso* ⓜ a·ko·so

harbour *puerto* ⓜ pwer·to

hard (not easy) *difícil* dee·fee·seel

hard (not soft) *duro/a* ⓜ/ⓕ doo·ro/a

hardware store *ferretería* ⓕ fe·re·te·ree·a

hash *hachís* ⓜ a·chees

hat *sombrero* ⓜ som·bre·ro

have *tener* te·ner

hay fever *alergia* ⓕ *de polén* a·ler·khya de po·len

he *él* el

head *cabeza* ⓕ ka·be·sa

headache *dolor* ⓜ *de cabeza* do·lor de ka·be·sa

headlights *faros* ⓜ pl fa·ros

health *salud* ⓕ sa·loo

hear *oír* o·eer

hearing aid *audífono* ⓜ ow·dee·fo·no

heart *corazón* ⓜ ko·ra·son

heart condition *condición* ⓕ *cardíaca* kon·dee·syon kar·dee·a·ka

heat *calor* ⓜ ka·lor

heater *estufa* ⓕ es·too·fa

heating *calefacción* ⓕ ka·le·fak·syon

heavy *pesado/a* ⓜ/ⓕ pe·sa·do/a

helmet *casco* ⓜ kas·ko

help *ayudar* a·yoo·dar

her *su* soo

hepatitis *hepatitis* ⓕ e·pa·tee·tees

herbalist *herborista* ⓜ&ⓕ er·bo·rees·ta

herbs *hierbas* ⓕ pl yer·bas

here *aquí* a·kee

heroin *heroína* ⓕ e·ro·ee·na

herring *arenque* ⓜ a·ren·ke

high *alto/a* ⓜ/ⓕ al·to/a

high school *instituto* ⓜ een·stee·too·to

hike *ir de excursión* eer de ek·skoor·syon

hiking *excursionismo* ⓜ ek·skoor·syo·nees·mo

hiking boots *botas* ⓕ pl *de montaña* bo·tas de mon·ta·nya

hiking route *camino* ⓜ *rural* ka·mee·no roo·ral

hill *colina* ⓕ ko·lee·na

Hindu *hindú* een·doo

hire *alquilar* al·kee·lar

his *su* soo

historical *histórico/a* ⓜ/ⓕ ees·to·ree·ko/a

hitchhike *hacer dedo* a·ser de·do

HIV positive *seropositivo/a* ⓜ/ⓕ se·ro·po·see·tee·vo/a

hockey *hockey* ⓜ kho·kee

holiday *día* ⓜ *festivo* dee·a fes·tee·vo

holidays *vacaciones* ⓕ pl va·ka·syo·nes

Holy Week *Semana* ⓕ *Santa* se·ma·na san·ta

home *casa* ⓕ ka·sa

homeless *sin techo* seen te·cho

homemaker *ama* ⓕ *de casa* a·ma de ka·sa

homosexual *homosexual* o·mo·sek·swal

Honduras *Honduras* ⓕ on·doo·ras

honey *miel* ⓕ myel

honeymoon *luna* ⓕ *de miel* loo·na de myel

horoscope *horóscopo* ⓜ o·ros·ko·po

horse *caballo* ⓜ ka·ba·lyo

horse riding *equitación* ⓕ e·kee·ta·syon

horseradish *rábano* ⓜ *picante* ra·ba·no pee·kan·te

hospital *hospital* ⓜ os·pee·tal

hospitality *hospitalidad* ⓕ os·pee·ta·lee·da

hot *caliente* ka·lyen·te

hot water *agua* ⓕ *caliente* a·gwa ka·lyen·te

hotel *hotel* ⓜ o·tel

house *casa* ⓕ ka·sa

how *como* ko·mo

how much *cuanto* kwan·to

hug *abrazo* ⓜ a·bra·so

huge *enorme* e·nor·me

human rights *derechos* ⓜ pl *humanos* de·re·chos oo·ma·nos

hummingbird *colibrí* ⓜ ko·lee·bree

(be) hungry *tener hambre* te·ner am·bre

hunting *caza* ⓕ ka·sa

(be in a) hurry *tener prisa* te·*ner* *pree*·sa

hurt *dañar* da·*nyar*

husband *esposo* ⓜ es·*po*·so

hut *cabaña* ① ka·*ba*·nya

I

I *yo* yo

ice *hielo* ⓜ *ye*·lo

ice axe *piolet* ⓜ pyo·*let*

ice cream *helado* ⓜ e·*la*·do

ice-cream parlour *heladería* ①
e·la·de·*ree*·a

ice hockey *hockey* ⓜ *sobre hielo*
kho·kee *so*·bre *ye*·lo

identification *identificación* ①
ee·den·tee·fee·ka·*syon*

identification card (ID) *cédula* ⓕ *de*
identidad se·*doo*·la de ee·den·tee·*da*

idiot *idiota* ⓜ&① ee·*dyo*·ta

if *si* see

ill *enfermo/a* ⓜ/① en·*fer*·mo/a

illegal *ilegal* ee·le·*gal*

immigration *inmigración* ①
een·mee·gra·*syon*

important *importante* eem·por·*tan*·te

impossible *imposible* eem·po·*see*·ble

included *incluido/a* ⓜ/①
een·kloo·*ee*·do/a

income tax *impuesto* ⓜ *sobre la renta*
eem·*pwes*·to *so*·bre la *ren*·ta

India *India* ① *een*·dya

indicators (car) *direccionales* ⓜ pl
dee·rek·syo·*na*·les

indigestion *indigestión* ①
een·dee·khes·*tyon*

industry *industria* ① een·*doos*·trya

infection *infección* ① een·fek·*syon*

inflammation *inflamación* ①
een·fla·ma·*syon*

information *información* ①
een·for·ma·*syon*

influenza *gripe* ① *gree*·pe

ingredient *ingrediente* ⓜ
een·gre·*dyen*·te

inhaler *inhalador* ⓜ ee·na·la·*dor*

inject *inyectarse* een·yek·*tar*·se

injection *inyección* ① een·yek·*syon*

injury *herida* ① e·*ree*·da

innocent *inocente* ee·no·*sen*·te

inside *adentro* a·*den*·tro

instructor *instructor/instructora* ⓜ/①
een·strook·*tor*/een·strook·*to*·ra

instructor (skiing) *monitor/monitora*
ⓜ/① mo·nee·*tor*/mo·nee·*to*·ra

insurance *seguro* ⓜ se·*goo*·ro

interesting *interesante*
een·te·re·*san*·te

intermission *descanso* ⓜ des·*kan*·so

international *internacional*
een·ter·na·syo·*nal*

Internet *Internet* ⓜ een·ter·*net*

Internet cafe *cibercafé* ⓜ see·ber·ka·*fe*

interpreter *intérprete* ⓜ&①
een·*ter*·pre·te

interview *entrevista* ① en·tre·*vees*·ta

invite *invitar* een·vee·*tar*

Ireland *Irlanda* ① eer·*lan*·da

iron (clothes) *plancha* ① *plan*·cha

island *isla* ① *ees*·la

IT *informática* ① een·for·*ma*·tee·ka

itch *picazón* ⓜ pee·ka·*son*

itemised *detallado/a* ⓜ/①
de·ta·*lya*·do/a

itinerary *itinerario* ① ee·tee·ne·*ra*·ryo

IUD (contraceptive device) *DIU* ⓜ
de ee oo

J

jacket *chaqueta* ① cha·*ke*·ta

jaguar *jaguar* ⓜ kha·*gwar*

jail *cárcel* ① *kar*·sel

jam *mermelada* ① mer·me·*la*·da

Japan *Japón* ⓜ kha·*pon*

jar *jarra* ① *kha*·ra

jaw *mandíbula* ① man·*dee*·boo·la

jealous *celoso/a* ⓜ/① se·*lo*·so/a

jeans *bluejeans* ⓜ pl *bloo*·jeens

jeep *yip* ⓜ yeep

jet lag *jet lag* dyet lag

jewellery *joyería* ① kho·ye·*ree*·a

Jewish *judío/a* ⓜ/① khoo·*dee*·o/a

job *trabajo* ⓜ tra·*ba*·kho
jockey *jockey* ⓜ *yo*·kee
jogging *footing* foo·*teen*
joke *broma* ⓕ *bro*·ma
journalist *periodista* ⓜ&ⓕ
  pe·ryo·*dees*·ta
judge *juez* ⓜ&ⓕ khwes
juice *jugo* ⓜ *khoo*·go
jump *saltar* sal·*tar*
jumper (sweater) *chompa* ⓕ *chom*·pa
jumper leads *cables* ⓜ pl *de arranque*
  ka·bles de a·*ran*·ke

K

ketchup *salsa* ⓕ *de tomate* *sal*·sa de
  to·*ma*·te
key *llave* ⓕ *lya*·ve
keyboard *teclado* ⓜ te·*kla*·do
kick *patada* ⓕ pa·*ta*·da
kick *dar una patada* dar *oo*·na pa·*ta*·da
kill *matar* ma·*tar*
kilogram *kilo* ⓜ *kee*·lo
kilometre *kilómetro* ⓜ kee·*lo*·me·tro
kind *amable* a·*ma*·ble
kindergarten *jardín* ⓜ *de infancia* •
  kinder ⓜ khar·*deen* de een·*fan*·sya •
  keen·der
king *rey* ⓜ ray
kiss *beso* ⓜ *be*·so
kiss *besar* be·*sar*
kitchen *cocina* ⓕ ko·*see*·na
kitten *gatito/a* ⓜ/ⓕ ga·*tee*·to/a
kiwifruit *kiwi* ⓜ *kee*·wee
knapsack *mochila* ⓕ mo·*chee*·la
knee *rodilla* ⓕ ro·*dee*·lya
knife *cuchillo* ⓜ koo·*chee*·lyo
know (someone) *conocer* ko·no·*ser*
know (something) *saber* sa·*ber*
kosher *kosher* *ko*·sher

L

labourer *obrero/a* ⓜ/ⓕ o·*bre*·ro/a
lace *encaje* ⓜ en·*ka*·khe
lager *cerveza* ⓕ *rubia* ser·*ve*·sa *roo*·bya
lake *lago* ⓜ *la*·go

lamb *cordero* ⓜ kor·*de*·ro
land *tierra* ⓕ *tye*·ra
landlady *propietaria* ⓕ pro·pye·*ta*·rya
landlord *propietario* ⓜ pro·pye·*ta*·ryo
language *idioma* ⓜ ee·*dyo*·ma
laptop *computadora* ⓕ *portátil*
  kom·poo·ta·*do*·ra por·*ta*·teel
lard *manteca* ⓕ *de cerdo* man·*te*·ka
  de *ser*·do
large *grande* *gran*·de
laser pointer *puntero* ⓜ *láser*
  poon·*te*·ro *la*·ser
late *tarde* *tar*·de
Latin America *Latinoamérica* ⓕ
  la·tee·no·a·*me*·ree·ka
Latin American *latinoamericano/a*
  ⓜ/ⓕ la·tee·no·a·me·ree·*ka*·no/a
laugh *reírse* re·*eer*·se
laundrette *lavandería* ⓕ la·van·de·*ree*·a
laundry *lavandería* ⓕ la·van·de·*ree*·a
law *ley* ⓕ lay
lawyer *abogado/a* ⓜ/ⓕ a·bo·*ga*·do/a
laxatives *laxantes* ⓜ pl lak·*san*·tes
lazy *perezoso/a* ⓜ/ⓕ pe·re·so·so/a
leader *jefe/a* ⓜ/ⓕ *khe*·fe/a
leaf *hoja* ⓕ *o*·kha
learn *aprender* a·pren·*der*
leather *cuero* ⓜ *kwe*·ro
leave *partir* par·*teer*
lecturer *profesor/profesora* ⓜ/ⓕ
  pro·fe·*sor*/pro·fe·*so*·ra
leek *puerro* ⓜ *pwe*·ro
left (direction) *izquierda* ⓕ ees·*kyer*·da
left luggage office *consigna* ⓕ
  kon·*seekh*·na
left-wing *izquierdista* ees·kyer·*dees*·ta
leg (body) *pierna* ⓕ *pyer*·na
legal *legal* le·*gal*
legislation *legislación* ⓕ
  le·khees·la·*syon*
lemon *limón* ⓜ lee·*mon*
lemonade *limonada* ⓕ lee·mo·*na*·da
lens *objetivo* ⓜ ob·khe·*tee*·vo
Lent *Cuaresma* ⓕ kwa·*res*·ma
lentils *lentejas* ⓕ pl len·*te*·khas
lesbian *lesbiana* ⓕ les·*bya*·na
less *de menos* de *me*·nos

letter *carta* ① *kar*·ta
lettuce *lechuga* ① le·*choo*·ga
liar *mentiroso/a* ⓜ/① men·tee·*ro*·so/a
library *biblioteca* ① bee·blyo·*te*·ka
lice *piojos* ⓜ pl *pyo*·khos
license plate number *matrícula* ①
   ma·*tree*·koo·la
lie (not stand) *tumbarse* toom·*bar*·se
life *vida* ① *vee*·da
lifejacket *chaleco* ⓜ *salvavidas*
   cha·*le*·ko sal·va·*vee*·das
lift (elevator) *ascensor* ⓜ a·sen·*sor*
lift *levantar* le·van·*tar*
light *luz* ① loos
light (colour) *claro/a* ⓜ/① *kla*·ro/a
light (not heavy) *ligero/a* ⓜ/①
   lee·*khe*·ro/a
light bulb *bombilla* ① bom·*bee*·lya
light meter *fotómetro* ⓜ fo·*to*·me·tro
lighter *encendedor* en·sen·de·*dor*
lights (on car) *faros* ⓜ pl *fa*·ros
like (affection) *gustar(le)* goos·*tar(le)*
lime *lima* ① *lee*·ma
line *línea* ① *lee*·ne·a
lip balm *bálsamo* ⓜ *de labios*
   bal·sa·mo de *la*·byos
lips *labios* ⓜ pl *la*·byos
lipstick *lápiz* ⓜ *de labios* *la*·pees de
   la·byos
liquor store *bodega* ① bo·*de*·ga
listen *escuchar* es·koo·*char*
live *vivir* vee·*veer*
liver *hígado* ⓜ *ee*·ga·do
lizard *lagartija* ① la·gar·*tee*·kha
local *local* lo·*kal*
lock (door) *cerradura* ① se·ra·*doo*·ra
lock *cerrar* se·*rar*
locked *cerrado/a* ⓜ/① *con llave*
   se·*ra*·do/a kon *lya*·ve
locker *lócker* ① *lo*·ker
lollies *caramelos* ⓜ pl ka·ra·*me*·los
long *largo/a* ⓜ/① *lar*·go/a
long-distance *larga distancia* *lar*·ga
   dees·*tan*·sya
look *mirar* mee·*rar*
look after *cuidar de* kwee·*dar* de
look for *buscar* boos·*kar*
lookout *mirador* ⓜ mee·ra·*dor*

loose change *monedas* ① pl *sueltas*
   mo·*ne*·das *swel*·tas
lose *perder* per·*der*
lost *perdido/a* ⓜ/① per·*dee*·do/a
lost property office *oficina* ① *de*
   objetos perdidos o·fee·*see*·na de
   ob·*khe*·tos per·*dee*·dos
loud *ruidoso/a* ⓜ/① rwee·*do*·so/a
love *querer* ke·*rer*
lover *amante* ⓜ&① a·*man*·te
low *bajo/a* ⓜ/① *ba*·kho/a
lubricant *lubricante* ⓜ loo·bree·*kan*·te
luck *suerte* ① *swer*·te
lucky *afortunado/a* ⓜ/①
   a·for·too·*na*·do/a
luggage *equipaje* ⓜ e·kee·*pa*·khe
luggage lockers *consigna* ①
   automática kon·*seeg*·na
   ow·to·*ma*·tee·ka
luggage tag *etiqueta* ① *de equipaje*
   e·tee·*ke*·ta de e·kee·*pa*·khe
lump *bulto* ⓜ *bool*·to
lunch *almuerzo* ⓜ al·*mwer*·so
lungs *pulmones* ⓜ pl pool·*mo*·nes
luxurious *de lujo* de *loo*·kho

M

macaw *papagayo* ⓜ pa·pa·*ga*·yo
machine *máquina* ① *ma*·kee·na
made of (cotton) *hecho/a* ⓜ/① *de*
   (algodón) e·cho/a de (al·go·*don*)
magazine *revista* ① re·*vees*·ta
magician *mago/a* ⓜ/① *ma*·go/a
mail *correo* ⓜ ko·*re*·o
mailbox *buzón* ⓜ boo·*son*
main *principal* preen·see·*pal*
make *hacer* a·*ser*
make-up *maquillaje* ⓜ ma·kee·*lya*·khe
malaria *malaria* ① ma·*la*·rya
mallet *mazo* ⓜ *ma*·so
mammogram *mamograma* ⓜ
   ma·mo·*gra*·ma
man *hombre* ⓜ *om*·bre
manager *director/directora* ⓜ/①
   dee·rek·*tor/*dee·rek·*to*·ra

mandarin *mandarina* ① man·da·*ree*·na
mango *mango* ⓜ *man*·go
manual *manual* ma·*nwal*
many *muchos/as* ⓜ/① pl *moo*·chos/as
map *mapa* ⓜ *ma*·pa
margarine *margarina* ① mar·ga·*ree*·na
marijuana *marihuana* ① ma·ree·*wa*·na
marital status *estado* ⓜ *civil* es·*ta*·do see·*veel*
market *mercado* ⓜ mer·*ka*·do
marmalade *mermelada* ① mer·me·*la*·da
marriage *matrimonio* ⓜ ma·tree·*mo*·nyo
married *casado/a* ⓜ/① ka·*sa*·do/a
marry *casarse* ka·*sar*·se
martial arts *artes* ⓜ pl *marciales ar*·tes mar·*sya*·les
mass (Catholic) *misa* ① *mee*·sa
massage *masaje* ⓜ ma·*sa*·khe
masseur/masseuse *masajista* ⓜ&① ma·sa·*khees*·ta
mat *esterilla* ① es·te·*ree*·lya
match (sport) *partido* ⓜ par·*tee*·do
matches *fósforos* ⓜ pl *fos*·fo·ros
matte (photos) *mate ma*·te
mattress *colchón* ⓜ kol·*chon*
maybe *quizás* kee·*sas*
mayonnaise *mayonesa* ① ma·yo·*ne*·sa
mayor *alcalde* ⓜ&① al·*kal*·de
measles *sarampión* ⓜ sa·ram·*pyon*
meat *carne* ① *kar*·ne
mechanic *mecánico/a* ⓜ/① me·*ka*·ne·ko/a
media *medios* ⓜ pl *de comunicación me*·dyos de ko·moo·nee·ka·*syon*
medicine *medicina* ① me·dee·*see*·na
meditation *meditación* ① me·dee·ta·*syon*
meet *encontrar* en·kon·*trar*
melon *melón* ⓜ me·*lon*
member *miembro* ⓜ&① *myem*·bro
menstruation *menstruación* ① mens·trwa·*syon*
menu *menú* ⓜ me·*noo*

message *mensaje* ⓜ men·*sa*·khe
metal *metal* ⓜ me·*tal*
metre (distance) *metro* ⓜ *me*·tro
metro *subterráneo* ⓜ soob·te·*ra*·ne·o
metro station *estación* ① *de subterráneo* es·ta·*syon* de soob·te·*ra*·ne·o
Mexico *México* ⓜ *me*·khee·ko
microwave oven *microondas* ⓜ mee·kro·*on*·das
midnight *medianoche* ① me·dya·*no*·che
migraine *migraña* ① mee·*gra*·nya
military *militares* ⓜ pl mee·lee·*ta*·res
military service *servicio* ⓜ *militar* ser·*vee*·syo mee·lee·*tar*
milk *leche* ① *le*·che
millimetre *milímetro* ⓜ mee·*lee*·me·tro
million *millón* ⓜ mee·*lyon*
mince (meat) *carne* ① *molida kar*·ne mo·*lee*·da
mind (look after) *cuidar* kwee·*dar*
mineral water *agua* ⓜ *mineral a*·gwa mee·ne·*ral*
mints *pastillas* ① pl *de menta* pas·*tee*·lyas de *men*·ta
minute *minuto* ⓜ mee·*noo*·to
mirror *espejo* ⓜ es·*pe*·kho
miscarriage *aborto* ⓜ *natural* a·*bor*·to na·too·*ral*
miss (feel absence of) *extrañar* ek·stra·*nyar*
mistake *error* ⓜ e·*ror*
mix *mezclar* mes·*klar*
mobile phone *teléfono* ⓜ *móvil/ celular* te·*le*·fo·no *mo*·veel/se·loo·*lar*
modem *módem* ⓜ *mo*·dem
moisturiser *crema* ① *hidratante kre*·ma ee·dra·*tan*·te
monastery *monasterio* ⓜ mo·nas·*te*·ryo
money *dinero* ⓜ dee·*ne*·ro
month *mes* ⓜ mes
monument *monumento* ⓜ mo·noo·*men*·to

moon *luna* ⓕ *loo*·na
more *más* mas
morning *mañana* ⓕ ma·*nya*·na
morning sickness *náuseas* ⓕ pl *del
embarazo* now·se·as del em·ba·*ra*·so
mosque *mezquita* ⓕ mes·*kee*·ta
mosquito *mosquito* ⓜ mos·*kee*·to
mosquito coil *espiral* ⓜ *repelente
contra mosquitos* es·pee·*ral
re·pe·len·te kon·tra mos·*kee*·tos
mosquito net *mosquitera* ⓕ
mos·kee·*te*·ra
mother *madre* ⓕ *ma*·dre
mother-in-law *suegra* ⓕ *swe*·gra
motorboat *motora* ⓕ mo·*to*·ra
motorcycle *motocicleta* ⓕ
mo·to·see·*kle*·ta
motorway *autopista* ⓕ ow·to·*pees*·ta
mountain *montaña* ⓕ mon·*ta*·nya
mountain bike *bicicleta* ⓕ *de montaña*
bee·see·*kle*·ta de mon·*ta*·nya
mountain path *sendero* ⓜ sen·*de*·ro
mountain range *cordillera* ⓕ
kor·dee·*lye*·ra
mountaineering *alpinismo* ⓜ
al·pee·*nees*·mo
mouse *ratón* ⓜ ra·*ton*
mouth *boca* ⓕ *bo*·ka
movie *película* ⓕ pe·*lee*·koo·la
MP3 player *reproductor* ⓜ *de MP3*
re·pro·dook·tor de *e*·me pe tres
mud *lodo* ⓜ *lo*·do
muesli *muesli* ⓜ *mwes*·lee
mum *mamá* ⓕ ma·*ma*
muscle *músculo* ⓜ *moos*·koo·lo
museum *museo* ⓜ moo·*se*·o
mushroom *champiñón* ⓜ
cham·pee·*nyon*
music *música* ⓕ *moo*·see·ka
musician *músico/a* ⓜ/ⓕ *moo*·see·ko/a
Muslim *musulmán/musulmana* ⓜ/ⓕ
moo·sool·*man*/moo·sool·*ma*·na
mussels *mejillones* ⓜ pl
me·khee·*lyo*·nes
mustard *mostaza* ⓕ mos·*ta*·sa
mute *mudo/a* ⓜ/ⓕ *moo*·do/a
my *mi* mee

N

nail clippers *cortauñas* ⓜ kor·ta·oo·nyas
name *nombre* ⓜ *nom*·bre
napkin *servilleta* ⓕ ser·vee·*lye*·ta
nappy *pañal* ⓜ pa·*nyal*
nappy rash *irritación* ⓕ *de pañal*
ee·rree·ta·syon de pa·*nyal*
national *nacional* na·syo·*nal*
national park *parque* ⓜ *nacional*
par·ke na·syo·*nal*
nationality *nacionalidad* ⓕ
na·syo·na·lee·*da*
nature *naturaleza* ⓕ na·too·ra·*le*·sa
naturopathy *naturopatia* ⓕ
na·too·ro·*pa*·tya
nausea *náusea* ⓕ *now*·se·a
near (to) *cerca (de)* ser·ka (de)
nearby *cerca* ser·ka
nearest *más cercano/a* ⓜ/ⓕ mas
ser·*ka*·no/a
necessary *necesario/a* ⓜ/ⓕ
ne·se·*sa*·ryo/a
neck *cuello* ⓜ *kwe*·lyo
need *necesitar* ne·se·see·*tar*
needle (sewing) *aguja* ⓕ a·*goo*·kha
needle (syringe) *jeringuilla* ⓕ
khe·reen·*gee*·lya
neither *tampoco* tam·*po*·ko
net *red* ⓕ re
Netherlands *Holanda* ⓕ o·*lan*·da
never *nunca* *noon*·ka
new *nuevo/a* ⓜ/ⓕ *nwe*·vo/a
New Year *Año Nuevo* ⓜ a·nyo *nwe*·vo
New Year's Day *dia de Año Nuevo* ⓜ
dee·a de a·nyo *nwe*·vo
New Year's Eve *Nochevieja* ⓕ
no·che·*vye*·kha
New Zealand *Nueva Zelanda* ⓕ
nwe·va se·*lan*·da
news *noticias* ⓕ pl no·*tee*·syas
newsagency *quiosco* ⓜ *kee*·os·ko
newspaper *periódico* ⓜ pe·*ryo*·dee·ko
next *próximo/a* ⓜ/ⓕ *prok*·see·mo/a
next to *al lado de* al *la*·do de
Nicaragua *Nicaragua* ⓕ nee·ka·*ra*·gwa
nice (object) *bueno/a* ⓜ/ⓕ *bwe*·no/a

nice (person) *simpático/a* ⓜ/ⓕ
seem·pa·tee·ko·a
nickname *apodo* ⓜ a·po·do
night *noche* ⓕ no·che
night life *vida* ⓕ *nocturna* vee·da
nok·toor·na
no *no* no
noisy *ruidoso/a* ⓜ/ⓕ rwee·do·so/a
non-direct *indirecto/a* een·dee·rek·to/a
none *nada* na·da
non-fiction *literatura* ⓕ *no novelesca*
lee·te·ra·too·ra no no·ve·les·ka
non-smoking *no fumadores* no
foo·ma·do·res
noodles *fideos* ⓜ pl fee·de·os
noon *mediodía* ⓜ me·dyo·dee·a
north *norte* ⓕ nor·te
nose *nariz* ⓕ na·rees
notebook *cuaderno* ⓜ kwa·der·no
nothing *nada* na·da
novel *novela* ⓕ no·ve·la
now *ahora* a·o·ra
nuclear energy *energía* ⓕ *nuclear*
e·ner·khee·a noo·kle·ar
nuclear testing *pruebas* ⓕ pl
nucleares prwe·bas noo·kle·a·res
nuclear waste *desperdicios* ⓜ pl
nucleares des·per·dee·syos
noo·kle·a·res
number *número* ⓜ noo·me·ro
nun *monja* ⓕ mon·kha
nurse *enfermero/a* ⓜ/ⓕ en·fer·me·ro/a
nut *nuez* ⓕ nwes

O

oats *avena* ⓕ a·ve·na
ocean *océano* ⓜ o·se·a·no
off (spoiled) *pasado/a* ⓜ/ⓕ pa·sa·do/a
office *oficina* ⓕ o·fee·see·na
office worker *oficinista* ⓜ&ⓕ
o·fee·see·nees·ta
often *a menudo* a me·noo·do
oil *aceite* ⓜ a·say·te
old *viejo/a* ⓜ/ⓕ vye·kho/a
olive *aceituna* ⓕ a·say·too·na
olive oil *aceite* ⓜ *de oliva* a·say·te de
o·lee·va

Olympic Games *juegos* ⓜ pl *olímpicos* khwe·gos o·leem·pee·kos
on *en* en
once *una vez* oo·na ves
one-way ticket *boleto* ⓜ *sencillo*
bo·le·to sen·see·lyo
onion *cebolla* ⓕ se·bo·lya
only *sólo* so·lo
open *abierto/a* ⓜ/ⓕ a·byer·to/a
open *abrir* a·breer
opening hours *horas* ⓕ pl *de
apertura* o·ras de a·per·too·ra
opera *ópera* ⓕ o·pe·ra
opera house *teatro* ⓜ *de la ópera*
te·a·tro de la o·pe·ra
operation (medical) *operación* ⓕ
o·pe·ra·syon
operator *operador/operadora* ⓜ/ⓕ
o·pe·ra·dor/o·pe·ra·do·ra
opinion *opinión* ⓕ o·pee·nyon
opposite *frente a* fren·te a
or *o* o
orange (fruit) *naranja* ⓕ na·ran·kha
orange (colour) *naranjo/a* ⓜ/ⓕ
na·ran·kho/a
orange juice *jugo* ⓜ *de naranja*
khoo·go de na·ran·kha
orchestra *orquesta* ⓕ or·kes·ta
orchid *orquídea* ⓕ or·kee·de·a
order (command) *orden* ⓕ or·den
order (placement) *orden* ⓜ or·den
order *ordenar* or·de·nar
ordinary *corriente* ko·ryen·te
orgasm *orgasmo* ⓜ or·gas·mo
original *original* o·ree·khee·nal
other *otro/a* ⓜ/ⓕ o·tro/a
our *nuestro/a* ⓜ/ⓕ nwes·tro/a
outside *exterior* ⓜ ek·ste·ryor
ovarian cyst *quiste* ⓜ *ovárico*
kees·te o·va·ree·ko
oven *horno* ⓜ or·no
over (above) *sobre* so·bre
overcoat *abrigo* ⓜ a·bree·go
overdose *sobredosis* ⓕ so·bre·do·sees
owner *dueño/a* ⓜ/ⓕ dwe·nyo/a
oxygen *oxígeno* ⓜ ok·see·khe·no
oyster *ostra* ⓕ os·tra
ozone layer *capa* ⓕ *de ozono* ka·pa
de o·so·no

P

pacemaker *marcapasos* ⓜ
mar·ka·*pa*·sos
pacifier *chupete* ⓜ choo·*pe*·te
package *paquete* ⓜ pa·*ke*·te
packet *paquete* ⓜ pa·*ke*·te
padlock *candado* ⓜ kan·*da*·do
page *página* ⓕ *pa*·khee·na
pain *dolor* ⓜ do·*lor*
painful *doloroso/a* ⓜ/ⓕ do·lo·ro·*so*/a
painkillers *analgésicos* ⓜ pl
a·nal·*khe*·see·kos
paint *pintar* peen·*tar*
painter *pintor/pintora* ⓜ/ⓕ
peen·*tor*/peen·*to*·ra
painting (art) *pintura* ⓕ peen·*too*·ra
painting (canvas) *cuadro* ⓜ *kwa*·dro
pair (couple) *pareja* ⓕ pa·*re*·kha
palace *palacio* ⓜ pa·*la*·syo
palm pilot *palm pilot* ⓜ palm pee·*lot*
pan *olla* ⓕ *o*·lya
panoramic *panorámico/a* ⓜ/ⓕ
pa·no·ra·*mee*·ko/a
Panama *Panamá* ⓕ pa·na·*ma*
panther *pantera* ⓕ pan·*te*·ra
pants *pantalones* ⓜ pl pan·ta·*lo*·nes
panty liners *salvaeslips* ⓜ pl
sal·va·e·*sleeps*
pantyhose *medias* ⓕ pl *me*·dyas
pap smear *citología* ⓕ
see·to·lo·*khee*·a
paper *papel* ⓜ pa·*pel*
paperwork *trabajo* ⓜ *administrativo*
tra·*ba*·kho ad·mee·nees·tra·*tee*·vo
Paraguay *Paraguay* ⓜ pa·ra·*gway*
parcel *paquete* ⓜ pa·*ke*·te
parents *padres* ⓜ pl *pa*·dres
park *parque* ⓜ *par*·ke
park (car) *estacionar* es·ta·syo·*nar*
parliament *parlamento* ⓜ par·la·*men*·to
parrot *loro* ⓜ *lo*·ro
part *parte* ⓕ *par*·te
partner (relationship) *pareja* ⓜ&ⓕ
pa·*re*·kha
part-time *a tiempo parcial* a *tyem*·po
par·*syal*
party (celebration) *fiesta* ⓕ *fyes*·ta
party (politics) *partido* ⓜ par·*tee*·do
pass (mountain) *paso* ⓜ *pa*·so
pass (permit) *pase* ⓜ *pa*·se
passenger *pasajero/a* ⓜ/ⓕ
pa·sa·*khe*·ro/a
passport *pasaporte* ⓜ pa·sa·*por*·te
passport number *número* ⓜ *de
pasaporte* noo·me·ro de pa·sa·*por*·te
past *pasado* ⓜ pa·*sa*·do
pasta *pasta* ⓕ *pas*·ta
pate (food) *paté* ⓜ pa·*te*
path *sendero* ⓜ sen·*de*·ro
pay *pagar* pa·*gar*
payment *pago* ⓜ *pa*·go
pea *guisante* ⓕ gee·*san*·te
peace *paz* ⓕ pas
peach *durazno* ⓜ doo·*ras*·no
peak *cumbre* ⓕ *koom*·bre
peanut *maní* ⓜ ma·*nee*
pear *pera* ⓕ *pe*·ra
pedal *pedal* ⓜ pe·*dal*
pedestrian *peatón* ⓜ&ⓕ pe·a·*ton*
pegs (tent) *estacas* ⓕ pl es·*ta*·kas
pen (ballpoint) *bolígrafo* ⓜ
bo·*lee*·gra·fo
pencil *lápiz* ⓜ *la*·pees
penis *pene* ⓜ *pe*·ne
penicillin *penicilina* ⓕ pe·nee·see·*lee*·na
penknife *navaja* ⓕ na·*va*·kha
pensioner *pensionado/a* ⓜ/ⓕ
pen·syo·*na*·do/a
people *gente* ⓕ *khen*·te
pepper (spice) *pimienta* ⓕ
pee·*myen*·ta
per (day) *por (día)* por (*dee*·a)
percent *por ciento* por *syen*·to
performance *actuación* ⓕ ak·twa·*syon*
perfume *perfume* ⓜ per·*foo*·me
period pain *dolor* ⓜ *menstrual* do·*lor*
mens·*trwal*
permission *permiso* ⓜ per·*mee*·so
permit *permiso* ⓜ per·*mee*·so
permit *permitir* per·mee·*teer*
person *persona* ⓕ per·*so*·na
perspire *sudar* soo·*dar*
Peru *Perú* ⓜ pe·*roo*
petition *petición* ⓕ pe·tee·*syon*

english–latin american spanish

petrol *gasolina* ① ga·so·*lee*·na

pharmacy *farmacia* ① far·*ma*·sya

pharmacist *farmacéutico/a* ⑩/① far·ma·see·oo·tee·ko/a

phone book *guía* ① *telefónica* gee·a te·le·fo·nee·ka

phone box *cabina* ① *telefónica* ka·*bee*·na te·le·*fo*·nee·ka

phone card *tarjeta* ① *de teléfono* tar·*khe*·ta de te·*le*·fo·no

photo *fotografía* ① fo·to·gra·*fee*·a

photocopier *fotocopiadora* ① fo·to·ko·pya·*do*·ra

photographer *fotógrafo/a* ⑩/① fo·*to*·gra·fo/a

photography *fotografía* ① fo·to·gra·*fee*·a

phrasebook *libro* ⑩ *de frases* *lee*·bro de *fra*·ses

pick (up) *levantar* le·van·tar

pickaxe *piqueta* ① pee·*ke*·ta

pickles *pepinillos* ⑩ pl pe·pee·*nee*·lyos

picnic *picnic* ⑩ *peek*·neek

pie *empanada* ① em·pa·*na*·da

piece *pedazo* ⑩ pe·*da*·so

pig *cerdo* ⑩ *ser*·do

pill *pastilla* ① pas·*tee*·lya

the Pill *la píldora* ① la *peel*·do·ra

pillow *almohada* ① al·mo·*a*·da

pillowcase *funda* ① *de almohada* *foon*·da de al·mo·*a*·da

pineapple *ananá(s)* ⑩ a·na·*na*(s)

pink *rosa* *ro*·sa

pistachio *pistacho* ⑩ pees·*ta*·cho

place *lugar* ⑩ loo·*gar*

place of birth *lugar* ⑩ *de nacimiento* loo·*gar* de na·see·*myen*·to

plane *avión* ⑩ a·*vyon*

planet *planeta* ⑩ pla·*ne*·ta

plant *planta* ① *plan*·ta

plant *sembrar* sem·brar

plastic *plástico* ⑩ *plas*·tee·ko

plate *plato* ⑩ *pla*·to

plateau *meseta* ① me·*se*·ta

platform *plataforma* ① pla·ta·*for*·ma

play *obra* ① *o*·bra

play (a game) *jugar* khoo·*gar*

play (the guitar) *tocar (la guitarra)* to·*kar* (la gee·*ta*·ra)

play (tennis) *jugar (al tenis)* khoo·gar (al *te*·nees)

plug (bath) *tapón* ⑩ ta·*pon*

plug (electricity) *enchufe* ⑩ en·*choo*·fe

plum *ciruela* ① see·rwe·la

pocket *bolsillo* ⑩ bol·*see*·lyo

poetry *poesía* ① po·e·*see*·a

point *punto* ⑩ *poon*·to

point *apuntar* a·poon·tar

poisonous *venenoso/a* ⑩/① ve·ne·*no*·so/a

police *policía* ① po·lee·*see*·a

police station *comisaría* ① ko·mee·sa·*ree*·a

policy *política* ① po·*lee*·tee·ka

policy (insurance) *póliza* ① *po*·lee·sa

politician *político/a* ⑩/① po·*lee*·tee·ko/a

politics *política* ① po·*lee*·tee·ka

pollen *polen* ⑩ *po*·len

polls *sondeos* ⑩ pl son·*de*·os

pollution *contaminación* ① kon·ta·mee·na·*syon*

pony *potro* ⑩ *po*·tro

pool (game) *billar* ⑩ bee·*lyar*

pool (swimming) *piscina* ① pee·*see*·na

poor *pobre* *po*·bre

popular *popular* po·poo·*lar*

pork *cerdo* ⑩ *ser*·do

port *puerto* ⑩ *pwer*·to

port (wine) *oporto* ⑩ o·*por*·to

portable CD player *reproductor* ⑩ *de compacts portátil* re·pro·dook·tor de *kom*·paks por·ta·teel

possible *posible* po·*see*·ble

post code *código* ⑩ *postal* *ko*·dee·go pos·tal

post office *correos* ⑩ pl ko·*re*·os

postage *franqueo* ① fran·*ke*·o

postcard *postal* ① pos·tal

pot (ceramic) *cacharro* ① ka·*cha*·ro

pot (kitchen) *olla* ① *o*·lya

pot (dope) *chocolate* ⑩ cho·ko·*la*·te

potato *papa* ① *pa*·pa

pottery *alfarería* ① al·fa·re·*ree*·a

pound (money) *libra* ① *lee*·bra

poverty *pobreza* ⒡ po·*bre*·sa

power *poder* ⓜ po·*der*

prawn *langostino* ⓜ lan·gos·*tee*·no

prayer *oración* ⒡ o·ra·*syon*

prefer *preferir* pre·fe·*reer*

pregnancy test kit *prueba* ⒡ *del embarazo* prwe·ba del em·ba·ra·so

pregnant *embarazada* em·ba·ra·*sa*·da

premenstrual tension *tensión* ⒡ *premenstrual* ten·*syon* pre·mens·*trwal*

prepare *preparar* pre·pa·*rar*

present (gift) *regalo* ⓜ re·*ga*·lo

presentation *presentación* ⒡ pre·sen·ta·*syon*

president *presidente/a* ⓜ/⒡ pre·see·*den*·te/a

pressure *presión* ⒡ pre·*syon*

pretty *bonito/a* ⓜ/⒡ bo·*nee*·to/a

prevent *prevenir* pre·ve·*neer*

price *precio* ⓜ *pre*·syo

priest *sacerdote* ⓜ sa·ser·*do*·te

prime minister (man) *primer ministro* ⓜ pree·mer mee·*nees*·tro

prime minister (woman) *primera ministra* ⒡ pree·me·ra mee·*nees*·tra

prison *cárcel* ⒡ *kar*·sel

prisoner *prisionero/a* ⓜ/⒡ pree·syo·ne·ro/a

private *privado/a* ⓜ/⒡ pree·*va*·do/a

produce *producir* pro·doo·*seer*

profit *beneficio* ⓜ be·ne·*fee*·syo

programme *programa* ⓜ pro·*gra*·ma

projector *proyector* ⓜ pro·yek·*tor*

promise *promesa* ⒡ pro·*me*·sa

proposal *propuesta* ⒡ pro·*pwes*·ta

protect *proteger* pro·te·*kher*

protected *protegido/a* ⓜ/⒡ pro·te·*khee*·do/a

protest *protesta* ⒡ pro·*tes*·ta

protest *protestar* pro·tes·*tar*

provisions *provisiones* ⒡ pl pro·vee·*syo*·nes

prune *ciruela* ⒡ *pasa* see·rwe·la *pa*·sa

pub *pub* ⓜ poob

public telephone *teléfono* ⓜ *público* te·*le*·fo·no *poo*·blee·ko

public toilet *baños* ⓜ pl *ba*·nyos

Puerto Rico *Puerto* ⓜ *Rico* pwer·to *ree*·ko

pull *jalar* kha·*lar*

pump *bomba* ⒡ *bom*·ba

pumpkin *calabaza* ⒡ ka·la·*ba*·sa

puncture *pinchar* peen·*char*

punish *castigar* kas·tee·*gar*

puppy *cachorro* ⓜ ka·*cho*·ro

pure *puro/a* ⓜ/⒡ *poo*·ro/a

purple *morado/a* ⓜ/⒡ mo·ra·do/a

push *empujar* em·poo·*khar*

put *poner* po·*ner*

Q

Q

qualifications *cualificaciones* ⒡ pl kwa·lee·fee·ka·*syo*·nes

quality *calidad* ⒡ ka·lee·*da*

quarantine *cuarentena* ⒡ kwa·ren·*te*·na

quarrel *pelea* ⒡ pe·*le*·a

quarter *cuarto* ⓜ *kwar*·to

queen *reina* ⒡ *ray*·na

question *pregunta* ⒡ pre·*goon*·ta

queue *cola* ⒡ *ko*·la

quick *rápido/a* ⓜ/⒡ *ra*·pee·do/a

quiet *tranquilo/a* ⓜ/⒡ tran·*kee*·lo/a

R

rabbit *conejo* ⓜ ko·*ne*·kho

race (people) *raza* ⒡ *ra*·sa

race (sport) *carrera* ⒡ ka·*re*·ra

racetrack (sport) *pista* ⒡ *pees*·ta

racing bike *bicicleta* ⒡ *de carreras* bee·see·*kle*·ta de ka·re·ras

racquet *raqueta* ⒡ ra·*ke*·ta

radiator *radiador* ⓜ ra·dya·*dor*

radish *rábano* ⓜ *ra*·ba·no

railway *ferrocarril* ⓜ fe·ro·ka·*reel*

railway station *estación* ⒡ *de tren* es·ta·*syon* de tren

rain *lluvia* ⒡ *lyoo*·vya

raincoat *impermeable* ⓜ eem·per·me·*a*·ble

raisin *pasa* ⒡ *de uva* pa·sa de *oo*·va

Q

rape *violar* vyo·*lar*
rare *raro/a* ⓜ/ⓕ ra·ro/a
rash *irritación* ⓕ ee·rree·ta·*syon*
raspberry *frambuesa* ⓕ fram·*bwe*·sa
rat *rata* ⓕ ra·ta
raw *crudo/a* ⓜ/ⓕ kroo·do/a
razor *afeitadora* ⓕ a·fay·ta·*do*·ra
razor blade *hoja* ⓕ *de afeitar* o·kha
  de a·fay·*tar*
read *leer* le·*er*
ready *listo/a* ⓜ/ⓕ *lees*·to/a
real estate agent *agente* ⓜ
  inmobiliario a·*khen*·te
  een·mo·be·*lya*·ryo
realistic *realista* re·a·*lees*·ta
reason *razón* ⓕ ra·*son*
receipt *recibo* ⓜ re·*see*·bo
receive *recibir* re·see·*beer*
recently *recientemente*
  re·syen·te·*men*·te
recognise *reconocer* re·ko·no·*ser*
recommend *recomendar*
  re·ko·men·*dar*
recording *grabación* ⓕ gra·ba·*syon*
recyclable *reciclable* re·see·*kla*·ble
recycle *reciclar* re·see·*klar*
red *rojo/a* ⓜ/ⓕ ro·kho/a
referee *árbitro* ⓜ *ar*·bee·tro
references (work) *referencias* ⓕ pl
  re·fe·*ren*·syas
refrigerator *refrigeradora* ⓕ
  re·free·khe·ra·*do*·ra
refugee *refugiado/a* ⓜ/ⓕ
  re·foo·*khya*·do/a
refund *reembolso* ⓜ re·em·*bol*·so
refuse *negar(se)* ne·*gar*(·se)
registered mail *correo* ⓜ *certificado*
  ko·*rre*·o ser·tee·fee·*ka*·do
relationship *relación* ⓕ re·la·*syon*
relax *relajarse* re·la·*khar*·se
relic *reliquia* ⓕ re·*lee*·kya
religion *religión* ⓕ re·lee·*khyon*
religious *religioso/a* ⓜ/ⓕ
  re·lee·*khyo*·so/a
remote *remoto/a* ⓜ/ⓕ re·*mo*·to/a
remote control *mando* ⓜ *a distancia*
  man·do a dees·*tan*·sya

rent *alquiler* ⓜ al·kee·*ler*
rent *alquilar* al·kee·*lar*
repair *reparar* re·pa·*rar*
republic *república* ⓕ re·*poo*·blee·ka
reservation *reserva* ⓕ re·*ser*·va
reserve *hacer una reserva* a·*ser* oo·na
  re·*ser*·va
rest *descansar* des·kan·*sar*
restaurant *restaurante* ⓜ res·tow·*ran*·te
resume *currículum* ⓜ koo·*rree*·koo·loom
retired *jubilado/a* ⓜ/ⓕ
  khoo·bee·*la*·do/a
return *volver* vol·*ver*
return ticket *boleto* ⓜ *de ida y vuelta*
  (bo·*le*·to) de ee·da ee *vwel*·ta
reverse charge call *llamada* ⓕ *a*
  cobro revertido lya·*ma*·da a *ko*·bro
  re·ver·*tee*·do
review *crítica* ⓕ *kree*·tee·ka
rhythm *ritmo* ⓜ *reet*·mo
rice *arroz* ⓜ a·*ros*
rich *rico/a* ⓜ/ⓕ *ree*·ko/a
ride *paseo* ⓜ pa·*se*·o
ride *montar* mon·*tar*
right (correct) *correcto/a* ⓜ/ⓕ
  ko·*rrek*·to/a
right (direction) *derecha* de·*re*·cha
right-wing *derechista* de·re·*chees*·ta
ring (on finger) *anillo* a·*nee*·lyo
ring (by phone) *llamar por teléfono*
  lya·*mar* por te·*le*·fo·no
rip-off *estafa* ⓕ es·*ta*·fa
risk *riesgo* ⓜ *ryes*·go
river *río* ⓜ *ree*·o
road *calle* ⓕ *ka*·lye
rob *robar* ro·*bar*
rock (stone) *roca* ⓕ *ro*·ka
rock (music) *rock* ⓜ rok
rock climbing *escalada* ⓕ es·ka·*la*·da
rock group *grupo* ⓜ *de rock* *groo*·po
  de rok
roll (bread) *bollo* ⓜ *bo*·lyo
romance novel *novela* ⓕ *rosa* no·*ve*·la
  ro·sa
romantic *romántico/a* ⓜ/ⓕ
  ro·man·*tee*·ko/a
roof *techo* ⓜ *te*·cho

room *habitación* ① a·bee·ta·*syon*
room number *numero* ⑩ *de habitación*
  noo·me·ro de a·bee·ta·*syon*
rope *cuerda* ① *kwer*·da
round *redondo/a* ⑩/① re·*don*·do/a
roundabout *glorieta* ① glo·*rye*·ta
route *ruta* ① *roo*·ta
rowing *remo* ⑩ *re*·mo
rubbish *basura* ① ba·*soo*·ra
rug *alfombra* ① al·*fom*·bra
rugby *rugby* ⑩ *roog*·bee
ruins *ruinas* ① pl *rwee*·nas
rules *reglas* ① pl *re*·glas
rum *ron* ⑩ ron
running (sport) *footing* ⑩ foo·*teen*

S

Sabbath *sábado* ⑩ *sa*·ba·do
sad *triste* *trees*·te
saddle *sillín* ⑩ see·*lyeen*
safe *caja* ① *fuerte* ka·kha fwer·te
safe *seguro/a* ⑩/① se·*goo*·ro/a
safe sex *sexo* ⑩ *seguro* sek·so
  se·*goo*·ro
sail *vela* ① *ve*·la
sailing boat *barco* ⑩ *de vela* bar·ko
  de *ve*·la
saint *santo/a* ⑩/① *san*·to/a
salad *ensalada* ① en·sa·*la*·da
salami *salami* ⑩ sa·*la*·mee
salary *salario* ⑩ sa·*la*·ryo
sales tax *IVA* ⑩ *ee*·va
salmon *salmón* ⑩ sal·*mon*
salt *sal* ① sal
same *igual* ee·*gwal*
sand *arena* ① a·*re*·na
sandals *sandalias* ① pl san·*da*·lyas
sandwich *sandwich* ⑩ *san*·weech
sanitary napkins *compresas* ① pl
  kom·*pre*·sas
saucepan *olla* ① *o*·lya
sauna *sauna* ① *sow*·na
sausage *salchicha* ① sal·*chee*·cha
say *decir* de·*seer*
scale (climb) *trepar* tre·*par*
scarf *bufanda* ① boo·*fan*·da
school *escuela* ① es·*kwe*·la

science *ciencia* ① *syen*·sya
science fiction *ciencia* ① *ficción*
  syen·sya feek·*syon*
scientist *científico/a* ⑩/①
  syen·*tee*·fee·ko/a
scissors *tijeras* ① pl tee·*khe*·ras
score *marcar* mar·*kar*
scoreboard *marcador* ⑩ mar·ka·*dor*
Scotland *Escocia* ① es·*ko*·sya
screen *pantalla* ① pan·*ta*·lya
sea *mar* ⑩ mar
seasickness *mareo* ⑩ ma·*re*·o
seaside *orilla* ① *del mar* o·*ree*·lya
  del mar
season *estación* ① es·ta·*syon*
seat *asiento* ⑩ a·*syen*·to
seatbelt *cinturón* ⑩ *de seguridad*
  seen·too·ron de se·goo·ree·*da*
second *segundo* ⑩ se·*goon*·do
second *segundo/a* ⑩/① se·*goon*·do/a
second-hand *de segunda mano* de
  se·*goon*·da ma·no
secretary *secretario/a* ⑩/①
  se·kre·*ta*·ryo/a
see *ver* ver
selfish *egoísta* ⑩&① e·go·*ees*·ta
self-service *autoservicio* ⑩
  ow·to·ser·*vee*·syo
sell *vender* ven·*der*
send *enviar* en·*vyar*
sensible *juicioso/a* ⑩/① khwee·*syo*·so/a
sensual *sensual* sen·*swal*
separate *separado/a* ⑩/① se·pa·*ra*·do/a
separate *separar* se·pa·*rar*
series *serie* ① *se*·rye
serious *serio/a* ⑩/① *se*·ryo/a
service charge *servicio* ⑩ ser·*vee*·syo
service station *gasolinera* ①
  ga·so·lee·*ne*·ra
several *varios/as* ⑩/① *va*·ryos/as
sew *coser* ko·*ser*
sex *sexo* ⑩ sek·so
sexism *sexismo* ⑩ sek·*sees*·mo
sexy *sexy* sek·see
shade *sombra* ① *som*·bra
shadow *sombra* ① *som*·bra

shampoo *champú* ⓜ cham·*poo*
shape *forma* ① *for*·ma
share (with) *compartir* kom·par·*teer*
shave *afeitarse* a·fay·*tar*·se
shaving cream *espuma* ① *de afeitar*
es·*poo*·ma de a·fay·*tar*
she *ella* e·lya
sheep *oveja* ① o·*ve*·kha
sheet (bed) *sábana* ① *sa*·ba·na
ship *barco* ⓜ *bar*·ko
shirt *camisa* ① ka·*mee*·sa
shoe shop *zapatería* ① sa·pa·te·*ree*·a
shoes *zapatos* ⓜ pl sa·*pa*·tos
shoot *disparar* dees·pa·*rar*
shop *tienda* ① *tyen*·da
(go) shopping *ir de compras* eer de
kom·pras
shopping centre *centro* ⓜ *comercial*
sen·tro ko·mer·*syal*
short (height) *bajo/a* ⓜ/① *ba*·kho/a
short (length) *corto/a* ⓜ/① *kor*·to/a
shortage *escasez* ① es·ka·*ses*
shorts *pantalones* ⓜ pl *cortos*
pan·ta·*lo*·nes *kor*·tos
short stories *cuentos* ⓜ pl *kwen*·tos
shoulders *hombros* ⓜ pl *om*·bros
shout *gritar* gree·*tar*
show *espectáculo* ⓜ es·pek·*ta*·koo·lo
show *mostrar* mos·*trar*
shower *ducha* ① *doo*·cha
shrine *capilla* ① ka·*pee*·lya
shut *cerrado/a* ⓜ/① se·*ra*·do/a
shy *tímido/a* ⓜ/① *tee*·mee·do/a
sick *enfermo/a* ⓜ/① en·*fer*·mo/a
side *lado* ⓜ *la*·do
sign *señal* ① se·*nyal*
signature *firma* ① *feer*·ma
silk *seda* ① *se*·da
silver *plata* ① *pla*·ta
SIM card *tarjeta* ① *SIM* tar·*khe*·ta seem
similar *similar* see·mee·*lar*
simple *sencillo/a* ⓜ/① sen·*see*·lyo/a
since (time) *desde* *des*·de
sing *cantar* kan·*tar*
Singapore *Singapur* ⓜ seen·ga·*poor*
singer *cantante* ⓜ&① kan·*tan*·te
single (unmarried) *soltero/a* ⓜ/①
sol·*te*·ro/a

single room *habitación* ① *individual*
a·bee·ta·*syon* een·dee·vee·*dwal*
singlet *camiseta* ① ka·mee·*se*·ta
sister *hermana* ① er·*ma*·na
sit *sentarse* sen·*tar*·se
size (clothes) *talla* ① *ta*·lya
size (general) *tamaño* ta·*ma*·nyo
skateboarding *monopatinaje* ⓜ
mo·no·pa·tee·*na*·khe
ski *esquiar* es·*kyar*
skiing *esquí* ⓜ es·*kee*
ski lift *telesquí* ① te·le·*skee*
skis *esquís* ⓜ pl es·*kees*
skimmed milk *leche* ① *desnatada*
le·che des·na·*ta*·da
skin *piel* ① pyel
skirt *falda* ① *fal*·da
sky *cielo* ⓜ *sye*·lo
sleep *dormir* dor·*meer*
sleeping bag *saco* ⓜ *de dormir* *sa*·ko
de dor·*meer*
sleeping car *coche* ⓜ *cama* *ko*·che
ka·ma
sleeping pills *pastillas* ① pl *para*
dormir pas·*tee*·lyas *pa*·ra dor·*meer*
(be) sleepy *tener sueño* te·*ner* *swe*·nyo
slide (film) *diapositiva* ①
dya·po·see·*tee*·va
slow *lento/a* ⓜ/① *len*·to/a
slowly *despacio* des·*pa*·syo
small *pequeño/a* ⓜ/① pe·*ke*·nyo/a
smell *olor* ⓜ o·*lor*
smile *sonreír* son·re·*eer*
smoke *fumar* foo·*mar*
SMS *SMS* e·se e·me e·se
snack *tentempié* ⓜ ten·tem·*pye*
snail *caracol* ⓜ ka·ra·*kol*
snake *serpiente* ① ser·*pyen*·te
snorkelling *buceo* ⓜ boo·*se*·o
snow *nieve* ① *nye*·ve
snowboarding *surf* ⓜ *sobre la nieve*
soorf *so*·bre la *nye*·ve
soap *jabón* ⓜ kha·*bon*
soap opera *telenovela* ① te·le·no·*ve*·la
soccer *fútbol* ⓜ *foot*·bol
social welfare *asistencia* ① *social*
a·sees·*ten*·sya so·*syal*

socialist *socialista* so·sya·*lees*·ta

socks *calcetines* ⓜ pl kal·se·*tee*·nes

soft drink *gaseosa* ⓕ ga·se·o·sa

soldier *soldado* ⓜ sol·*da*·do

some *algún* al·*goon*

someone *alguien* al·gyen

something *algo* al·go

sometimes *de vez en cuando* de ves en *kwan*·do

son *hijo* ⓜ ee·kho

song *canción* ⓕ kan·*syon*

soon *pronto* *pron*·to

sore *dolorido/a* ⓜ/ⓕ do·lo·*ree*·do/a

soup *sopa* ⓕ so·pa

sour cream *crema* ⓕ *agria* kre·ma a·grya

south *sur* ⓜ soor

South America *Sudamérica* ⓕ soo·da·*me*·ree·ka

South American *sudamericano/a* ⓜ/ⓕ soo·da·me·ree·*ka*·no/a

souvenir *recuerdo* ⓜ re·*kwer*·do

souvenir shop *tienda* ⓕ *de recuerdos* tyen·da de re·*kwer*·dos

soy milk *leche* ⓕ *de soya* le·che de so·ya

soy sauce *salsa* ⓕ *de soya* sal·sa de so·ya

space *espacio* ⓜ es·*pa*·syo

spade *pala* ⓕ *pa*·la

Spain *España* ⓕ es·*pa*·nya

speak *hablar* a·*blar*

special *especial* es·pe·*syal*

specialist *especialista* ⓜ&ⓕ es·pe·sya·*lees*·ta

speed *velocidad* ⓕ ve·lo·see·*da*

speed limit *límite* ⓜ *de velocidad* *lee*·mee·te de ve·lo·see·*da*

speedometer *velocímetro* ⓜ ve·lo·*see*·me·tro

spermicide *espermicida* ⓕ es·per·mee·*see*·da

spider *araña* ⓕ a·*ra*·nya

spinach *espinacas* ⓕ pl es·pee·*na*·kas

spoon *cuchara* ⓕ koo·*cha*·ra

sport *deportes* ⓜ pl de·*por*·tes

sports store *tienda* ⓕ *deportiva* tyen·da de·por·*tee*·va

sportsperson *deportista* ⓜ&ⓕ de·por·*tees*·ta

sprain *torcedura* ⓕ tor·se·*doo*·ra

spring (mechanical) *muelle* ⓜ mwe·lye

spring (season) *primavera* ⓕ pree·ma·*ve*·ra

square (shape) *cuadrado* ⓜ kwa·*dra*·do

square (town) *plaza* ⓕ *pla*·sa

stadium *estadio* ⓜ es·*ta*·dyo

stage *escenario* ⓜ e·se·*na*·ryo

stairway *escalera* ⓕ es·ka·*le*·ra

stamp *sello* ⓜ *se*·lyo

standby ticket *boleto* ⓜ *de lista de espera* bo·*le*·to de *lees*·ta de es·*pe*·ra

stars *estrellas* ⓕ pl es·*tre*·lyas

start *comenzar* ko·men·*sar*

station *estación* ⓕ es·ta·*syon*

statue *estatua* ⓕ es·*ta*·twa

stay (at a hotel) *alojarse* a·lo·*khar*·se

stay (remain) *quedarse* ke·*dar*·se

STD (sexually transmitted disease) *enfermedad* ⓕ *de transmisión sexual* en·fer·me·*da* de trans·mee·*syon* sek·*swal*

steak (beef) *bistec* ⓜ bees·*tek*

steal *robar* ro·*bar*

steep *escarpado/a* ⓜ/ⓕ es·kar·*pa*·do/a

step *paso* ⓜ *pa*·so

stereo *equipo* ⓜ *estereofónico* e·*kee*·po es·te·re·o·*fo*·nee·ko

stingy *tacaño/a* ⓜ/ⓕ ta·*ka*·nyo/a

stockings *medias* ⓕ pl *me*·dyas

stomach *estómago* ⓜ es·*to*·ma·go

stomachache *dolor* ⓜ *de estómago* do·*lor* de es·*to*·ma·go

stone *piedra* ⓕ *pye*·dra

stoned (drugged) *volado/a* ⓜ/ⓕ vo·*la*·do/a

stop *parada* ⓕ pa·*ra*·da

stop *parar* pa·*rar*

storm *tormenta* ⓕ tor·*men*·ta

story *cuento* ⓜ *kwen*·to

stove *estufa* ⓕ es·*too*·fa

straight *recto/a* ⓜ/ⓕ *rek*·to/a

strange *extraño/a* ⓜ/ⓕ ek·*stra*·nyo/a
stranger *extraño/a* ⓜ/ⓕ ek·*stra*·nyo/a
strawberry *frutilla* ⓕ froo·*tee*·lya
stream *arroyo* ⓜ a·*ro*·yo
street *calle* ⓕ *ka*·lye
street market *feria* ⓕ *fe*·rya
string *cuerda* ⓕ *kwer*·da
strong *fuerte* *fwer*·te
stubborn *testarudo/a* ⓜ/ⓕ tes·ta·*roo*·do/a
student *estudiante* ⓜ&ⓕ es·too·*dyan*·te
studio *estudio* ⓜ es·*too*·dyo
stupid *estúpido/a* ⓜ/ⓕ es·*too*·pee·do/a
style *estilo* ⓜ es·*tee*·lo
subtitles *subtítulos* ⓜ pl soob·*tee*·too·los
suburb *barrio* ⓜ *ba*·ryo
subway *subteráneo* soob·te·*ra*·ne·o
sugar *azúcar* ⓜ a·*soo*·kar
sugar cane *caña de azúcar* *ka*·nya de a·*soo*·kar
suit *traje* ⓜ *tra*·khe
suitcase *maleta* ⓕ ma·*le*·ta
summer *verano* ⓜ ve·*ra*·no
sun *sol* ⓜ sol
sunblock *crema solar* *kre*·ma so·*lar*
sunburn *quemadura de sol* ke·ma·*doo*·ra de sol
sunglasses *anteojos de sol* ⓜ pl an·te·o·khos de sol
sunny *soleado/a* ⓜ/ⓕ so·le·*a*·do/a
sunrise *amanecer* ⓜ a·ma·ne·*ser*
sunset *puesta del sol* ⓕ *pwes*·ta del sol
sunstroke *insolación* ⓕ een·so·la·*syon*
supermarket *supermercado* ⓜ soo·per·mer·*ka*·do
superstition *superstición* ⓕ soo·per·stee·*syon*
supporters *hinchas* ⓜ&ⓕ pl *een*·chas
surf *hacer surf* a·ser soorf
surface mail *por vía terrestre* por *vee*·a te·*res*·tre
surf *hacer surfing* ⓜ a·ser *soorf*·een
surfboard *tabla de surf* ta·bla de soorf
surname *apellido* ⓜ a·pe·*lyee*·do
surprise *sorpresa* ⓕ sor·*pre*·sa
sweater (jumper) *jersey* ⓜ *kher*·say

sweet *dulce* *dool*·se
swim *nadar* na·*dar*
swimming pool *piscina* ⓕ pee·*see*·na
swimsuit *traje de baño* ⓜ *tra*·khe de *ba*·nyo
synagogue *sinagoga* ⓕ see·na·*go*·ga
synthetic *sintético/a* ⓜ/ⓕ seen·te·tee·ko/a
syringe *jeringa* ⓕ khe·*reen*·ga

T

table *mesa* ⓕ *me*·sa
table tennis *ping pong* ⓜ peen pon
tablecloth *mantel* ⓜ man·*tel*
tail *rabo* ⓜ *ra*·bo
tailor *sastre* ⓜ *sas*·tre
take *tomar* to·*mar*
talk *hablar* a·*blar*
tall *alto/a* ⓜ/ⓕ *al*·to/a
tampons *tampones* ⓜ pl tam·*po*·nes
tanning lotion *bronceador* ⓜ bron·se·a·*dor*
tap (faucet) *grifo* ⓜ *gree*·fo
tapir *danta* ⓕ *dan*·ta
tasty *sabroso/a* ⓜ/ⓕ sa·*bro*·so/a
tax *impuesto* ⓜ eem·*pwes*·to
taxi *taxi* ⓜ *tak*·see
taxi stand *parada de taxis* ⓕ pa·*ra*·da de *tak*·sees
tea *té* ⓜ te
teacher *profesor/profesora* ⓜ/ⓕ pro·fe·*sor*/pro·fe·*so*·ra
team *equipo* ⓜ e·*kee*·po
teaspoon *cucharita* ⓕ koo·cha·*ree*·ta
teeth *dientes* ⓜ pl *dyen*·tes
telegram *telegrama* ⓜ te·le·*gra*·ma
telephone *teléfono* ⓜ te·*le*·fo·no
telephone *llamar (por teléfono)* lya·*mar* (por te·*le*·fo·no)
telephone centre *central telefónica* ⓕ sen·*tral* te·le·*fo*·nee·ka
telephoto lens *teleobjetivo* ⓜ te·le·ob·khe·*tee*·vo
television *televisión* ⓕ te·le·vee·*syon*
tell *decir* de·*seer*
temperature (fever) *fiebre* ⓕ *fye*·bre

temperature (weather) *temperatura* ① tem·pe·ra·*too*·ra

temple *templo* ⓜ *tem*·plo

tennis *tenis* ⓜ *te*·nees

tennis court *cancha* ① *de tenis* *kan*·cha de te·nees

tent *carpa* ① *kar*·pa

tent pegs *estacas* ① *de carpa* es·*ta*·kas de *kar*·pa

terrible *terible* te·*ree*·ble

test *prueba* ① *prwe*·ba

testimonial literature *literatura* ① *testimonial* lee·te·ra·*too*·ra tes·tee·mo·*nyal*

thank *dar gracias* dar *gra*·syas

the Pill *píldora* ① *peel*·do·ra

theatre *teatro* ⓜ te·*a*·tro

their *su* soo

they *ellos/ellas* ⓜ/① pl *e*·lyos/*e*·lyas

thief *ladrón/ladrona* ⓜ/① la·*dron*/la·*dro*·na

thin *delgado/a* ⓜ/① del·*ga*·do/a

think *pensar* pen·*sar*

third *tercio* ⓜ *ter*·syo

thirst *sed* ① se

(be) thirsty *tener sed* ① te·*ner* se

this *éste/a* ⓜ/① *es*·te/a

throat *garganta* ① gar·*gan*·ta

thrush (medical) *aftas* ① pl *af*·tas

ticket *boleto* ⓜ bo·*le*·to

ticket collector *revisor/revisora* ⓜ/① re·vee·*sor*/re·vee·*so*·ra

ticket machine *máquina* ① *de boletos* *ma*·kee·na de bo·*le*·tos

ticket office (theatre, cinema) *taquilla* ① ta·*kee*·lya

ticket office (general) *boletería* ① bo·le·te·*ree*·a

tide *marea* ① ma·*re*·a

tight *apretado/a* ⓜ/① a·pre·*ta*·do/a

time (hour) *hora* ① *o*·ra

time (period) *tiempo* ⓜ *tyem*·po

timetable *horario* ⓜ o·*ra*·ryo

tin (can) *lata* ① *la*·ta

tin opener *abrelatas* ⓜ a·bre·*la*·tas

tiny *pequeñito/a* ⓜ/① pe·ke·*nyee*·to/a

tip (gratuity) *propina* ① pro·*pee*·na

tired *cansado/a* ⓜ/① kan·*sa*·do/a

tissues *pañuelos* ⓜ pl *de papel* pa·*nywe*·los de pa·*pel*

toast *tostada* ① tos·*ta*·da

toaster *tostadora* ① tos·ta·*do*·ra

tobacco *tabaco* ⓜ ta·*ba*·ko

tobacconist *estanquero* ⓜ es·tan·*ke*·ro

tobogganing *ir en tobogán* eer en to·bo·*gan*

today *hoy* oy

toe *dedo* ⓜ *del pie* *de*·do del pye

tofu *tofú* ⓜ to·*foo*

together *juntos/as* ⓜ/① pl *khoon*·tos/as

toilet *baño* ⓜ • *servicio* ⓜ *ba*·nyo • ser·*vee*·syo

toilet paper *papel* ⓜ *higiénico* pa·*pel* ee·*khye*·nee·ko

tomato *tomate* ⓜ to·*ma*·te

tomato sauce *salsa* ① *de tomate* *sal*·sa de to·*ma*·te

tomorrow *mañana* ① ma·*nya*·na

tonight *esta noche* es·ta *no*·che

too (expensive) *demasiado (caro/a)* ⓜ/① de·ma·*sya*·do (*ka*·ro/a)

tooth (back) *muela* ① *mwe*·la

toothache *dolor* ⓜ *de muelas* do·*lor* de *mwe*·las

toothbrush *cepillo* ⓜ *de dientes* se·*pee*·lyo de *dyen*·tes

toothpaste *pasta* ① *dentífrica* *pas*·ta den·*tee*·free·ka

toothpick *palillo* ⓜ pa·*lee*·lyo

torch (flashlight) *linterna* ① leen·*ter*·na

touch *tocar* to·*kar*

tour *excursión* ① ek·skoor·*syon*

tourist *turista* ⓜ&① too·*rees*·ta

tourist office *oficina* ① *de turismo* o·fee·*see*·na de too·*rees*·mo

towards *hacia* *a*·sya

towel *toalla* ① to·*a*·lya

tower *torre* ① *to*·re

toxic waste *residuos* ⓜ pl *tóxicos* re·*see*·dwos *tok*·see·kos

toy shop *juguetería* ① khoo·ge·te·ree·a
track (path) *camino* ⓜ ka·mee·no
track (sports) *pista* ① pees·ta
trade *comercio* ⓜ ko·mer·syo
traffic *tráfico* ⓜ tra·fee·ko
traffic lights *semáforos* ⓜ pl se·ma·fo·ros
trail *camino* ⓜ ka·mee·no
train *tren* ⓜ tren
train station *estación* ① de tren es·ta·syon de tren
tram *tranvía* ⓜ tran·vee·a
transit lounge *sala* ① de tránsito sa·la de tran·see·to
translate *traducir* tra·doo·seer
transport *transporte* ⓜ trans·por·te
travel *viajar* vya·khar
travel agency *agencia* ① de viajes a·khen·sya de vya·khes
travel books *libros* ⓜ pl de viajes lee·bros de vya·khes
travel sickness *mareo* ⓜ ma·re·o
travellers cheque *cheque* ⓜ de viajero che·ke de vya·khe·ro
tree *árbol* ⓜ ar·bol
trip *viaje* ⓜ vya·khe
trousers *pantalones* ⓜ pl pan·ta·lo·nes
truck *camión* ⓜ ka·myon
trust *confianza* ① kon·fyan·sa
trust *confiar* kon·fyar
try (attempt) *probar* pro·bar
T-shirt *camiseta* ① ka·mee·se·ta
tube (tyre) *cámara* ① de aire ka·ma·ra de ai·re
tuna *atún* ⓜ a·toon
tune *melodía* ① me·lo·dee·a
turkey *pavo* ⓜ pa·vo
turn *doblar* do·blar
TV *tele* ① te·le
tweezers *pinzas* ① pl peen·sas
twice *dos veces* dos ve·ses
twin beds *dos camas* ① pl dos ka·mas
twins *gemelos/as* ⓜ/① pl khe·me·los/as
type *tipo* ⓜ tee·po
typical *típico/a* ⓜ/① tee·pee·ko/a
tyre *llanta* ① lyan·ta

U

ultrasound *ecografía* ① e·ko·gra·fee·a
umbrella *paraguas* ⓜ pa·ra·gwas
umpire *árbitro/a* ⓜ/① ar·bee·tro/a
uncle *tío* ⓜ tee·o
uncomfortable *incómodo/a* ⓜ/① een·ko·mo·do/a
underpants (men) *calzoncillos* ⓜ pl kal·son·see·lyos
underpants (women) *bragas* ① pl bra·gas
understand *entender* en·ten·der
underwater camera *cámara* ① submarina ka·ma·ra soob·ma·ree·na
underwear *ropa* ① interior ro·pa een·te·ryor
unemployed *desempleado/a* ⓜ/① des·em·ple·a·do/a
unfair *injusto/a* ⓜ/① een·khoos·to/a
uniform *uniforme* ⓜ oo·nee·for·me
universe *universo* ⓜ oo·nee·ver·so
university *universidad* ① oo·nee·ver·see·da
unleaded *sin plomo* seen plo·mo
unsafe *inseguro/a* ⓜ/① een·se·goo·ro/a
until *hasta* as·ta
unusual *extraño/a* ⓜ/① ek·stra·nyo/a
up *arriba* a·ree·ba
uphill *cuesta arriba* kwes·ta a·ree·ba
urgent *urgente* oor·khen·te
Uruguay *Uruguay* ⓜ oo·roo·gway
USA *Los Estados* ⓜ pl Unidos los es·ta·dos oo·nee·dos
useful *útil* oo·teel

V

vacant *vacante* va·kan·te
vacation *vacaciones* ① pl va·ka·syo·nes
vaccination *vacuna* ① va·koo·na
vagina *vagina* ① va·khee·na
vaginal discharge *flujo* ⓜ vaginal floo·kho va·khee·nal
validate *validar* va·lee·dar
valley *valle* ⓜ va·lye
valuable *valioso/a* ⓜ/① va·lyo·so/a

value *valor* ⓜ va·*lor*

van *caravana* ⓕ ka·ra·*va*·na

veal *ternera* ⓕ ter·*ne*·ra

vegan *vegetariano/a estricto/a* ⓜ/ⓕ ve·khe·ta·*rya*·no/a es·*treek*·to/a

vegetable *verdura* ⓕ ver·*doo*·ra

vegetable garden *huerta* ⓕ *wer*·ta

vegetarian *vegetariano/a* ⓜ/ⓕ ve·khe·ta·*rya*·no/a

vein *vena* ⓕ *ve*·na

venereal disease *enfermedad* ⓕ *venérea* en·fer·me·*da* ve·ne·re·a

Venezuela *Venezuela* ⓕ ve·ne·*swe*·la

venue *local* ⓜ lo·*kal*

very *muy* mooy

video *vídeo* ⓜ *vee*·de·o

video tape *cinta* ⓕ *de vídeo* *seen*·ta de *vee*·de·o

view *vista* ⓕ *vees*·ta

village *pueblo* ⓜ *pwe*·blo

vinegar *vinagre* ⓜ vee·*na*·gre

vineyard *viñedo* ⓜ vee·*nye*·do

virus *virus* ⓜ *vee*·roos

visa *visado* ⓜ *vee*·sa·do

visit *visitar* vee·see·*tar*

vitamins *vitaminas* ⓕ pl vee·ta·*mee*·nas

voice *voz* ⓕ vos

volleyball *vóleibol* ⓜ *vo*·lay·bol

vote *votar* vo·*tar*

vulture *buitre* ⓜ *bwee*·tre

W

wage *sueldo* ⓜ *swel*·do

wait *esperar* es·pe·*rar*

waiter *camarero/a* ⓜ/ⓕ ka·ma·*re*·ro/a

waiting room *sala* ⓕ *de espera* *sa*·la de es·*pe*·ra

wake up *despertarse* des·per·*tar*·se

walk *caminar* ka·mee·*nar*

wall (inside) *pared* ⓕ pa·*re*

wallet *cartera* ⓕ kar·*te*·ra

want *querer* ke·*rer*

WAP *WAP* ⓜ gwap

WAP-enabled *capacidad* ⓕ *de WAP* ka·pa·see·*da* de gwap

war *guerra* ⓕ *ge*·ra

wardrobe *vestuario* ⓜ ves·*twa*·ryo

warm *templado/a* ⓜ/ⓕ tem·*pla*·do/a

warn *advertir* ad·ver·*teer*

wash (oneself) *lavarse* la·*var*·se

wash (something) *lavar* la·*var*

wash cloth (flannel) *toallita* ⓕ to·a·*lyee*·ta

washing machine *lavadora* ⓕ la·va·*do*·ra

watch *reloj* ⓜ *de pulsera* re·*lokh* de pool·*se*·ra

watch *mirar* mee·*rar*

water *agua* ⓕ *a*·gwa

 boiled water *agua* ⓕ *hervida* *a*·gwa er·*vee*·da

 still water *agua* ⓕ *sin gas* *a*·gwa seen gas

 tap water *agua* ⓕ *del grifo* *a*·gwa del *gree*·fo

water bottle *cantimplora* ⓕ kan·teem·*plo*·ra

waterfall *cascada* ⓕ kas·*ka*·da

watermelon *sandía* ⓕ san·*dee*·a

waterproof *impermeable* eem·per·me·*a*·ble

waterskiing *esquí* ⓜ *acuático* es·*kee* a·*kwa*·tee·ko

water skis *esquís* ⓜ pl *acuáticos* es·*kees* a·*kwa*·tee·kos

wave *ola* ⓕ *o*·la

way *camino* ⓜ ka·*mee*·no

we *nosotros/as* ⓜ/ⓕ no·so·tros/as

weak *débil* de·beel

wealthy *rico/a* ⓜ/ⓕ *ree*·ko/a

wear *llevar* lye·*var*

weather *tiempo* ⓜ *tyem*·po

wedding *boda* ⓕ *bo*·da

wedding cake *tarta* ⓕ *nupcial* *tar*·ta noop·*syal*

wedding present *regalo* ⓜ *de bodas* re·*ga*·lo de *bo*·das

week *semana* ⓕ se·*ma*·na

weekend *fin* ⓜ *de semana* feen de se·*ma*·na

weight *peso* ⓜ *pe*·so

welcome *dar la bienvenida* dar la byen·ve·*nee*·da

welfare *bienestar* ⓜ byen·es·*tar*

well *bien* byen
well (water) *pozo* ⓜ po·so
west *oeste* ⓜ o·es·te
wet *mojado/a* ⓜ/ⓕ mo·kha·do/a
what *que* ke
wheel *rueda* ⓕ rwe·da
wheelchair *silla* ⓕ *de ruedas* see·lya de rwe·das
when *cuando* kwan·do
where *donde* don·de
white *blanco/a* ⓜ/ⓕ blan·ko/a
whiteboard *pizarra* ⓕ *blanca* pee·sa·ra blan·ka
who *quien* kyen
why *por qué* por ke
wide *ancho/a* ⓜ/ⓕ an·cho/a
widow *viuda* ⓕ vyoo·da
widower *viudo* ⓜ vyoo·do
wife *esposa* ⓕ es·po·sa
win *ganar* ga·nar
wind *viento* ⓜ vyen·to
window *ventana* ⓕ ven·ta·na
window-shopping *mirar escaparates* mee·rar es·ka·pa·ra·tes
windscreen *parabrisas* ⓜ pa·ra·bree·sas
windsurfing *hacer windsurfing* a·ser gween·soorf·een
wine *vino* ⓜ vee·no
  red wine *vino* ⓜ *tinto* vee·no teen·to
  sparkling wine *vino* ⓜ *espumoso* vee·no es·poo·mo·so
  white wine *vino* ⓜ *blanco* vee·no blan·ko
winery *bodega* ⓕ bo·de·ga
wings *alas* ⓕ pl a·las
winner *ganador/ganadora* ⓜ/ⓕ ga·na·dor/ga·na·do·ra
winter *invierno* ⓜ een·vyer·no
wire *alambre* ⓕ a·lam·bre
wish *desear* de·se·ar
with *con* kon
within (an hour) *dentro de (una hora)* den·tro de (oo·na o·ra)
without *sin* seen
woman *mujer* ⓕ moo·kher
wonderful *maravilloso/a* ⓜ/ⓕ ma·ra·vee·lyo·so/a
wood *madera* ⓕ ma·de·ra

wool *lana* ⓕ la·na
word *palabra* ⓕ pa·la·bra
work (occupation) *trabajo* ⓜ tra·ba·kho
work (of art) *obra* ⓕ o·bra
work experience *experiencia* ⓕ *laboral* ek·spe·ryen·sya la·bo·ral
work permit *permiso* ⓜ *de trabajo* per·mee·so de tra·ba·kho
workout *entreno* ⓜ en·tre·no
workshop *taller* ⓜ ta·lyer
world *mundo* ⓜ moon·do
World Cup *La Copa* ⓕ *Mundial* la ko·pa moon·dyal
worried *preocupado/a* ⓜ/ⓕ pre·o·koo·pa·do/a
worship (pray) *rezar* re·sar
wrist *muñeca* ⓕ moo·nye·ka
write *escribir* es·kree·beer
writer *escritor/escritora* ⓜ/ⓕ es·kree·tor/es·kree·to·ra
wrong *equivocado/a* ⓜ/ⓕ e·kee·vo·ka·do/a

(this) year *(este) año* (es·te) a·nyo

Y

yellow *amarillo/a* ⓜ/ⓕ a·ma·ree·lyo/a
yellow fever *fiebre* ⓕ *amarilla* fye·bre a·ma·ree·lya
yes *sí* see
(not) yet *todavía (no)* to·da·vee·a (no)
yesterday *ayer* a·yer
yoga *yoga* ⓜ yo·ga
yogurt *yogur* ⓜ yo·goor
you sg inf *tú* too
you sg pol *usted* oos·te
you pl inf&pol *ustedes* oos·te·des
young *joven* kho·ven
youth hostel *albergue* ⓜ *juvenil* al·ber·ge khoo·ve·neel

Z

zodiac *zodíaco* ⓜ so·dee·a·ko
zoo *zoológico* ⓜ so·o·lo·khee·ko
zoom lens *zoom* ⓜ soom

Nouns in the dictionary have their gender indicated by ⓜ or ⓕ.
If it's a plural noun, you'll also see pl. When a word that could be
either a noun or a verb has no gender indicated, it's a verb.

A

a bordo a *bor*·do *aboard*

a larga distancia a *lar*·ga dees·*tan*·sya
long-distance

a menudo a me·*noo*·do *often*

a tiempo a *tyem*·po *on time*

a través a tra·*ves across*

abajo a·*ba*·kho *below*

abarrotado/a ⓜ/ⓕ a·ba·ro·*ta*·do/a
crowded

abeja ⓕ a·*be*·kha *bee*

abierto/a ⓜ/ⓕ a·*byer*·to/a *open*

abogado/a ⓜ/ⓕ a·bo·*ga*·do/a *lawyer*

aborto ⓜ a·*bor*·to *abortion*

— natural na·too·*ral miscarriage*

abrazo ⓜ a·*bra*·so *hug*

abrebotellas ⓜ a·bre·bo·*te*·lyas *bottle
opener*

abrelatas ⓜ a·bre·*la*·tas *can opener •
tin opener*

abrigo ⓜ a·*bree*·go *overcoat*

abrir a·*breer open*

abuela ⓕ a·*bwe*·la *grandmother*

abuelo ⓜ a·*bwe*·lo *grandfather*

aburrido/a ⓜ/ⓕ a·boo·*ree*·do/a
boring

acabar a·ka·*bar end*

acampar a·kam·*par camp*

acantilado ⓜ a·kan·tee·*la*·do *cliff*

accidente ⓜ ak·see·*den*·te *accident*

aceite ⓜ a·*say*·te *oil*

— de oliva de o·*lee*·va *olive oil*

aceituna ⓕ a·say·*too*·na *olive*

aceptar a·sep·*tar accept*

acera ⓕ a·*se*·ra *footpath*

acondicionador ⓜ
a·kon·dee·syo·na·*dor conditioner*

aconsejar a·kon·se·*khar advise*

acoso ⓜ a·*ko*·so *harassment*

activista ⓜ&ⓕ ak·tee·*vees*·ta *activist*

actuación ⓕ ak·twa·*syon gig •
performance*

acupuntura ⓕ a·koo·poon·*too*·ra
acupuncture

adaptador ⓜ a·dap·ta·*dor adaptor*

addicto/a ⓜ/ⓕ a·*deek*·to/a *addicted*

adentro a·*den*·tro *inside*

adivinar a·dee·vee·*nar guess*

administración ⓕ
ad·mee·nees·tra·*syon administration*

admitir ad·mee·*teer admit • accept •
acknowledge*

aduana ⓕ a·*dwa*·na *customs*

adulto/a ⓜ/ⓕ a·*dool*·to/a *adult*

advertir ad·ver·*teer warn*

aeróbic ⓜ a·e·ro·*beek aerobics*

aerolínea ⓕ a·e·ro·*lee*·ne·a *airline*

aeropuerto ⓜ a·e·ro·*pwer*·to *airport*

afeitadora ⓕ a·fay·ta·*do*·ra *razor*

afeitarse a·fay·*tar*·se *shave*

afortunado/a ⓜ/ⓕ a·for·too·*na*·do/a
lucky

África ⓕ a·*free*·ka *Africa*

agencia de viajes a·*khen*·sya de
vya·khes *travel agency*

agenda ⓕ a·*khen*·da *diary*

agente ⓜ **inmobiliario** a·*khen*·te
een·mo·bee·*lya*·ryo *real estate agent*

agresivo/a ⓜ/ⓕ a·gre·*see*·vo/a
aggressive

agricultor(a) ⓜ/ⓕ a·gree·kool·*tor*/
a·gree·kool·*to*·ra *farmer*
agricultura ⓕ a·gree·kool·*too*·ra
agriculture
agua ⓕ *a*·gwa *water*
— **caliente** ka·*lyen*·te *hot water*
— **del grifo** del *gree*·fo *tap water*
— **hervida** er·*vee*·da *boiled water*
— **mineral** mee·ne·*ral* mineral water
— **sin gas** seen gas *still water*
aguja ⓕ a·*goo*·kha *needle (sewing)*
ahora a·*o*·ra *now*
aire ⓜ *ai*·re *air*
— **acondicionado**
a·kon·dee·syo·*na*·do *air-conditioning*
ajedrez ⓜ a·khe·*dres* *chess*
ají ⓜ a·*khee* *chilli*
ajo ⓜ *a*·kho *garlic*
al fondo de al *fon*·do de *at the bottom*
al lado de al *la*·do de *next to*
alambre ⓜ a·*lam*·bre *wire*
alas ⓕ pl *a*·las *wings*
albergue ⓜ **juvenil** al·*ber*·ge
khoo·ve·*neel* *youth hostel*
alcalde ⓜ&ⓕ al·*kal*·de *mayor*
alcohol ⓜ al·*kol* *alcohol*
Alemania a·le·*ma*·nya *Germany*
alergia ⓕ a·*ler*·khya *allergy*
alfarería ⓕ al·fa·re·*ree*·a *pottery*
alfombra ⓕ al·*fom*·bra *rug*
algo *al*·go *something*
algodón ⓜ al·go·*don* *cotton*
alguien *al*·gyen *someone*
algún al·*goon* *some*
alguno/a ⓜ/ⓕ sg al·*goo*·no/a
any (singular)
algunos/as ⓜ/ⓕ pl al·*goo*·nos/as
any (plural)
almacén ⓜ al·ma·*sen* *general store*
almendra ⓕ al·*men*·dra *almond*
almohada ⓕ al·mo·*a*·da *pillow*
almuerzo ⓜ al·*mwer*·so *lunch*
alojamiento ⓜ a·lo·kha·*myen*·to
accommodation
alojarse a·lo·*khar*·se *stay (at a hotel)*
alpinismo ⓜ al·pee·*nees*·mo
mountaineering

alquilar al·kee·*lar* *hire • rent*
— **un carro** oon ka·ro *hire a car*
alquiler ⓜ al·kee·*ler* *hire • rental*
altar ⓜ al·*tar* *altar*
alto/a ⓜ/ⓕ *al*·to/a *high • tall*
altura ⓕ al·*too*·ra *altitude*
alucinar a·loo·see·*nar* *hallucinate*
ama ⓕ **de casa** *a*·ma de *ka*·sa
homemaker
amable a·*ma*·ble *kind*
amanecer a·ma·ne·*ser* *sunrise*
amante ⓜ&ⓕ a·*man*·te *lover*
amarillo/a ⓜ/ⓕ a·ma·*ree*·lyo/a *yellow*
amateur ⓜ&ⓕ a·ma·*toor* *amateur*
ambulancia ⓕ am·boo·*lan*·sya
ambulance
América ⓕ a·*me*·ree·ka *America*
amigo/a ⓜ/ⓕ a·*mee*·go/a *friend*
ampolla ⓕ am·*po*·lya *blister*
analgésicos ⓜ pl a·nal·*khe*·see·kos
painkillers
análisis ⓜ **de sangre** a·*na*·lee·sees de
san·gre *blood test*
ananas a·na·*nas* *pineapple*
anaranjado/a ⓜ/ⓕ a·na·ran·*kha*·do/a
orange (colour)
anarquista ⓜ&ⓕ a·nar·*kees*·ta
anarchist
ancho/a ⓜ/ⓕ *an*·cho/a *wide*
andar an·*dar* *walk*
— **en bicicleta** en bee·see·*kle*·ta
cycle
anillo ⓜ a·*nee*·lyo *ring (on finger)*
animal ⓜ a·nee·*mal* *animal*
año *a*·nyo *year*
Año Nuevo ⓜ *a*·nyo *nwe*·vo *New Year*
anteayer an·te·a·*yer* *day before
yesterday*
anteojos ⓜ pl an·te·*o*·khos *glasses •
goggles*
— **de sol** de sol *sunglasses*
antes *an*·tes *before*
antibióticos ⓜ pl an·tee·*byo*·tee·kos
antibiotics
anticonceptivo ⓜ
an·tee·kon·sep·*tee*·vo *contraceptive*
antigüedad ⓕ an·tee·gwe·*da* *antique*

antiguo/a ⓜ/ⓕ an·*tee*·gwo/a *ancient*
antihistamínicos ⓜ pl an·tee·ees·ta·*mee*·nee·kos *antihistamines*
antinuclear an·tee·noo·kle·*ar antinuclear*
antiséptico ⓜ an·tee·*sep*·tee·ko *antiseptic*
anuncio ⓜ a·*noon*·syo *advertisement*
apellido ⓜ a·pe·*lyee*·do *family name • surname*
apéndice ⓕ a·*pen*·dee·se *appendix*
apodo ⓜ a·*po*·do *nickname*
aprender a·pren·*der learn*
apretado/a ⓜ/ⓕ a·pre·*ta*·do/a *tight*
apuesta ⓕ a·*pwes*·ta *bet*
apuntar a·poon·*tar point*
aquí a·*kee here*
araña ⓕ a·*ra*·nya *spider*
árbitro ⓜ *ar*·bee·tro *referee*
árbol ⓜ *ar*·bol *tree*
arena ⓕ a·*re*·na *sand*
arenque a·*ren*·ke *herring*
Argentina ⓕ ar·khen·*tee*·na *Argentina*
armadillo ⓜ ar·ma·*dee*·lyo *armadillo*
armario ⓜ ar·*ma*·ryo *cupboard*
arqueológico/a ⓜ/ⓕ ar·ke·o·*lo*·khee·ko/a *archaeological*
arquitecto/a ⓜ/ⓕ ar·kee·*tek*·to/a *architect*
arquitectura ⓕ ar·kee·*tek*·too·ra *architecture*
arrendar a·ren·*dar hire • rent*
arriba a·*ree*·ba *above • up*
arroyo ⓜ a·*ro*·yo *stream*
arroz a·*ros rice*
arte ⓜ *ar*·te *art*
artes ⓜ pl **marciales** *ar*·tes mar·*sya*·les *martial arts*
artesanía ⓕ ar·te·sa·*nee*·a *craft • handicraft*
artista ⓜ&ⓕ ar·*tees*·ta *artist*
  — **callejero/a** ⓜ/ⓕ ka·lye·*khe*·ro/a *busker*
arveja ⓕ ar·*ve*·kha *pea*
ascensor ⓜ a·sen·*sor elevator • lift*
Asia *a*·sya *Asia*

asiento ⓜ a·*syen*·to *seat*
  — **de seguridad para bebés** de se·goo·ree·*da* para be·*bes child's car seat*
asistencia ⓕ **social** a·sees·*ten*·sya so·*syal social welfare*
asma ⓜ *as*·ma *asthma*
aspirina ⓕ as·pee·*ree*·na *aspirin*
atascado/a ⓜ/ⓕ a·tas·*ka*·do/a *blocked*
atletismo ⓜ at·le·*tees*·mo *athletics*
atmósfera ⓕ at·*mos*·fe·ra *atmosphere*
atún ⓜ a·*toon tuna*
audífono ⓜ ow·*dee*·fo·no *hearing aid*
Australia ⓕ ows·*tra*·lya *Australia*
auto ⓜ *ow*·to *car*
autobús ⓜ ow·to·*boos bus (city)*
automático/a ⓜ/ⓕ ow·to·*ma*·tee·ko/a *automatic*
autopista ⓕ ow·to·*pees*·ta *motorway*
autoservicio ⓜ ow·to·ser·*vee*·syo *self-service*
avena ⓕ a·*ve*·na *oats*
avenida ⓕ a·ve·*nee*·da *avenue*
avergonzado/a ⓜ/ⓕ a·ver·gon·*sa*·do/a *embarrassed*
averiado/a ⓜ/ⓕ a·ve·*rya*·do/a *broken down (machine)*
avión ⓜ a·*vyon plane*
ayer a·*yer yesterday*
ayudar a·yoo·*dar help*
azúcar ⓜ a·*soo*·kar *sugar*
azul a·*sool blue*

B

babysitter ⓜ&ⓕ be·bee·*see*·ter *babysitter*
baila ⓕ *bai*·la *dance*
bailar bai·*lar dance*
bajo/a ⓜ/ⓕ *ba*·kho/a *low • short (height)*
balcón ⓜ bal·*kon balcony*
balde ⓜ *bal*·de *bucket*
ballet ⓜ ba·*le ballet*
bálsamo ⓜ **de labios** *bal*·sa·mo de *la*·byos *lip balm*
banco ⓜ *ban*·ko *bank (money)*
bandera ⓕ ban·*de*·ra *flag*

baño ⓜ ba-nye-ra *bath • bathroom • toilet*

baños ⓜ pl ba-nyos *toilets*

bar ⓜ bar *bar*

barato/a ⓜ/ⓕ ba-ra-to/a *cheap*

barbero ⓜ bar-be-ro *barber*

barco ⓜ bar-ko *boat • ship*
— **de vela** de ve-la *sailing boat*

barrio ⓜ ba-ryo *suburb*

basquetbol ⓜ bas-ket-bol *basketball*

basura ⓕ ba-soo-ra *rubbish*

batería ⓕ ba-te-ree-a *battery (car) • drums*

bautizo ⓜ bow-tee-so *baptism*

bebé ⓜ&ⓕ be-be *baby*

béisbol ⓜ bays-bol *baseball*

Belice ⓕ be-lee-se *Belize*

bello/a ⓜ/ⓕ be-lyo/a *beautiful*

beneficio ⓜ be-ne-fee-syo *profit*

berenjena ⓕ be-ren-khe-na *aubergine • eggplant*

besar be-sar *kiss*

beso ⓜ be-so *kiss*

biblia ⓕ bee-blya *bible*

biblioteca ⓕ bee-blyo-te-ka *library*

bicho ⓜ bee-cho *bug*

bici ⓕ bee-see *bike*

bicicleta ⓕ bee-see-kle-ta *bicycle*
— **de carreras** de ka-re-ras *racing bike*
— **de montaña** de mon-ta-nya *mountain bike*

bien byen *well*

bienestar ⓜ byen-es-tar *welfare*

billar ⓜ bee-lyar *pool (game)*

billetes ⓜ pl **de banco** bee-lye-tes de ban-ko *banknotes*

biodegradable byo-de-gra-da-ble *biodegradable*

biografía ⓕ byo-gra-fya *biography*

birome ⓕ bee-ro-me *ballpoint pen (Arg)*

bistec ⓜ bees-tek *steak (beef)*

blanco y negro blan-ko e ne-gro *B&W (film)*

blanco/a ⓜ/ⓕ blan-ko/a *white*

bluejeans ⓜ pl bloo-jeens *jeans*

boca ⓕ bo-ka *mouth*

boda ⓕ bo-da *wedding*

bodega ⓕ bo-de-ga *liquor store • winery*

bol ⓜ bol *bowl*

bolas ⓕ pl **de algodón** bo-las de al-go-don *cotton balls*

boletería ⓕ bo-le-te-ree-a *ticket office*

boleto ⓜ bo-le-to *ticket*
— **de ida y vuelta** de ee-da ee vwel-ta *return ticket*
— **de lista de espera** de lees-ta de es-pe-ra *standby ticket*
— **sencillo** sen-see-lyo *one-way ticket*

bolígrafo ⓜ bo-lee-gra-fo *pen (ballpoint)*

Bolivia ⓕ bo-lee-vya *Bolivia*

bollos ⓜ pl bo-lyos *bread rolls*

bolsa ⓕ **de compras** bol-sa de kom-pras *shopping bag*

bolsillo ⓜ bol-see-lyo *pocket*

bolso ⓜ bol-so *bag (general) • handbag*

bomba ⓕ bom-ba *pump • bomb*

bombillo ⓜ bom-bee-lyo *light bulb*

bondadoso/a ⓜ/ⓕ bon-da-do-so/a *caring*

bonito/a ⓜ/ⓕ bo-nee-to/a *pretty*

bosque ⓜ bos-ke *forest*

botas ⓕ pl bo-tas *boots*
— **de montaña** de mon-ta-nya *hiking boots*

botella ⓕ bo-te-lya *bottle*

botón ⓜ bo-ton *button*

boxeo ⓜ bok-se-o *boxing*

bragas ⓕ pl bra-gas *underpants (women)*

Braille ⓜ bray-e-le *Braille*

Brasil ⓜ bra-seel *Brazil*

brazo ⓜ bra-so *arm*

briliante bree-lyan-te *brilliant • glossy*

broma ⓕ bro-ma *joke*

bronceador ⓜ bron-se-a-dor *tanning lotion*

bronquitis ⓕ bron-kee-tees *bronchitis*

brújula ⓕ broo-khoo-la *compass*

brumoso/a ⓜ/ⓕ broo-mo-so/a *foggy*

buceo ⓜ boo-se-o *snorkelling*

budista ⓜ&ⓕ boo-dees-ta *Buddhist*

bueno/a ⓜ/ⓕ bwe·no/a *good • nice*
bufanda ⓕ boo·fan·da *scarf*
buffet ⓜ boo·fe *buffet (meal)*
bulto ⓜ bool·to *lump*
burro ⓜ boo·ro *donkey*
buscar boos·kar *look for*
buzón ⓜ boo·son *mailbox*

C

caballo ⓜ ka·ba·lyo *horse*
cabaña ⓕ ka·ba·nya *hut*
cabeza ⓕ ka·be·sa *head*
cabina ⓕ **telefónica** ka·bee·na te·le·fo·nee·ka *phone box*
cable ⓜ ka·ble *cable*
cables ⓜ pl **de arranque** ka·bles de a·ran·ke *jumper leads*
cabra ⓕ ka·bra *goat*
cacao ⓜ ka·kow *cocoa*
cacharro ⓜ ka·cha·ro *pot (ceramic)*
cachorro ⓜ ka·cho·ro *puppy*
cacto ⓜ kak·to *cactus*
cada ka·da *each*
cadena ⓕ ka·de·na *chain*
  — de bici de bee·see *bike chain*
café ⓜ ka·fe *cafe • coffee*
cafetería ⓕ ka·fe·te·ree·a *cafe*
caída ⓕ ka·ee·da *fall (tumble)*
caja ⓕ ka·kha *box*
  — fuerte fwer·te *safe*
  — registradora re·khees·tra·do·ra *cash register*
cajero ⓜ **automático** ka·khe·ro ow·to·ma·tee·ko *automatic teller machine*
cajero/a ⓜ/ⓕ ka·khe·ro/a *cashier*
cajón ⓜ **con llave** ka·khon kon lya·ve *locker*
calabacín ⓜ ka·la·ba·seen *courgette*
calabaza ⓕ ka·la·ba·sa *pumpkin*
calcetines ⓜ pl kal·se·tee·nes *socks*
calculadora ⓕ kal·koo·la·do·ra *calculator*
calefacción ⓕ ka·le·fak·syon *heating*
  — central sen·tral *central heating*
calendario ⓜ ka·len·da·ryo *calendar*

calidad ⓕ ka·lee·da *quality*
caliente ka·lyen·te *hot*
calle ⓕ ka·lye *road*
calor ⓜ ka·lor *heat*
calzoncillos ⓜ pl kal·son·see·lyos *underpants (men)*
cama ⓕ ka·ma *bed*
  — de matrimonio de ma·tree·mo·nyo *double bed*
cámara ⓕ **(fotográfica)** ka·ma·ra (fo·to·gra·fee·ka) *camera*
  — de aire de ai·re *tube (tyre)*
  — descartable des·kar·ta·ble *disposable camera*
  — digital de·khee·tal *digital camera*
  — submarina soob·ma·ree·na *underwater camera*
camarero/a ⓜ/ⓕ ka·ma·re·ro/a *waiter*
cambiar kam·byar *change • exchange*
cambio ⓜ kam·byo *change (coins) • exchange*
  — de dinero de dee·ne·ro *currency exchange*
caminar ka·mee·nar *walk*
camino ⓜ ka·mee·no *track • trail • way*
  — de bici de bee·see *bike path*
  — rural roo·ral *hiking route*
camión ⓜ ka·myon *truck*
camisa ⓕ ka·mee·sa *shirt*
camiseta ⓕ ka·mee·se·ta *singlet • T-shirt*
cámping ⓜ kam·peen *campsite*
campo ⓜ kam·po *countryside*
caña ⓕ **de azúcar** ka·nya de a·soo·kar *sugar cane*
Canadá ka·na·da *Canada*
canasta ⓕ ka·nas·ta *basket*
cancelar kan·se·lar *cancel*
cáncer ⓜ kan·ser *cancer*
cancha ⓕ **de golf** kan·cha de golf *golf course*
cancha ⓕ **de tenis** kan·cha de te·nees *tennis court*
canción ⓕ kan·syon *song*
candado ⓜ kan·da·do *padlock*
candidiasis ⓜ kan·dee·dya·sees *thrush (medical)*

cansado/a ⓜ/ⓕ kan·*sa*·do/a *tired*

cantalupo ⓜ kan·ta·*loo*·po *cantaloupe*

cantante ⓜ&ⓕ kan·*tan*·te *singer*

cantar kan·*tar sing*

cantidad ⓕ kan·tee·*da amount*

cantimplora ⓕ kan·teem·*plo*·ra *water bottle*

capa ⓕ **de ozono** *ka*·pa de o·*so*·no *ozone layer*

capacidad ⓕ **de SMS** ka·pa·see·*da* de e·se em·e e·se *SMS capability*

capacidad ⓕ **de WAP** ka·pa·see·*da* de gwap *WAP-enabled*

capilla ⓕ ka·*pee*·lya *shrine*

capote ⓜ ka·*po*·te *cloak*

cara ⓕ *ka*·ra *face*

caracol ⓜ ka·ra·*kol snail*

caramelos ⓜ pl ka·ra·*me*·los *lollies*

caravana ⓕ ka·ra·*va*·na *caravan • van*

cárcel ⓕ *kar*·sel *jail • prison*

caries ⓕ *ka*·ryes *cavity (tooth)*

carne ⓕ *kar*·ne *meat*
— **de vaca** de *va*·ka *beef*
— **molida** mo·*lee*·da *mince*

carnet ⓜ kar·*net drivers licence*

carnicería ⓕ kar·nee·se·*ree*·a *butcher's shop*

caro/a ⓜ/ⓕ *ka*·ro/a *expensive*

carpa ⓕ *kar*·pa *tent*

carpintero ⓜ kar·peen·*te*·ro *carpenter*

carrera ⓕ ka·*re*·ra *race (sport)*

carro ⓜ *ka*·ro *car*

carta ⓕ *kar*·ta *letter*

cartas ⓕ pl *kar*·tas *cards*

cartera ⓕ kar·*te*·ra *wallet*

cartón ⓜ kar·*ton carton*

cartucho ⓜ **de gas** kar·*too*·cho de gas *gas cartridge*

casa ⓕ *ka*·sa *house • home*

casado/a ⓜ/ⓕ ka·*sa*·do/a *married*

casarse ka·*sar*·se *marry*

cascada ⓕ kas·*ka*·da *waterfall*

casco ⓜ *kas*·ko *helmet*

casete ⓜ ka·*set cassette*

casi *ka*·see *almost*

casino ⓜ ka·*see*·no *casino*

castaña ⓕ **de cajú** kas·*ta*·nya de ka·*khoo cashew*

castigar kas·tee·*gar punish*

castillo ⓜ kas·*tee*·lyo *castle*

catedral ⓕ ka·te·*dral cathedral*

católico/a ⓜ/ⓕ ka·*to*·lee·ko/a *Catholic*

caza ⓕ *ka*·sa *hunting*

cebolla ⓕ se·*bo*·lya *onion*

cédula ⓕ **de identidad** *se*·doo·la de ee·den·tee·*da identification card (ID)*

celebración ⓕ se·le·bra·*syon celebration*

celoso/a ⓜ/ⓕ se·*lo*·so/a *jealous*

cementerio ⓜ se·men·*te*·ryo *cemetery*

cena ⓕ *se*·na *dinner*

cenicero ⓜ se·nee·*se*·ro *ashtray*

centavo ⓜ sen·*ta*·vo *cent*

centímetro ⓜ sen·*tee*·me·tro *centimetre*

central ⓕ **telefónica** sen·*tral* te·le·fo·nee·ka *telephone centre*

centro ⓜ *sen*·tro *centre*
— **comercial** ko·mer·*syal shopping centre*
— **de la ciudad** de la syoo·*da city centre*

Centroamérica ⓕ sen·tro·a·*me*·ree·ka *Central America*

centroamericano/a ⓜ/ⓕ sen·tro·a·me·ree·*ka*·no/a *Central American*

cepillo ⓜ **de dientes** se·*pee*·lyo de *dyen*·tes *toothbrush*

cerámica ⓕ se·*ra*·mee·ka *ceramic*

cerca ⓕ *ser*·ka *fence*

cerca *ser*·ka *near • nearby*

cerdo ⓜ *ser*·do *pig • pork*

cereales ⓜ se·re·*a*·les *cereal*

cerrado/a ⓜ/ⓕ se·*ra*·do/a *closed • shut • locked*
— **con llave** kon *lya*·ve *locked*

cerradura ⓕ se·ra·*doo*·ra *lock (door)*

cerrar se·*rar close • lock • shut*

certificado ⓜ ser·tee·fee·*ka*·do *certificate*

cerveza ⓕ ser·*ve*·sa *beer*
— **rubia** *roo*·bya *lager*

chaleco ⓜ **salvavidas** cha·*le*·ko sal·va·*vee*·das *life jacket*

champiñón ⓜ cham·pee·*nyon* *mushroom*

champú ⓜ cham·*poo* *shampoo*

chancho ⓜ *chan*·cho *pig • pork*

chaqueta ⓕ cha·*ke*·ta *jacket*

cheque ⓜ *che*·ke *cheque*
— **de viajero** de vya·*khe*·ro *travellers cheque*

chica ⓕ *chee*·ka *girl*

chicle ⓜ *chee*·kle *chewing gum*

chico ⓜ *chee*·ko *boy*

Chile ⓜ *chee*·le *Chile*

chocolate ⓜ cho·ko·*la*·te *chocolate • pot (dope)*

choque ⓜ *cho*·ke *crash (accident)*

chupete ⓜ choo·*pe*·te *dummy • pacifier*

cibercafé ⓜ see·ber·ka·*fe* *Internet cafe*

ciclismo ⓜ see·*klees*·mo *cycling*

ciclista ⓜ&ⓕ see·*klees*·ta *cyclist*

ciego/a ⓜ/ⓕ *sye*·go/a *blind*

cielo ⓜ *sye*·lo *sky*

ciencia ⓕ *syen*·sya *science*
— **ficción** feek·*syon* *science fiction*

científico/a ⓜ/ⓕ syen·*tee*·fee·ko/a *scientist*

cigarillo ⓜ see·ga·*ree*·lyo *cigarette*

cigarro ⓜ see·*ga*·ro *cigar*

cine ⓜ *see*·ne *cinema*

cinta ⓕ **de vídeo** *seen*·ta de *vee*·de·o *video tape*

cinturón ⓜ **de seguridad** seen·too·*ron* de se·goo·ree·*da* *seatbelt*

circo ⓜ *seer*·ko *circus*

ciruela ⓕ see·*rwe*·la *plum*
— **pasa** *pa*·sa *prune*

cistitis ⓕ sees·*tee*·tees *cystitis*

cita ⓕ *see*·ta *appointment • date*

citología ⓕ see·to·lo·*khee*·a *pap smear*

ciudad ⓕ syoo·*da* *city*

ciudadanía ⓕ syoo·da·da·*nee*·a *citizenship*

claro/a ⓜ/ⓕ *kla*·ro/a *light (colour)*

clase ⓕ *kla*·se *class*
— **preferente** pre·fe·*ren*·te *business class*
— **turística** too·*rees*·tee·ka *economy class*

clásico/a ⓜ/ⓕ *kla*·see·ko/a *classical*

cliente/a ⓜ/ⓕ *klyen*·te/a *client*

cobrar (un cheque) ko·*brar* (oon *che*·ke) *cash (a cheque)*

coca ⓕ *ko*·ka *coke (drug) • coca plant*

cocaína ⓕ ko·ka·*ee*·na *cocaine*

coche ⓜ **cama** *ko*·che *ka*·ma *sleeping car*

cocina ⓕ ko·*see*·na *kitchen • cuisine*

cocinar ko·see·*nar* *cook*

cocinero/a ⓜ/ⓕ ko·see·*ne*·ro/a *chef • cook*

coco ⓜ *ko*·ko *coconut*

cocodrilo ⓜ ko·ko·*dree*·lo *crocodile*

codeína ⓕ ko·de·*ee*·na *codeine*

código ⓜ **postal** *ko*·dee·go pos·*tal* *post code*

coima ⓕ *koy*·ma *bribe*

coimear koy·me·*ar* *bribe*

cola ⓕ *ko*·la *queue*

colchón ⓜ kol·*chon* *mattress*

colega ⓜ&ⓕ ko·*le*·ga *colleague*

cólera ⓕ *ko*·le·ra *cholera*

coles ⓜ pl **de Bruselas** *ko*·les de broo·*se*·las *Brussels sprouts*

colibrí ⓜ ko·lee·*bree* *hummingbird*

coliflor ko·lee·*flor* *cauliflower*

colina ⓕ ko·*lee*·na *hill*

Colombia ⓕ ko·*lom*·bya *Colombia*

color ⓜ ko·*lor* *colour*

comedia ⓕ ko·*me*·dya *comedy*

comenzar ko·men·*sar* *begin • start*

comer ko·*mer* *eat*

comerciante ⓜ&ⓕ ko·mer·*syan*·te *business person*

comercio ⓜ ko·*mer*·syo *trade*

cómics ⓜ pl *ko*·meeks *comics*

comida ⓕ ko·*mee*·da *food*
— **de bebé** de be·*be* *baby food*

comisaría ⓕ ko·mee·sa·*ree*·a *police station*

como *ko*·mo *how*

cómodo/a ⓜ/ⓕ ko·mo·do/a *comfortable*

cómpact ⓜ *kom*·pakt *CD*

compañero/a ⓜ/ⓕ kom·pa·*nye*·ro/a *companion*

compañía ⓕ kom·pa·*nyee*·a *company*

compartir kom·par·*teer* *share (with)*

comprar kom·*prar* *buy*

compresas ⓕ pl kom·*pre*·sas *sanitary napkins*

compromiso ⓜ kom·pro·*mee*·so *engagement (marriage)*

computadora ⓕ kom·poo·ta·*do*·ra *computer*
— **portátil** por·ta·teel *laptop*

comunión ⓕ ko·moo·*nyon* *communion*

comunista ⓜ&ⓕ ko·moo·*nees*·ta *communist*

con kon *with*
— **filtro** *feel*·tro *filtered*

coñac ko·*nyak* *brandy*

concierto ⓜ kon·*syer*·to *concert*

condición ⓕ **cardíaca** kon·dee·*syon* kar·*dee*·a·ka *heart condition*

condon ⓜ kon·*don* *condom*

cóndor ⓜ kon·dor *condor*

conducir kon·doo·*seer* *drive*

conejo ⓜ ko·*ne*·kho *rabbit*

conexión ⓕ ko·nek·*syon* *connection*

confesión ⓕ kon·fe·*syon* *confession*

confianza ⓕ kon·*fyan*·sa *trust*

confiar kon·*fyar* *trust*

confirmar kon·feer·*mar* *confirm*

congelación ⓕ kon·khe·la·*syon* *frostbite*

conocer ko·no·*ser* *know (a person)*

conocido/a ⓜ/ⓕ ko·no·*see*·do/a *famous*

consejo ⓜ kon·*se*·kho *advice*

conservador(a) ⓜ/ⓕ kon·ser·va·*dor*/kon·ser·va·*do*·ra *conservative*

consigna ⓕ kon·*see*·nya *left luggage office*
— **automática** ow·to·ma·*tee*·ka *luggage lockers*

construir kon·stroo·*eer* *build*

consulado ⓜ kon·soo·*la*·do *consulate*

contaminación ⓕ kon·ta·mee·na·*syon* *pollution*

contar kon·*tar* *count*

contemporáneo/a ⓜ/ⓕ kon·tem·po·*ra*·ne·o/a *contemporary*

contestador ⓜ **automático** kon·tes·ta·*dor* ow·to·ma·*tee*·ko *answering machine*

contrato ⓜ kon·*tra*·to *contract*

control ⓜ kon·*trol* *checkpoint*

convento ⓜ kon·*ven*·to *convent*

copa ⓕ *ko*·pa *drink*

Copa ⓕ **Mundial** *ko*·pa moon·*dyal* *World Cup*

copos ⓜ pl **de maíz** *ko*·pos de ma·*ees* *cornflakes*

corazón ⓜ ko·ra·*son* *heart*

cordero ⓜ kor·*de*·ro *lamb*

cordillera ⓕ kor·dee·*lye*·ra *mountain range*

corpiño ⓜ kor·*pee*·nyo *bra (Arg)*

correcto/a ⓜ/ⓕ ko·*rek*·to/a *right (correct)*

correo ⓜ ko·*re*·o *mail*
— **aereo** a·e·re·o *airmail*
— **certificado** ser·tee·fee·*ka*·do *registered mail*
— **urgente** oor·*khen*·te *express mail*

correos ⓜ pl ko·*re*·os *post office*

corrida ⓕ ko·*ree*·da *bullfight*

corriente ko·*ryen*·te *current*

corriente ko·*ryen*·te *ordinary*

corrupto/a ⓜ/ⓕ ko·*roop*·to/a *corrupt*

cortar kor·*tar* *cut*

cortaúñas ⓜ kor·ta·*oo*·nyas *nail clippers*

corte ⓜ **de pelo** *kor*·te de *pe*·lo *haircut*

corto/a ⓜ/ⓕ *kor*·to/a *short (length)*

cosecha ⓕ ko·*se*·cha *crop • harvest*

coser ko·*ser* *sew*

costa ⓕ *kos*·ta *coast*

Costa Rica ⓕ *kos*·ta *ree*·ka *Costa Rica*

costar kos·*tar* *cost*

crecer kre·*ser* *grow*

crema ⓕ *kre*·ma *cream*
— **agria** a·grya *sour cream*
— **hidratante** ee·dra·*tan*·te *moisturiser*
— **solar** so·*lar* *sunblock*

críquet ⓜ *kree·ket cricket (sport)*
cristiano/a ⓜ/ⓕ *krees·tya·no/a Christian*
crítica ⓕ *kree·tee·ka review*
crudo/a ⓜ/ⓕ *kroo·do/a raw*
cuaderno ⓜ *kwa·der·no notebook*
cuadrado ⓜ *kwa·dra·do square (place)*
cuadro ⓜ *kwa·dro painting (canvas)*
cualificaciones ⓕ pl *kwa·lee·fee·ka·syo·nes qualifications*
cuando *kwan·do when*
cuanto *kwan·to how much*
cuarentena ⓕ *kwa·ren·te·na quarantine*
Cuaresma ⓕ *kwa·res·ma Lent*
cuarto ⓜ *kwar·to quarter*
Cuba ⓕ *koo·ba Cuba*
cubiertos ⓜ pl *koo·byer·tos cutlery*
cucaracha ⓕ *koo·ka·ra·cha cockroach*
cuchara ⓕ *koo·cha·ra spoon*
cucharita ⓕ *koo·cha·ree·ta teaspoon*
cuchillo ⓜ *koo·chee·lyo knife*
cuenta ⓕ *kwen·ta bill • check*
— **bancaria** *ban·ka·rya bank account*
cuento ⓜ *kwen·to story • short story*
cuerda ⓕ *kwer·da rope • string*
— **para tender la ropa** *pa·ra ten·der la ro·pa clothes line*
cuero ⓜ *kwe·ro leather*
cuerpo ⓜ *kwer·po body*
cuervo ⓜ *kwer·vo vulture*
cuesta abajo *kwes·ta a·ba·kho downhill*
cuesta arriba *kwes·ta a·ree·ba uphill*
cueva ⓕ *kwe·va cave*
cuidar *kwee·dar care for • mind (an object)*
culo ⓜ *koo·lo bum (ass)*
culpa ⓕ *kool·pa (someone's) fault*
culpable *kool·pa·ble guilty*
cumbre ⓕ *koom·bre peak*
cumpleaños ⓜ *koom·ple·a·nyos birthday*
cupón ⓜ *koo·pon coupon*
curitas ⓕ pl *koo·ree·tas Band-Aids*
currículum ⓜ *koo·ree·koo·loom resume*
curry ⓜ *koo·ree curry*
— **en polvo** *en pol·vo curry powder*
cuy ⓜ *kooy guinea pig*

D

damasco *da·mas·ko apricot*
dañar *da·nyar hurt*
danta ⓕ *dan·ta tapir*
dar *dar give*
— **gracias** *gra·syas thank*
— **la bienvenida** *la byen·ve·nee·da welcome*
— **una patada** *oo·na pa·ta·da kick*
de *de from*
— **cercanías** *ser·ka·nee·as local*
— **(cuatro) estrellas** *(kwa·tro) es·tre·lyas (four-)star*
— **derecha** *de·re·cha right-wing*
— **izquierda** *ees·kyer·da left-wing*
— **lujo** *loo·kho luxurious*
— **menos** *me·nos less*
— **segunda mano** *se·goon·da ma·no second-hand*
— **vez en cuando** *ves en kwan·do sometimes*
débil *de·beel weak*
decidir *de·see·deer decide*
decir *de·seer say • tell*
dedo ⓜ *de·do finger*
— **del pie** *del pye toe*
defectuoso/a ⓜ/ⓕ *de·fek·two·so/a faulty*
deforestación ⓕ *de·fo·res·ta·syon deforestation*
dejar entrar *de·khar en·trar admit (allow to enter)*
delgado/a ⓜ/ⓕ *del·ga·do/a thin*
demasiado (caro/a) ⓜ/ⓕ *de·ma·sya·do (ka·ro/a) too (expensive)*
democracia ⓕ *de·mo·kra·see·a democracy*
demora ⓕ *de·mo·ra delay*
dentista ⓜ&ⓕ *den·tees·ta dentist*
dentro de (una hora) *den·tro de (oo·na o·ra) within (an hour)*
deportes ⓜ pl *de·por·tes sport*
deportista ⓜ&ⓕ *de·por·tees·ta sportsperson*
depósito ⓜ *de·po·see·to deposit (bank)*
derecha *de·re·cha right (direction)*
derechista *de·re·chees·ta right-wing*

derechos ⓜ pl de·*re*·chos *rights*
— **civiles** see·*vee*·les *civil rights*
— **de animales** de a·nee·*ma*·les *animal rights*
— **humanos** oo·*ma*·nos *human rights*
desayuno ⓜ de·sa·*yoo*·no *breakfast*
descansar des·kan·*sar rest*
descanso ⓜ des·*kan*·so *intermission*
descendiente ⓜ de·sen·*dyen*·te *descendant*
descomponerse des·kom·po·*ner*·se *break down*
descubrir des·koo·*breer discover*
descuento ⓜ des·*kwen*·to *discount*
desde *des*·de *since (time)*
desear de·se·*ar wish*
desempleado/a ⓜ/ⓕ des·em·*ple*·a·do/a *unemployed*
desierto ⓜ de·*syer*·to *desert*
desodorante ⓜ de·so·do·*ran*·te *deodorant*
despacio des·*pa*·syo *slowly*
desperdicios ⓜ pl nucleares des·per·*dee*·syos noo·kle·*a*·res *nuclear waste*
despertador ⓜ des·per·ta·*dor alarm clock*
despertarse des·per·*tar*·se *wake up*
después de des·*pwes* de *after*
destino ⓜ des·*tee*·no *destination*
detallado/a ⓜ/ⓕ de·ta·*lya*·do/a *itemised*
detalle ⓜ de·*ta*·lye *detail*
detener de·te·*ner arrest*
detrás de de·*tras* de *behind*
día ⓜ *dee*·a *day*
— **de Año Nuevo** de *a*·nyo *nwe*·vo *New Year's Day*
— **festivo** fes·*tee*·vo *holiday*
diabetes ⓕ dya·*be*·tes *diabetes*
diafragma ⓜ dya·*frag*·ma *diaphragm*
diapositiva ⓕ dya·po·see·*tee*·va *slide (film)*
diariamente dya·rya·*men*·te *daily*
diarrea ⓕ dya·*re*·a *diarrhoea*
dibujar dee·boo·*khar draw*
diccionario ⓜ deek·syo·*na*·ryo *dictionary*

dientes ⓜ pl *dyen*·tes *teeth*
diferencia ⓕ **de horas** dee·fe·*ren*·sya de *o*·ras *time difference*
diferente dee·fe·*ren*·te *different*
difícil dee·*fee*·seel *difficult*
dinero ⓜ dee·*ne*·ro *money*
— **en efectivo** en e·fek·*tee*·vo *cash*
dios dyos *god (general)*
dirección ⓕ dee·rek·*syon address*
direccionales ⓜ pl dee·rek·syo·*na*·les *indicators (car)*
directo/a ⓜ/ⓕ dee·*rek*·to/a *direct*
director(a) ⓜ/ⓕ dee·rek·*tor*/ dee·rek·to·ra *director*
disco ⓜ *dees*·ko *disk*
discoteca ⓕ dees·ko·*te*·ka *disco*
discriminación ⓕ dees·kree·mee·na·*syon discrimination*
discutir dees·koo·*teer argue*
diseño ⓜ dee·*se*·nyo *design*
disentería ⓕ dees·en·te·*ree*·a *dysentry*
disparar dees·pa·*rar shoot*
DIU ⓜ de·ee·oo *IUD (contraceptive device)*
diversión ⓕ dee·ver·*syon fun*
divertirse dee·ver·*teer*·se *enjoy (oneself)*
doblar do·*blar turn*
doble *do*·ble *double*
docena ⓕ do·*se*·na *dozen*
dólar ⓜ *do*·lar *dollar*
dolor ⓜ do·*lor pain*
— **de cabeza** de ka·*be*·sa *headache*
— **de estómago** de es·*to*·ma·go *stomachache*
— **de muelas** de *mwe*·las *toothache*
— **menstrual** mens·*trwal period pain*
dolorido/a ⓜ/ⓕ do·lo·*ree*·do/a *sore*
doloroso/a ⓜ/ⓕ do·lo·*ro*·so/a *painful*
donde *don*·de *where*
dormir dor·*meer sleep*
dos ⓜ/ⓕ dos *two*
— **camas** ⓕ pl *ka*·mas *twin beds*
— **copias** ⓕ pl *ko*·pyas *double copies (photos)*
— **veces** *ve*·ses *twice*

drama ⓜ *dra·ma* drama
droga ⓕ *dro·ga* drug (illegal)
drogadicción ⓕ *dro·ga·deek·syon* drug addiction
drogas ⓕ pl *dro·gas* drugs (illegal)
ducha ⓕ *doo·cha* shower
dueño/a ⓜ/ⓕ *dwe·nyo/a* owner
dulce ⓕ *dool·se* sweet • candy
durante *doo·ran·te* during
durazno ⓜ *doo·ras·no* peach
duro/a ⓜ/ⓕ *doo·ro/a* hard (not soft)

E

ecografía ⓕ *e·ko·gra·fee·a* ultrasound
Ecuador ⓜ *e·kwa·dor* Ecuador
eczema ⓕ *ek·se·ma* eczema
edad ⓕ *e·da* age
edificio ⓜ *e·dee·fee·syo* building
educación ⓕ *e·doo·ka·syon* education
egoísta ⓜ&ⓕ *e·go·ees·ta* selfish
ejemplo ⓜ *e·khem·plo* example
ejército ⓜ *e·kher·see·to* army
él ⓜ *el* he
El Salvador ⓜ *el sal·va·dor* El Salvador
elecciones ⓕ pl *e·lek·syo·nes* elections
electricidad ⓕ *e·lek·tree·see·da* electricity
electricista ⓜ&ⓕ *e·lek·tree·sees·ta* electrician
ella ⓕ *e·lya* she
ellos/ellas ⓜ/ⓕ pl *e·lyos/e·lyas* they
embajada ⓕ *em·ba·kha·da* embassy
embajador(a) ⓜ/ⓕ *em·ba·kha·dor/ em·ba·kha·do·ra* ambassador
embarazada *em·ba·ra·sa·da* pregnant
embarcarse *em·bar·kar·se* board (plane, ship)
emborrachado/a ⓜ/ⓕ *em·bo·ra·cha·do/a* drunk
embrague ⓜ *em·bra·ge* clutch
emergencia ⓕ *e·mer·khen·sya* emergency
emocional *e·mo·syo·nal* emotional
empanada ⓕ *em·pa·na·da* pie

empleado/a ⓜ/ⓕ *em·ple·a·do/a* employee
empujar *em·poo·khar* push
en *on* • in
 — **el extranjero** el ek·stran·khe·ro abroad
encaje ⓜ *en·ka·khe* lace
encantador(a) ⓜ/ⓕ *en·kan·ta·dor/ en·kan·ta·do·ra* charming
encendedor ⓜ *en·sen·de·dor* lighter
enchufe ⓜ *en·choo·fe* plug (electricity)
encía ⓕ *en·see·a* gum (mouth)
encontrar *en·kon·trar* find • meet
energía ⓕ **nuclear** *e·ner·khee·a noo·kle·ar* nuclear energy
enfadado/a ⓜ/ⓕ *en·fa·da·do/a* angry
enfermedad ⓕ *en·fer·mee·da* disease
 — **de transmisión sexual** de trans·mee·syon sek·swal STD (sexually transmitted disease)
 — **venérea** ve·ne·re·a venereal disease
enfermero/a ⓜ/ⓕ *en·fer·me·ro/a* nurse
enfermo/a ⓜ/ⓕ *en·fer·mo/a* sick
enorme *e·nor·me* huge
ensalada ⓕ *en·sa·la·da* salad
entender *en·ten·der* understand
entrar *en·trar* enter
entre *en·tre* among • between
entregar *en·tre·gar* deliver
entrenador(a) ⓜ/ⓕ *en·tre·na·dor/ en·tren·na·do·ra* coach
entreno ⓜ *en·tre·no* workout
entrevista ⓕ *en·tre·vees·ta* interview
enviar *en·vyar* send
epilepsia ⓕ *e·pee·lep·sya* epilepsy
equipaje ⓜ *e·kee·pa·khe* luggage
equipo ⓜ *e·kee·po* equipment • team
 — **de inmersión** de een·mer·syon diving equipment
 — **estereofónico** es·te·re·o·fo·nee·ko stereo
equitación ⓕ *e·kee·ta·syon* horse riding
equivocado/a ⓜ/ⓕ *e·kee·vo·ka·do/a* wrong
error ⓜ *e·ror* mistake
escalada ⓕ *es·ka·la·da* rock climbing

escalera ① es·ka·le·ra *stairway*
— **electrica** e·lek·tree·ka *escalator*
escape ⓜ es·ka·pe *exhaust (car)*
escarcha ① es·kar·cha *frost*
escarpado/a ⓜ/① es·kar·pa·do/a *steep*
escasez ① es·ka·ses *shortage*
escenario ⓜ e·se·na·ryo *stage*
Escocia es·ko·sya *Scotland*
escoger es·ko·kher *choose*
escribir es·kree·beer *write*
escritor(a) ⓜ/① es·kree·tor/
es·kree·to·ra *writer*
escuchar es·koo·char *listen*
escuela ① es·kwe·la *school*
esgrima ① es·gree·ma *fencing (sport)*
espacio ⓜ es·pa·syo *space*
espalda ① es·pal·da *back (body)*
España es·pa·nya *Spain*
especial es·pe·syal *special*
especialista ⓜ&① es·pe·sya·lees·ta
specialist
especies ① pl **en peligro de
extinción** es·pe·syes en pe·lee·gro
de ek·steen·syon *endangered species*
espectáculo ⓜ es·pek·ta·koo·lo *show*
espejo ⓜ es·pe·kho *mirror*
esperar es·pe·rar *wait*
espermicida ① es·per·mee·see·da
spermicide
espinacas ① pl es·pee·na·kas *spinach*
espiral ⓜ **repelente contra
mosquitos** es·pee·ral re·pe·len·te
kon·tra mos·kee·tos *mosquito coil*
esposa ① es·po·sa *wife*
esposo ⓜ es·po·so *husband*
espuma ① **de afeitar** es·poo·ma de
a·fay·tar *shaving cream*
esquí ⓜ es·kee *skiing*
— **acuático** a·kwa·tee·ko
waterskiing
esquiar es·kyar *ski*
esquina ① es·kee·na *corner*
esquís ⓜ pl es·kees *skis*
— **acuáticos** a·kwa·tee·kos *water skis*
esta noche es·ta no·che *tonight*
estacas ① pl es·ta·kas *pegs (tent)*

estación ① es·ta·syon *station • season*
— **de tren** de tren *railway station*
— **de autobuses** de ow·to·boo·ses
bus station (city)
— **de ómnibuses** de om·nee·boo·ses
bus station (inter-city)
— **de subterráneo** de
soob·te·ra·ne·o *metro station*
estacionamiento ⓜ
es·ta·syo·na·myen·to *car park*
estacionar es·ta·syo·nar *park (car)*
estadio ⓜ es·ta·dyo *stadium*
estado ⓜ **civil** es·ta·do see·veel
marital status
estafa ① es·ta·fa *rip-off*
estanquero ⓜ es·tan·ke·ro *tobacconist*
estar es·tar *be*
— **aburrido/a** ⓜ/① a·boo·ree·do/a
be bored
— **de acuerdo** de a·kwer·do *agree*
estatua ① es·ta·twa *statue*
este ⓜ es·te *east*
éste/a ⓜ/① es·te/a *this*
esterilla ① es·te·ree·lya *mat*
esteticista ⓜ&① es·te·tee·sees·ta
beautician
estilo ⓜ es·tee·lo *style*
estómago ⓜ es·to·ma·go *stomach*
estrellas ① pl es·tre·lyas *stars*
estreñimiento ⓜ es·tre·nyee·myen·to
constipation
estudiante ⓜ&① es·too·dyan·te
student
estudio ⓜ es·too·dyo *studio*
estufa ① es·too·fa *heater • stove*
estúpido/a ⓜ/① es·too·pee·do/a
stupid
etiqueta ① **de equipaje** e·tee·ke·ta
de e·kee·pa·khe *luggage tag*
euro ⓜ e·oo·ro *euro*
Europa ① e·oo·ro·pa *Europe*
eutanasia ① e·oo·ta·na·sya *euthanasia*
excelente ek·se·len·te *excellent*
exceso ⓜ **de equipaje** ek·se·so de
e·kee·pa·khe *excess baggage*
excursión ① ek·skoor·syon *tour*

excursionismo ⓜ
ek·skoor·syo·*nees*·mo *hiking*

experiencia ⓕ ek·spe·*ryen*·sya
experience

— **laboral** la·bo·*ral* *work experience*

explotación ⓕ ek·splo·ta·*syon*
exploitation

exposición ⓕ ek·spo·see·*syon*
exhibition

expreso/a ⓜ/ⓕ ek·*spre*·so/a *express*

exterior ⓜ ek·ste·*ryor* *outside*

extrañar ek·stra·*nyar*
miss (feel absence of)

extranjero/a ⓜ/ⓕ ek·stran·*khe*·ro/a
foreigner

extranjero/a ⓜ/ⓕ ek·stran·*khe*·ro/a
foreign

extraño/a ⓜ/ⓕ ek·*stra*·nyo/a *stranger*

extraño/a ⓜ/ⓕ ek·*stra*·nyo/a
strange · unusual

F

fábrica ⓕ *fa*·bree·ka *factory*

fácil *fa*·seel *easy*

facturación ⓕ fak·too·ra·*syon* *check-in (airport)*

— **de equipaje** de e·kee·*pa*·khe
check-in (luggage)

falda ⓕ *fal*·da *skirt*

familia ⓕ fa·*mee*·lya *family*

fantastico/a ⓜ/ⓕ fan·*tas*·tee·ko/a
fantasy · great

farmacia ⓕ far·*ma*·sya *chemist · pharmacy*

faros ⓜ *fa*·ros *headlights*

fastidiado/a ⓜ/ⓕ fas·tee·*dya*·do/a
annoyed

fecha ⓕ *fe*·cha *date (day)*

— **de nacimiento** de na·see·*myen*·to
date of birth

feliz fe·*lees* *happy*

feria ⓕ *fe*·rya *street market*

ferretería ⓕ fe·re·te·*ree*·a *hardware store*

festival ⓜ fes·tee·*val* *festival*

ficción ⓕ feek·*syon* *fiction*

fideos ⓜ pl fee·*de*·os *noodles*

fiebre ⓕ *fye*·bre *fever*

— **amarilla** a·ma·*ree*·lya *yellow fever*

— **del dengue** del *den*·ge *dengue fever*

— **del heno** del *e*·no *hay fever*

— **glandular** glan·doo·*lar* *glandular fever*

fiesta ⓕ *fyes*·ta *party (celebration)*

film ⓜ feelm *film (cinema)*

fin ⓜ feen *end*

— **de semana** de se·*ma*·na *weekend*

firma ⓕ *feer*·ma *signature*

flamenco ⓜ fla·*men*·ko *flamingo · flamenco (dance)*

flash flash *flash (camera)*

flor ⓕ flor *flower*

florista ⓜ&ⓕ flo·*rees*·ta *florist*

flujo ⓜ *floo*·kho va·khee·*nal* *vaginal discharge*

foco ⓜ *fo*·ko *lightbulb*

footing foo·*teen* *jogging*

forma ⓕ *for*·ma *shape*

fósforos ⓜ pl *fos*·fo·ros *matches*

fotocopiadora ⓕ fo·to·ko·pee·a·*do*·ra
photocopier

fotografía ⓕ fo·to·gra·*fee*·a *photo · photography*

fotógrafo/a ⓜ/ⓕ fo·to·gra·*fo*/a
photographer

fotómetro ⓜ fo·to·*me*·tro *light meter*

frágil *fra*·kheel *fragile*

frambuesa ⓕ fram·*bwe*·sa *raspberry*

Francia ⓕ *fran*·sya *France*

franqueo ⓜ fran·*ke*·o *postage*

frazada ⓕ fra·*sa*·da *blanket*

freír fre·*eer* *fry*

freno ⓜ pl *fre*·no *brake*

frente a *fren*·te a *opposite*

frigorífico ⓜ free·go·*ree*·fee·ko *fridge*

frijoles ⓜ pl free·*kho*·les *beans*

frío/a ⓜ/ⓕ *free*·o/a *cold*

frontera ⓕ fron·*te*·ra *border (frontier)*

fruta ⓕ *froo*·ta *fruit*

frutilla ⓕ froo·*tee*·lya *strawberry*

fuego ⓜ *fwe*·go *fire*

fuerte *fwer*·te *strong*

fumar foo·*mar* *smoke*

G

funda ① **de almohada** *foon-*da de al-mo-*a*-da *pillowcase*

funeral ⓜ foo-ne-*ral funeral*

fútbol ⓜ *foot-*bol *football · soccer*

futuro ⓜ foo-*too-*ro *future*

galleta ① ga-*lye-*ta *biscuit · cookie*

ganador(a) ⓜ/① ga-na-*dor*/ ga-na-*do-*ra *winner*

ganar ga-*nar earn · win*

garage ⓜ ga-*ra-*khe *garage (car shelter)*

garbanzos ⓜ pl gar-*ban-*sos *chickpeas*

garganta ① gar-*gan-*ta *throat*

gas ⓜ gas *gas (for cooking)*

gasolina ① ga-so-*lee-*na *gas · petrol*

gasolinera ① ga-so-lee-*ne-*ra *service station*

gastroenteritis ① gas-tro-en-te-*ree-*tees *gastroenteritis*

gatito/a ⓜ/① ga-*tee-*to/a *kitten*

gato/a ⓜ/① ga-*to/a cat*

gay gay *gay*

gemelos/as ⓜ/① pl khe-*me-*los/as *twins*

general khe-ne-*ral general*

gente ① *khen-*te *people*

gimnasia ① kheem-*na-*sya *gymnastics*

ginecólogo/a ⓜ/① khe-ne-*ko-*lo-go/a *gynaecologist*

glorieta ① glo-*rye-*ta *roundabout*

gobierno ⓜ go-*byer-*no *government*

goma ① *go-*ma *gum (chewing)*

gordo/a ⓜ/① *gor-*do/a *fat*

gotas ① pl **para los ojos** *go-*tas *pa-*ra los o-khos *eye drops*

grabación ① gra-ba-*syon recording*

gracioso/a ⓜ/① gra-*syo-*so/a *funny*

gramos ⓜ pl *gra-*mos *grams*

grande *gran-*de *big*

grandes almacenes ⓜ pl *gran-*des al-ma-*se-*nes *department store*

granizo ⓜ gra-*nee-*so *hail*

granja ① *gran-*kha *farm*

gratis *gra-*tees *free (gratis)*

grifo ⓜ *gree-*fo *tap · faucet*

gripe ① *gree-*pe *influenza*

gris grees *grey*

gritar gree-*tar shout*

grupo ⓜ *groo-*po *group · band (music)*
— **de rock** de rok *rock group*
— **sanguíneo** san-*gwee-*ne-o *blood group*

guantes ⓜ pl *gwan-*tes *gloves*

guardarropa ⓜ gwar-da-*ro-*pa *cloakroom*

guardería ① gwar-de-*ree-*a *childminding service · creche*

Guatemala ① gwa-te-*ma-*la *Guatemala*

guerra ① *ge-*ra *war*

guía ① *gee-*a *guidebook*
— **audio** *ow-*dyo *audio guide*
— **de espectáculos** de es-pek-*ta-*koo-los *entertainment guide*
— **telefónica** te-le-*fo-*nee-ka *phone book*

guía ⓜ&① *gee-*a *a guide (person)*

guitarra ① gee-*ta-*ra *guitar*

gustar(le) goos-*tar(le) like*

H

habitación a-bee-ta-*syon room · bedroom*
— **doble** *do-*ble *double room*
— **individual** een-dee-vee-*dwal single room*

hablar a-*blar speak · talk*

hacer a-*ser do · make*
— **dedo** *de-*do *hitchhike*
— **surf** soorf *surf*
— **windsurf** *gween-*soorf *windsurfing*

hachís ⓜ a-*chees hash*

hacia a-sya *towards*
— **abajo** a-*ba-*kho *down*

halal a-*lal halal*

hamaca ① a-*ma-*ka *hammock*

harina ① a-*ree-*na *flour*

hasta *as-*ta *until*

hecho/a ⓜ/ⓕ *e*·cho/a *made*
— **a mano** a *ma*·no *handmade*
— **de (algodón)** de (al·go·*don*)
  made of (cotton)
heladería ⓕ e·la·de·*ree*·a *ice-cream
  parlour*
helado ⓜ e·*la*·do *ice cream*
helar e·*lar freeze*
hepatitis ⓕ e·pa·*tee*·tees *hepatitis*
herborista ⓜ&ⓕ er·bo·*rees*·ta *herbalist*
herida ⓕ e·*ree*·da *injury*
hermana ⓕ er·*ma*·na *sister*
hermano ⓜ er·*ma*·no *brother*
hermoso/a ⓜ/ⓕ er·*mo*·so/a
  handsome
heroína ⓕ e·ro·*ee*·na *heroin*
hielo ⓜ *ye*·lo *ice*
hierba ⓕ *yer*·ba *grass*
hierbas ⓕ pl *yer*·bas *herbs*
hígado ⓜ *ee*·ga·do *liver*
higo ⓜ *ee*·go *fig*
hija ⓕ *ee*·kha *daughter*
hijo ⓜ *ee*·kho *son*
hilo ⓜ *ee*·lo *thread*
— **dental** den·*tal dental floss*
hinchas ⓜ&ⓕ pl *een*·chas *fans
  (supporters)*
hindú een·*doo Hindu*
historial ⓜ **profesional** ees·to·*ryal*
  pro·fe·syo·*nal CV*
histórico/a ⓜ/ⓕ ees·*to*·ree·ko/a
  historical
hockey ⓜ *kho*·kee *hockey*
— **sobre hielo** so·bre ye·lo *ice hockey*
hoja ⓕ *o*·kha *leaf*
— **de afeitar** de a·fay·*tar razor blade*
Holanda ⓕ o·*lan*·da *Netherlands*
hombre ⓜ *om*·bre *man*
hombros ⓜ pl *om*·bros *shoulders*
homosexual o·mo·sek·*swal
  homosexual*
Honduras ⓕ on·*doo*·ras *Honduras*
hora ⓕ *o*·ra *time*
horario ⓜ o·*ra*·ryo *timetable*
horas ⓕ pl **de abrir** o·ras de a·*breer
  opening hours*
hormiga ⓕ or·*mee*·ga *ant*

horno ⓜ *or*·no *oven*
horóscopo ⓜ o·*ros*·ko·po *horoscope*
hospital ⓜ os·pee·*tal hospital*
hostelería ⓕ os·te·le·*ree*·a *hospitality*
hotel ⓜ o·*tel hotel*
hoy oy *today*
huerta ⓕ *wer*·ta *vegetable garden*
hueso ⓜ *we*·so *bone*
huevo ⓜ *we*·vo *egg*

I

I

identificación ⓕ
  ee·den·tee·fee·ka·*syon identification*
idioma ⓜ ee·*dyo*·ma *language*
idiota ⓜ&ⓕ ee·*dyo*·ta *idiot*
iglesia ⓕ ee·*gle*·sya *church*
igual ee·*gwal same*
igualdad ⓕ ee·gwal·*da equality*
ilegal ee·le·*gal illegal*
impermeable ⓜ eem·per·me·*a*·ble
  raincoat
impermeable eem·per·me·*a*·ble
  waterproof
importante eem·por·*tan*·te *important*
imposible eem·po·*see*·ble *impossible*
impuesto ⓜ eem·*pwes*·to *tax*
— **sobre la renta** so·bre la *ren*·ta
  income tax
incluido/a ⓜ/ⓕ een·kloo·ee·do/a
  included
incómodo/a ⓜ/ⓕ een·*ko*·mo·do/a
  uncomfortable
India een·dya *India*
indigestión ⓕ een·dee·khes·*tyon
  indigestion*
industria ⓕ een·*doos*·trya *industry*
infección ⓕ een·fek·*syon infection*
inflamación ⓕ een·fla·ma·*syon
  inflammation*
información ⓕ een·for·ma·*syon
  information*
informática ⓕ een·for·*ma*·tee·ka *IT*
informativo ⓜ een·for·ma·*tee*·vo
  current affairs
ingeniería ⓕ een·khe·nye·*ree*·a
  engineering

ingeniero/a ⓜ/ⓕ een·khe·*nye*·ro/a
   engineer
Inglaterra een·gla·*te*·ra *England*
inglés ⓜ een·*gles* *English (language)*
inglés(a) ⓜ/ⓕ een·*gles*/een·*gle*·sa
   English
ingrediente ⓜ een·gre·*dyen*·te
   ingredient
inhalador ⓜ een·a·la·*dor* *inhaler*
injusto/a ⓜ/ⓕ een·*khoos*·to/a *unfair*
inmigración ⓕ een·mee·gra·*syon*
   immigration
inocente ee·no·*sen*·te *innocent*
inseguro/a ⓜ/ⓕ een·se·*goo*·ro/a
   unsafe
insolación ⓕ een·so·la·*syon* *sunstroke*
instituto ⓜ een·stee·*too*·to *high
   school*
instructor(a) ⓜ/ⓕ een·strook·*tor*/
   een·strook·*to*·ra *instructor*
interesante een·te·re·*san*·te
   interesting
internacional een·ter·na·syo·*nal*
   international
Internet ⓜ&ⓕ een·ter·*net* *Internet*
intérprete ⓜ&ⓕ een·*ter*·pre·te
   interpreter
intoxicación ⓕ **alimenticia**
   een·tok·see·ka·*syon*
   a·lee·men·*tee*·sya *food poisoning*
inundación ⓕ ee·noon·da·*syon* *flood*
invierno ⓜ een·*vyer*·no *winter*
invitar een·vee·*tar* *invite*
inyección ⓕ een·yek·*syon* *injection*
inyectarse een·yek·*tar*·se *inject*
ir eer *go*
   — **de compras** de *kom*·pras *shop*
   — **de excursión** de ek·skoor·*syon*
   hike
   — **en tobogán** en to·bo·*gan*
   tobogganing
Irlanda ⓕ eer·*lan*·da *Ireland*
irritación ⓕ ee·ree·ta·*syon*
   irritation · rash
   — **de pañal** de pa·*nyal* *nappy rash*
isla ⓕ *ees*·la *island*
itinerario ⓜ ee·tee·ne·*ra*·ryo *itinerary*
IVA ⓜ *ee*·va *sales tax*
izquierda ⓕ ees·*kyer*·da *left (direction)*

jabón ⓜ kha·*bon* *soap*
jaguar ⓜ kha·*gwar* *jaguar*
jalar kha·*lar* *pull*
jamón ⓜ kha·*mon* *ham*
Japón ⓜ kha·*pon* *Japan*
jarabe ⓜ kha·*ra*·be *cough medicine*
jardín ⓜ khar·*deen* *garden*
   — **botánico** bo·*ta*·nee·ko *botanic
   garden*
   — **de infantes** de een·*fan*·tes
   kindergarten
jardinería ⓕ khar·dee·ne·*ree*·a
   gardening
jarra ⓕ *kha*·ra *jar*
jefe/a ⓜ/ⓕ *khe*·fe/a *boss · leader ·
   manager*
jengibre ⓜ khen·*khee*·bre *ginger*
jeringa ⓕ khe·*reen*·ga *syringe*
jersey ⓜ kher·*say* *sweater · jumper*
jet lag ⓜ dyet lag *jet lag*
jockey ⓜ kho·*kay* *jockey*
joven kho·ven *young*
joyería ⓕ kho·ye·*ree*·a *jewellery*
jubilado/a ⓜ/ⓕ khoo·bee·*la*·do/a
   retired
judío/a ⓜ/ⓕ khoo·*dee*·o/a *Jewish*
juego ⓜ *khwe*·go *game (play)*
   — **de computadora** de
   kom·poo·ta·*do*·ra *computer game*
juegos ⓜ pl **olímpicos** *khwe*·gos
   o·*leem*·pee·kos *Olympic Games*
juez ⓜ&ⓕ khwes *judge*
jugar khoo·*gar* *play (a game)*
   — **al tenis** al te·*nees* *play tennis*
jugo ⓜ *khoo*·go *juice*
   — **de naranja** de na·*ran*·kha *orange
   juice*
juguetería ⓕ khoo·ge·te·*ree*·a *toy shop*
juicioso/a ⓜ/ⓕ khwee·*syo*·so/a *sensible*
juntos/as ⓜ/ⓕ pl *khoon*·tos/as *together*

kilo ⓜ *kee*·lo *kilogram*
kilómetro ⓜ kee·*lo*·me·tro *kilometre*
kiwi *kee*·wee *kiwifruit*
kosher ko·*sher* *kosher*

L

La Copa ① **Mundial** la *ko*·pa moon·*dyal* the World Cup
la píldora ① la *peel*·do·ra the Pill
labios ⓜ pl *la*·byos lips
lado ⓜ *la*·do side
ladrón(a) ⓜ/① la·*dron*/la·*dro*·na thief
lagartija ① la·gar·*tee*·kha lizard
lago ⓜ *la*·go lake
lana ① *la*·na wool
langostino ⓜ lan·gos·*tee*·no prawn
lápiz ⓜ *la*·pees pencil
— **de labios** de *la*·byos lipstick
largo/a ⓜ/① *lar*·go/a long
lata ① *la*·ta can · tin
Latinoamérica ① la·tee·no·a·*me*·ree·ka Latin America
latinoamericano/a ⓜ/① la·tee·no·a·me·ree·*ka*·no/a Latin American
lavadora ① la·va·*do*·ra washing machine
lavandería ① la·van·de·*ree*·a laundrette · laundry
lavar la·*var* wash (something)
lavarse la·*var*·se wash (oneself)
laxantes ⓜ pl lak·*san*·tes laxatives
leche ① *le*·che milk
— **de soya** de *so*·ya soy milk
— **semi** *se*·mee skimmed milk
lechuga ① le·*choo*·ga lettuce
leer le·*er* read
legal le·*gal* legal
legislación ① le·khees·la·*syon* legislation
lejos *le*·khos far
leña ① *le*·nya firewood
lenteja ① pl len·*te*·kha lentil
lentes ⓜ pl *len*·tes lenses
— **de contacto** de kon·*tak*·to contact lenses
lento/a ⓜ/① *len*·to/a slow
lesbiana ① les·*bya*·na lesbian
levantar le·van·*tar* lift
levantarse le·van·*tar*·se get up

ley ① lay law
libra ① *lee*·bra pound (money)
libre *lee*·bre free (not bound)
librería ① lee·bre·*ree*·a bookshop
libro ⓜ *lee*·bro book
— **de frases** de *fra*·ses phrasebook
libros ⓜ pl **de viajes** *lee*·bros de *vya*·khes travel books
ligar lee·*gar* chat up
ligero/a ⓜ/① lee·*khe*·ro/a light (not heavy)
lila *lee*·la purple
lima ① *lee*·ma lime
límite ⓜ *lee*·mee·te limit
— **de equipaje** de e·kee·*pa*·khe baggage allowance
— **de velocidad** de ve·lo·see·*da* speed limit
limón ⓜ lee·*mon* lemon
limonada ① lee·mo·*na*·da lemonade
limpio/a ⓜ/① *leem*·pyo/a clean
línea ① *lee*·ne·a line
linterna ① leen·*ter*·na flashlight · torch
listo/a ⓜ/① *lees*·to/a ready
literatura ① lee·te·ra·*too*·ra literature
— **de ficción** de feek·*syon* fiction (literature)
— **no novelesca** no no·ve·*les*·ka non-fiction (literature)
llamada ① lya·*ma*·da phone call
— **a cobro revertido** a *ko*·bro re·ver·*tee*·do collect call
llamar lya·*mar* call
— **por telefono** por te·*le*·fo·no ring (by phone)
llano/a ⓜ/① *lya*·no/a flat
llanta ① *lyan*·ta tyre
llave ① *lya*·ve key
llegadas ① pl lye·*ga*·das arrivals
llegar lye·*gar* arrive
lleno/a ⓜ/① *lye*·no/a full · booked out
llevar lye·*var* carry · wear
lluvia ① *lyoo*·vya rain
local ⓜ lo·*kal* venue

loción ⓕ lo·*syon lotion*
— **para después del afeitado**
*pa·*ra des·*pwes* del a·*fay·ta·do
aftershave
loco/a ⓜ/ⓕ *lo·ko/a crazy*
lodo ⓜ *lo·do mud*
loro ⓜ *lo·ro parrot*
Los Estados ⓜ pl **Unidos** los es·*ta·dos
oo·*nee·dos the USA*
los/las dos ⓜ/ⓕ pl los/las dos *both*
lubricante ⓜ loo·bree·*kan·te
lubricant*
lucha ⓕ *loo·cha fight*
lugar ⓜ loo·*gar place*
— **de nacimiento** de
na·see·*myen·to place of birth*
luna ⓕ *loo·na moon*
— **llena** *lye·na full moon*
— **de miel** de myel *honeymoon*
luz ⓕ loos *light*

M

madera ⓕ ma·*de·ra wood*
madre ⓕ *ma·dre mother*
madrugada ⓕ ma·droo·*ga·da dawn*
mago/a ⓜ/ⓕ *ma·go/a magician*
maíz ⓜ ma·*ees corn*
malaria ⓕ ma·*la·rya malaria*
maleta ⓕ ma·*le·ta suitcase*
maletín ⓜ ma·le·*teen briefcase*
— **de primeros auxilios**
de pree·*me·ros ow·*see·lyos
first-aid kit
malla ⓕ *ma·lya bathing suit*
malo/a ⓜ/ⓕ *ma·lo/a bad*
mamá ⓕ ma·*ma mum*
mamograma ⓜ ma·mo·*gra·ma
mammogram*
mañana ⓕ ma·*nya·na tomorrow •
morning*
mandarina ⓕ man·da·*ree·na
mandarin*
mandíbula ⓕ man·*dee·boo·la jaw*
mando ⓜ **a distancia** *man·do a
dees·*tan·sya remote control*

mango ⓜ *man·go mango*
maní ⓜ ma·*nee groundnut • peanut*
manifestación ⓕ ma·nee·fes·ta·*syon
demonstration (protest)*
manillar ⓜ ma·nee·*lyar handlebar*
mano ⓕ *ma·no hand*
manteca ⓕ **de cerdo** man·*te·ka de
ser·do lard*
mantel ⓜ man·*tel tablecloth*
mantequilla ⓕ man·te·*kee·lya butter*
manual ma·*nwal manual*
manzana ⓕ man·*sa·na apple*
mapa ⓜ *ma·pa map*
maquillaje ⓜ ma·kee·*lya·khe make-up*
máquina ⓕ *ma·kee·na machine*
— **de boletos** de bo·*le·tos ticket
machine*
mar ⓜ mar *sea*
maravilloso/a ⓜ/ⓕ ma·ra·vee·*lyo·so/a
wonderful*
marcador ⓜ mar·ka·*dor scoreboard*
marcapasos ⓜ mar·ka·*pa·sos
pacemaker*
marcar mar·*kar score*
marchas ⓕ pl *mar·chas gears*
marcos ⓜ pl *mar·kos borders
(photography)*
marea ⓕ ma·*re·a tide*
mareado/a ⓜ/ⓕ ma·re·*a·do/a dizzy*
mareo ⓜ ma·*re·o seasickness • travel
sickness*
margarina ⓕ mar·ga·*ree·na margarine*
marihuana ⓕ ma·ree·*wa·na marijuana*
mariposa ⓕ ma·ree·*po·sa butterfly*
marrón ma·*ron brown*
martillo ⓜ mar·*tee·lyo hammer*
más mas *more • most*
más cercano/a ⓜ/ⓕ mas ser·*ka·no
nearest*
masaje ⓜ ma·*sa·khe massage*
masajista ⓜ&ⓕ ma·sa·*khees·ta
masseur/masseuse*
matar ma·*tar kill*
mate ⓜ *ma·te type of tea popular in
South America*
mate *ma·te matte (photos)*

matrícula ① ma·*tree*·koo·la *car registration* • *license plate number*

matrimonio ⓜ ma·tree·mo·nyo *marriage*

mayonesa ① ma·yo·*ne*·sa *mayonnaise*

mazo ⓜ *ma*·so *mallet*

mecánico/a ⓜ/① me·*ka*·nee·ko/a *mechanic*

mechero ⓜ me·*che*·ro *cigarette lighter*

medianoche ① me·dya·*no*·che *midnight*

medias ① pl *me*·dyas *pantyhose* • *stockings*

medicina ① me·dee·*see*·na *drug (medicinal)* • *medicine*

medico/a ⓜ/① me·dee·ko/a *doctor*

medio ⓜ **ambiente** *me*·dyo am·*byen*·te *environment*

medio/a ⓜ/① *me*·dyo/a *half*

mediodía ⓜ me·dyo·*dee*·a *noon*

medios ⓜ pl *me*·dyos *resources*
— **de comunicación** de ko·moo·nee·ka·*syon media*
— **de transporte** de trans·*por*·te *transport*

meditación ① me·dee·ta·*syon meditation*

mejillones ⓜ pl me·khee·*lyo*·nes *mussels*

mejor me·*khor best* • *better*

melodía ① me·lo·*dee*·a *tune*

melón ⓜ me·*lon melon*

mendigo/a ⓜ/① men·*dee*·go/a *beggar*

mensaje ⓜ men·*sa*·khe *message*

menstruación ① mens·trwa·*syon menstruation*

mentiroso/a ⓜ/① men·tee·ro·so/a *liar*

menú ⓜ me·*noo menu*
a menudo a me·noo·do *often*

mercado ⓜ mer·*ka*·do *market*
— **de artesanía** de ar·te·sa·*nee*·a *craft market*

mermelada ① mer·me·*la*·da *jam* • *marmalade*

mes ⓜ mes *month*

mesa ① *me*·sa *table*

meseta ① me·*se*·ta *plateau*

metal ⓜ me·*tal metal*

metro ⓜ *me*·tro *metre (distance)*

México ⓜ *me*·khee·ko *Mexico*

mezclar mes·*klar mix*

mezquita ① mes·*kee*·ta *mosque*

microondas ⓜ mee·kro·*on*·das *microwave oven*

miel ① myel *honey*

miembro ⓜ&① *myem*·bro *member*

migraña ① mee·*gra*·nya *migraine*

milímetro ⓜ mee·*lee*·me·tro *millimetre*

militares ⓜ pl mee·lee·*ta*·res *military*

millón ⓜ mee·*lyon million*

minusválido/a ⓜ/① mee·noos·va·*lee*·do/a *disabled*

minuto ⓜ mee·*noo*·to *minute*

mirador ⓜ mee·ra·*dor lookout*

mirar mee·*rar look* • *watch*
— **las vidrieras** las vee·*drye*·ras *window-shopping*

misa ① *mee*·sa *mass (Catholic)*

mochila ① mo·*chee*·la *backpack*

módem ⓜ *mo*·dem *modem*

mojado/a ⓜ/① mo·*kha*·do/a *wet*

monasterio ⓜ mo·nas·*te*·ryo *monastery*

monedas ① pl mo·*ne*·das *coins*
— **sueltas** swel·tas *loose change*

monitor(a) ⓜ/① mo·nee·*tor*/ mo·nee·*to*·ra *(skiing) instructor*

monja ① *mon*·kha *nun*

monopatinaje ⓜ mo·no·pa·tee·*na*·khe *skateboarding*

montaña ① mon·*ta*·nya *mountain*

montar mon·*tar ride*

monumento ⓜ mo·noo·*men*·to *monument*

mordedura ① mor·de·*doo*·ra *bite (dog)*

moretón ⓜ mo·re·*ton bruise*

morir mo·*reer die*

mosca ① *mos*·ka *fly*

mosquitera ① mos·kee·*te*·ra *mosquito net*

mosquito ⓜ mos·*kee*·to *mosquito*
mostaza ⓕ mos·*ta*·sa *mustard*
mostrador ⓜ mos·tra·*dor* *counter (shop)*
mostrar mos·*trar* *show*
motocicleta ⓕ mo·to·see·*kle*·ta
  motorcycle
motor ⓜ mo·*tor* *engine*
motora ⓕ mo·*to*·ra *motorboat*
muchos/as ⓜ/ⓕ pl *moo*·chos/as
  many
mudo/a ⓜ/ⓕ *moo*·do/a *mute*
muebles ⓜ pl *mwe*·bles *furniture*
muela ⓕ *mwe*·la *tooth (back)*
muelle ⓜ *mwe*·lye *spring*
muerto/a ⓜ/ⓕ *mwer*·to/a *dead*
muesli ⓜ *mwes*·lee *muesli*
mujer ⓕ moo·*kher* *woman*
multa ⓕ *mool*·ta *fine (payment)*
mundo ⓜ *moon*·do *world*
muñeca ⓕ moo·*nye*·ka *doll • wrist*
músculo ⓜ *moos*·koo·lo *muscle*
museo ⓜ moo·*se*·o *museum*
  — de arte de *ar*·te *art gallery*
música ⓕ *moo*·see·ka *music*
músico/a ⓜ/ⓕ *moo*·see·ko/a
  musician
musulmán(a) ⓜ/ⓕ moo·sool·*man*/
  moo·sool·*ma*·na *Muslim*
muy mooy *very*

N

nacional na·syo·*nal* *national*
nacionalidad ⓕ na·syo·na·lee·*da*
  nationality
nada *na*·da *none • nothing*
nadar na·*dar* *swim*
naranja ⓕ na·*ran*·kha *orange (fruit)*
nariz ⓕ na·*rees* *nose*
naturaleza ⓕ na·too·ra·*le*·sa *nature*
naturopatia ⓕ na·too·ro·*pa*·tya
  naturopathy
náusea ⓕ *now*·se·a *nausea*
náuseas ⓕ pl **del embarazo**
  now·se·as del em·ba·*ra*·so
  morning sickness
navaja ⓕ na·*va*·kha *penknife*

Navidad ⓕ na·vee·*da* *Christmas*
necesario/a ⓜ/ⓕ ne·se·*sa*·ryo/a
  necessary
necesitar ne·se·see·*tar* *need*
negar(se) ne·*gar*·(se) *refuse*
negocio ⓜ ne·*go*·syo *business*
  — de artículos básicos de
  ar·*tee*·koo·los ba·*see*·kos
  convenience store
negro/a ⓜ/ⓕ ne·gro/a *black*
Nicaragua ⓕ nee·ka·*ra*·gwa
  Nicaragua
nieto/a ⓜ/ⓕ nye·to/a *grandchild*
nieve ⓕ *nye*·ve *snow*
niño/a ⓜ/ⓕ *nee*·nyo/a *child*
no no *no*
  — fumadores foo·ma·*do*·res
  non-smoking
  — incluido/a ⓜ/ⓕ
  een·kloo·*ee*·do/a *excluded*
noche ⓕ *no*·che *evening • night*
Nochebuena ⓕ no·che·*bwe*·na
  Christmas Eve
Nochevieja ⓕ no·che·*vye*·kha
  New Year's Eve
nombre ⓜ *nom*·bre *name*
norte ⓜ *nor*·te *north*
nosotros/as ⓜ/ⓕ no·*so*·tros/as *we*
noticias ⓕ pl no·*tee*·syas *news*
novela ⓕ no·*ve*·la *novel*
  — negra ne·gra *detective novel*
  — rosa ro·sa *romance novel*
novia ⓕ *no*·vya *girlfriend*
novio ⓜ *no*·vyo *boyfriend*
nube ⓕ *noo*·be *cloud*
nublado/a ⓜ/ⓕ noo·*bla*·do/a
  cloudy
nuestro/a ⓜ/ⓕ nwes·tro/a *our*
Nueva Zelandia ⓕ nwe·va se·*lan*·dya
  New Zealand
nuevo/a ⓜ/ⓕ nwe·vo/a *new*
nuez ⓕ nwes *nut*
número ⓜ *noo*·me·ro *number*
  — de habitación de ha·bee·ta·*syon*
  room number
  — de pasaporte de pa·sa·*por*·te
  passport number
nunca *noon*·ka *never*

O

o o *or*

objetivo m ob·khe·*tee*·vo *lens*

obra f o·bra *play (theatre)* • *work (of art)*

obrero/a m/f o·*bre*·ro/a *factory worker* • *labourer*

océano m o·*se*·a·no *ocean*

ocupado/a m/f o·koo·*pa*·do/a *busy*

oeste m o·*es*·te *west*

oficina f o·fee·*see*·na *office*

— **de objetos perdidos** de ob·*khe*·tos per·*dee*·dos *lost property office*

— **de turismo** de too·*rees*·mo *tourist office*

oficinista m&f o·fee·see·*nees*·ta *office worker*

oír o·*eer* *hear*

ojo m o·kho *eye*

ola f o·la *saucepan* • *wave*

olor m o·lor *smell*

olvidar ol·vee·*dar* *forget*

ómnibus m om·*nee*·boos *bus (intercity)*

ópera f o·pe·ra *opera*

operación f o·pe·ra·*syon* *operation (medical)*

operador(a) m/f o·pe·ra·*dor*/ o·pe·ra·*do*·ra *operator*

opinión f o·pee·*nyon* *opinion*

oporto m o·*por*·to *port (wine)*

oportunidad f o·por·too·nee·*da* *chance*

oración f o·ra·*syon* *prayer*

orden m or·den *order (placement)*

orden f or·den *order (command)*

ordenar or·de·*nar* *order (give command)*

oreja f o·*re*·kha *ear*

orgasmo m or·*gas*·mo *orgasm*

original o·ree·khee·*nal* *original*

orilla f **del mar** o·*ree*·lya del mar *seaside*

oro m o·ro *gold*

orquesta f or·*kes*·ta *orchestra*

orquídea f or·*kee*·de·a *orchid*

oscuro/a m/f os·*koo*·ro/a *dark*

ostra f os·tra *oyster*

otoño m o·*to*·nyo *autumn*

otra vez o·tra ves *again*

otro/a m/f o·tro/a *other*

oveja f o·*ve*·kha *sheep*

oxígeno m ok·*see*·khe·no *oxygen*

P

padre m *pa*·dre *father*

padres m pl *pa*·dres *parents*

pagar pa·*gar* *pay*

página f *pa*·khee·na *page*

pago m *pa*·go *payment*

país m pa·*ees* *country (nation)*

pájaro m *pa*·kha·ro *bird*

pala f *pa*·la *spade*

palabra f pa·*la*·bra *word*

palacio m pa·*la*·syo *palace*

palillo m pa·*lee*·lyo *toothpick*

paloma f pa·*lo*·ma *dove*

palm m palm *palm pilot*

palma f **de coco** *pal*·ma de *ko*·ko *coconut palm*

palta f *pal*·ta *avocado*

pan m pan *bread*

— **blanco** *blan*·ko *white bread*

— **de centeno** de sen·*te*·no *rye bread*

— **de masa fermentada** de *ma*·sa fer·men·*ta*·da *sourdough bread*

— **integral** een·te·*gral* *wholemeal bread*

panadería f pa·na·de·*ree*·a *bakery*

pañal m pa·*nyal* *nappy* • *diaper*

Panamá f pa·na·*ma* *Panama*

panorámico/a m/f pa·no·ra·*mee*·ko/a *panoramic*

pantalla f pan·*ta*·lya *screen*

pantalones m pl pan·ta·*lo*·nes *pants* • *trousers*

— **cortos** *kor*·tos *shorts*

pantera f pan·*te*·ra *panther*

pañuelo m pa·*nywe*·lo *handkerchief*

— **de papel** de pa·*pel* *tissue*

papa f *pa*·pa *potato*

papá m pa·*pa* *dad*

papagayo m pa·pa·*ga*·yo *macaw*

papel ⓜ pa·*pel* paper
— **higiénico** ee·*khye*·nee·ko *toilet paper*
papeles ⓜ pl **del auto** pa·*pe*·les del *ow*·to *car owner's title*
paquete ⓜ pa·*ke*·te *package • packet • parcel*
para siempre pa·ra *syem*·pre *forever*
parabrisas ⓜ pa·ra·*bree*·sas *windscreen*
parada ① pa·*ra*·da *stop*
— **de autobús** de ow·to·*boos bus stop (city)*
— **de ómnibus** de *om*·nee·boos *bus stop (intercity)*
— **de subteráneo** de soob·te·*ra*·ne·o *metro stop*
— **de taxis** de *tak*·sees *taxi stand*
paraguas ⓜ pa·ra·gwas *umbrella*
Paraguay ⓜ pa·ra·*gway* Paraguay
para pa·ra *for*
parar pa·*rar* stop
pared ① pa·*re*·wall *(inside)*
pareja ① pa·*re*·kha *partner • pair (couple)*
parlamento ⓜ par·*la*·men·to *parliament*
parque ⓜ *par*·ke *park*
— **nacional** na·syo·*nal* national park
parte ① *par*·te *part*
partida ① **de nacimiento** par·*tee*·da de na·see·*myen*·to *birth certificate*
partido ⓜ par·*tee*·do *match (sport) • party (politics)*
partir par·*teer* leave
pasa ① **de uva** *pa*·sa de oo·va *raisin*
pasado ⓜ pa·*sa*·do *past*
— **mañana** ma·*nya*·na *day after tomorrow*
pasado/a ⓜ/① pa·*sa*·do/a *off (spoiled)*
pasajero/a ⓜ/① pa·sa·*khe*·ro/a *passenger*
pasaporte ⓜ pa·sa·*por*·te *passport*
Pascua ① *pas*·kwa *Easter*
pase ⓜ *pa*·se *pass (permit)*
paseo ⓜ pa·*se*·o *ride • street*

pasillo ⓜ pa·*see*·lyo *aisle (plane, train)*
paso ⓜ *pa*·so *step • pass (mountain)*
pasta ① *pas*·ta *pasta*
— **dentífrica** den·*tee*·free·ka *toothpaste*
pastelería ① pas·te·le·*ree*·a *cake shop*
pastillas ① pl pas·*tee*·lyas *pills*
— **antipalúdicas** an·tee·pa·*loo*·dee·kas *antimalarial tablets*
— **de menta** de *men*·ta *mints*
— **para dormir** pa·ra dor·*meer* *sleeping pills*
paté ⓜ pa·*te* pate *(food)*
pato ⓜ *pa*·to *duck*
patrón/patrona ⓜ/① pa·*tron*/pa·*tro*·na *employer*
pavo ⓜ *pa*·vo *turkey*
paz ① pas *peace*
peatón ⓜ&① pe·a·*ton* *pedestrian*
pecho ⓜ *pe*·cho *chest*
pedal ⓜ pe·*dal* *pedal*
pedazo ⓜ pe·*da*·so *piece*
pedir pe·*deer* ask (for something) • *borrow*
peine ⓜ *pay*·ne *comb*
pelea ① pe·*le*·a *quarrel*
película ① pe·*lee*·koo·la *film (for camera) • movie*
peligroso/a ⓜ/① pe·lee·*gro*·so/a *dangerous*
pelo ⓜ *pe*·lo *hair*
pelota ① pe·*lo*·ta *ball*
— **de golf** de golf *golf ball*
peluquero/a ⓜ/① pe·loo·*ke*·ro/a *hairdresser*
pene ⓜ *pe*·ne *penis*
penicilina ① pe·nee·see·*lee*·na *penicillin*
pensar pen·*sar* *think*
pensión ① pen·*syon* *boarding house*
pensionado/a ⓜ/① pen·syo·na·do/a *pensioner*
pepinillos ⓜ pl pe·pee·*nee*·lyos *pickles*
pepino ⓜ pe·*pee*·no *cucumber*
pequeñito/a ⓜ/① pe·ke·*nee*·to/a *tiny*
pequeño/a ⓜ/① pe·*ke*·nyo/a *small*

pera ① *pe*·ra pear
perder per·*der* lose
perdido/a ⑩/① per·*dee*·do/a lost
perdonar per·do·*nar* forgive
perezoso/a ⑩/① pe·re·so·so/a lazy
perfume ⑩ per·*foo*·me perfume
periódico ⑩ pe·*ryo*·dee·ko newspaper
periodista ⑩&① pe·ryo·*dees*·ta
  journalist
permiso ⑩ per·*mee*·so
  permission • permit
  — de trabajo de tra·*ba*·kho work
  permit
permitir per·mee·*teer* allow
pero *pe*·ro but
perro/a ⑩/① *pe*·ro/a dog
  — guía *gee*·a guide dog
persona ① per·*so*·na person
Perú ⑩ pe·*roo* Peru
pesado/a ⑩/① pe·*sa*·do/a heavy
pesca ① *pes*·ka fishing
pescadería ① pes·ka·de·*ree*·a fish shop
pescado ⑩ pes·*ka*·do fish (as food)
peso ⑩ *pe*·so weight
petición ① pe·tee·*syon* petition
pez ⑩ pes fish
picadura ① pee·ka·*doo*·ra bite (insect)
picazón ① pee·ka·*son* itch
picnic ⑩ peek·*neek* picnic
pie ⑩ pye foot
piedra ① *pye*·dra stone
piel ① pyel skin
pierna ① *pyer*·na leg (body)
pila ① *pee*·la battery (small)
píldora ① *peel*·do·ra pill • the Pill
pimienta ① pee·*myen*·ta pepper
pimiento ⑩ pee·*myen*·to capsicum •
  bell pepper
pinchar peen·*char* puncture
ping pong ⑩ peen pon table tennis
pintar peen·*tar* paint
pintor(a) ⑩/① peen·*tor*/peen·*to*·ra
  painter
pintura ① peen·*too*·ra painting (art)
pinzas ① pl *peen*·sas tweezers
piojos ⑩ pl *pyo*·khos lice
piolet ⑩ pyo·*let* ice axe

piqueta ① pee·*ke*·ta pickaxe
piscina ① pee·*see*·na swimming pool
piso ⑩ *pee*·so floor (storey)
pista ① *pees*·ta sports track • tennis court
pistacho ⑩ pees·*ta*·cho pistachio
pizarra ① blanca pee·*sa*·ra *blan*·ka
  whiteboard
plancha ① *plan*·cha iron (clothes)
planeta ⑩ pla·*ne*·ta planet
planta ① *plan*·ta plant
plástico ⑩ *plas*·tee·ko plastic
plata ① *pla*·ta silver
plataforma ① pla·ta·*for*·ma platform
plátano ⑩ *pla*·ta·no banana
plato ⑩ *pla*·to plate
playa ① *pla*·ya beach
plaza ① *pla*·sa square
  — de toros de *to*·ros bullring
pobre *po*·bre poor
pobreza ① po·*bre*·sa poverty
pocos/as ⑩/① pl *po*·kos/as few
poder ⑩ po·*der* power
poder po·*der* can (be able)
poesía ① po·e·*see*·a poetry
polen ⑩ *po*·len pollen
policía ① po·lee·*see*·a police
política ① po·*lee*·tee·ka policy • politics
político/a ⑩/① po·*lee*·tee·ko/a politician
póliza ① *po*·lee·sa policy (insurance)
pollo ⑩ *po*·lyo chicken
pomelo ⑩ po·*me*·lo grapefruit
poner po·*ner* put
popular po·poo·*lar* popular
por por for
por (día) por (*dee*·a) per (day)
por ciento por *syen*·to percent
por qué por ke why
por vía aérea por *vee*·a a·*e*·re·a by airmail
por vía terrestre por *vee*·a te·*res*·tre
  surface mail
porque por·*ke* because
posible po·*see*·ble possible
potable po·*ta*·ble drinkable
potro ⑩ *po*·tro pony
pozo ⑩ *po*·so well (water)

precio ⓜ *pre·*syo *price*
— **de entrada** de en·*tra·*da *admission price*
— **del cubierto** del koo·*byer·*to *cover charge (restaurant)*
preferir pre·fe·*reer prefer*
pregunta ⓕ pre·*goon·*ta *question*
preguntar pre·goon·*tar ask (a question)*
preocupado/a ⓜ/ⓕ
pre·o·koo·*pa·*do/a *worried*
preocuparse por pre·o·koo·*par·*se por *care (about something)*
preparar pre·pa·*rar prepare*
presentación ⓕ pre·sen·ta·*syon presentation*
presidente/a ⓜ/ⓕ pre·see·*den·*te/a *president*
presión ⓕ pre·*syon pressure*
— **arterial** ar·te·*ryal blood pressure*
presupuesto ⓜ pre·soo·*pwes·*to *budget*
prevenir pre·ve·*neer prevent*
primavera ⓕ pree·ma·*ve·*ra *spring (season)*
primer ministro/a ⓜ/ⓕ pree·mer mee·*nees·*tro/a *prime minister*
primera clase ⓕ pree·*me·*ra *kla·*se *first class*
primero/a ⓜ/ⓕ pree·*me·*ro/a *first*
primo/a ⓜ/ⓕ *pree·*mo/a *cousin*
principal preen·see·*pal main*
prisionero/a ⓜ/ⓕ pree·syo·ne·ro/a *prisoner*
privado/a ⓜ/ⓕ pree·*va·*do/a *private*
probar pro·*bar try (attempt)*
producir pro·doo·*seer produce*
productos ⓜ pl **congelados** pro·*dook·*tos kon·khe·*la·*dos *frozen foods*
profesor(a) pro·fe·*sor/*pro·fe·*so·*ra *teacher · lecturer*
profundo/a ⓜ/ⓕ pro·*foon·*do/a *deep · profound*
programa ⓜ pro·*gra·*ma *programme*
prolongación ⓕ pro·lon·ga·*syon extension (visa)*
promesa ⓕ pro·*me·*sa *promise*
prometida ⓕ pro·me·*tee·*da *fiancee*
prometido ⓜ pro·me·*tee·*do *fiance*

pronto *pron·*to *soon*
propietaria ⓕ pro·pye·*ta·*rya *landlady*
propietario ⓜ pro·pye·*ta·*ryo *landlord*
propina ⓕ pro·*pee·*na *tip (gratuity)*
proteger pro·te·*kher protect*
propuesta ⓕ pro·*pwes·*ta *proposal*
protegido/a ⓜ/ⓕ pro·te·*khee·*do/a *protected*
protesta ⓕ pro·*tes·*ta *protest*
protestar pro·tes·*tar protest*
provisiones ⓕ pl pro·vee·*syo·*nes *provisions*
proximo/a ⓜ/ⓕ *prok·*see·mo/a *next*
proyector ⓜ pro·yek·*tor projector*
prueba ⓕ *prwe·*ba *test*
— **del embarazo** del em·ba·*ra·*so *pregnancy test kit*
pruebas ⓕ pl **nucleares** *prwe·*bas noo·kle·*a·*res *nuclear testing*
pub ⓜ poob *pub*
pueblo ⓜ *pwe·*blo *village*
puente ⓜ *pwen·*te *bridge*
puerro ⓜ *pwe·*ro *leek*
puerta ⓕ *pwer·*ta *door*
puerto ⓜ *pwer·*to *port · harbour*
Puerto ⓜ **Rico** *pwer·*to *ree·*ko *Puerto Rico*
puesta ⓕ **del sol** *pwes·*ta del sol *sunset*
pulga ⓕ *pool·*ga *flea*
pulmones ⓜ pl pool·*mo·*nes *lungs*
puntero ⓜ **láser** poon·*te·*ro *la·*ser *laser pointer*
punto ⓜ *poon·*to *point · dot · full stop*
puro/a ⓜ/ⓕ *poo·*ro/a *pure*

Q

que ke *what*
quedar ke·*dar stay (remain)*
quedarse ke·*dar·*se *stay (remain)*
quejarse ke·*khar·*se *complain*
quemadura ⓕ ke·ma·*doo·*ra *burn*
— **de sol** de sol *sunburn*
quemar ke·*mar burn*
querer ke·*rer love · want*
queso ⓜ *ke·*so *cheese*
— **crema** *kre·*ma *cream cheese*

quien kyen *who*
quincena ⓕ keen·*se*·na *fortnight*
quiosco ⓜ kee·*os*·ko *newsagency*
quiste ⓜ **ovárico** kees·te o·*va*·ree·ko *ovarian cyst*
quizás kee·*sas* *maybe*

R

rábano ⓜ *ra*·ba·no *radish*
— **picante** pee·*kan*·te *horseradish*
rabo ⓜ *ra*·bo *tail*
radiador ⓜ ra·dya·*dor* *radiator*
rana ⓕ *ra*·na *frog*
rápido/a ⓜ/ⓕ *ra*·pee·do/a *fast*
raqueta ⓕ ra·*ke*·ta *racquet*
raro/a ⓜ/ⓕ *ra*·ro/a *rare*
rata ⓕ *ra*·ta *rat*
ratón ⓜ ra·*ton* *mouse*
ratonero ⓜ ra·to·*ne*·ro *buzzard*
razón ⓕ ra·*son* *reason*
realista re·a·*lees*·ta *realistic*
rebajado ⓜ *reembolso* re·em·*bol*·so *refund*
recibir re·see·*beer* *receive*
recibo ⓜ re·*see*·bo *receipt*
reciclable re·see·*kla*·ble *recyclable*
reciclar re·see·*klar* *recycle*
recientemente re·syen·te·*men*·te *recently*
recogida ⓕ **de equipajes** re·ko·*khee*·da de e·kee·*pa*·khes *baggage claim*
recolección ⓕ **de fruta** re·ko·lek·*syon* de froo·ta *fruit picking*
recomendar re·ko·men·*dar* *recommend*
reconocer re·ko·no·*ser* *acknowledge* · *recognise*
recorrido ⓜ **guiado** re·ko·*ree*·do gee·*a*·do *guided tour*
recto/a ⓜ/ⓕ *rek*·to/a *straight*
recuerdo ⓜ re·*kwer*·do *souvenir*
recuerdos ⓜ pl re·*kwer*·dos *memories*
red ⓕ re *net*
redondo/a ⓜ/ⓕ re·*don*·do/a *round*
reembolso ⓜ re·em·*bol*·so *refund*
referencias ⓕ pl re·fe·*ren*·syas *references (work)*
refrigeradora ⓕ re·free·khe·ra·*do*·ra *refrigerator*

refugiado/a ⓜ/ⓕ re·foo·*khya*·do/a *refugee*
regalo ⓜ re·*ga*·lo *gift*
— **de bodas** de bo·das *wedding present*
régimen ⓜ *re*·khee·men *diet*
registrar re·khees·*trar* *check-in (hotel)*
reglas ⓕ pl *re*·glas *rules*
reina ⓕ *ray*·na *queen*
reírse re·*eer*·se *laugh*
relación ⓕ re·la·*syon* *relationship*
relajarse re·la·*khar*·se *relax*
religión ⓕ re·lee·*khyon* *religion*
religioso/a ⓜ/ⓕ re·lee·*khyo*·so/a *religious*
reliquia ⓕ re·*lee*·kya *relic*
reloj ⓜ re·*lokh* *clock*
— **de pulsera** de pool·*se*·ra *watch*
remo ⓜ *re*·mo *rowing*
remolacha ⓕ re·mo·*la*·cha *beetroot*
remoto/a ⓜ/ⓕ re·*mo*·to/a *remote*
reparar re·pa·*rar* *repair*
repollo ⓜ re·*po*·lyo *cabbage*
reproductor ⓜ **de compacts portátil** re·pro·dook·*tor* de *kom*·pakts por·*ta*·teel *portable CD player*
reproductor ⓜ **de MP3** re·pro·dook·*tor* de *e*·me pe tres *MP3 player*
república ⓕ re·*poo*·blee·ka *republic*
República ⓕ **Dominicana** re·*poo*·blee·ka do·mee·nee·*ka*·na *Dominican Republic*
requesón ⓜ re·ke·*son* *cottage cheese*
reserva ⓕ re·*ser*·va *reservation*
reservar re·ser·*var* *book (reserve)*
residencia ⓕ **de estudiantes** re·see·*den*·sya de es·too·*dyan*·tes *college*
residuos ⓜ pl **tóxicos** re·*see*·dwos *tok*·see·kos *toxic waste*
respirar res·pee·*rar* *breathe*
respuesta ⓕ res·*pwes*·ta *answer*
restaurante ⓜ res·tow·*ran*·te *restaurant*
revisar re·vee·*sar* *check*
revisor(a) ⓜ/ⓕ re·vee·*sor*/re·vee·*so*·ra *ticket collector*

revista ⓕ re·vees·ta *magazine*
rey ⓜ ray *king*
rezar re·sar *worship (pray)*
rico/a ⓜ/ⓕ ree·ko/a *rich*
riesgo ⓜ ryes·go *risk*
río ⓜ ree·o *river*
ritmo ⓜ reet·mo *rhythm*
robar ro·bar *rob*
roca ⓕ ro·ka *rock (stone)*
rock ⓜ rok *rock (music)*
rodilla ⓕ ro·dee·lya *knee*
rojo/a ⓜ/ⓕ ro·kho/a *red*
romántico/a ⓜ/ⓕ ro·man·tee·ko/a *romantic*
romper rom·per *break*
ron ⓜ ron *rum*
ropa ⓕ ro·pa *clothing*
— **de cama** de ka·ma *bedding*
— **interior** een·te·ryor *underwear*
rosa ro·sa *pink*
roto/a ⓜ/ⓕ ro·to/a *broken*
rueda ⓕ rwe·da *wheel*
rugby ⓜ roog·bee *rugby*
ruidoso/a ⓜ/ⓕ rwee·do·so/a *loud*
ruinas ⓕ pl rwee·nas *ruins*
ruta ⓕ roo·ta *route*

S

sábado ⓜ sa·ba·do *Sabbath*
sábana ⓕ sa·ba·na *sheet (bed)*
saber sa·ber *know (how to)*
sabroso/a ⓜ/ⓕ sa·bro·so/a *tasty*
sacacorchos ⓜ sa·ka·kor·chos *corkscrew*
sacerdote ⓜ sa·ser·do·te *priest*
saco ⓜ sa·ko *coat*
— **de dormir** de dor·meer *sleeping bag*
sal ⓕ sal *salt*
sala ⓕ sa·la *room*
— **de espera** de es·pe·ra *waiting room*
— **de tránsito** de tran·see·to *transit lounge*
salami ⓜ sa·la·mee *salami*
salario ⓜ sa·la·ryo *salary*
salchicha ⓕ sal·chee·cha *sausage*

saldo ⓜ sal·do *balance (account)*
salida ⓕ sa·lee·da *departure · exit*
salir sa·leer *go out (exit)*
salir con sa·leer kon *date (a person)*
salir de sa·leer de *depart*
salmón ⓜ sal·mon *salmon*
salón de belleza sa·lon de be·lye·sa *beauty salon*
salsa ⓕ sal·sa *sauce*
— **de ají** de a·khee *chilli sauce*
— **de soya** de so·ya *soy sauce*
— **de tomate** de to·ma·te *tomato sauce · ketchup*
saltar sal·tar *jump*
salud ⓕ sa·loo *health*
salvaeslips ⓜ pl sal·va·e·sleeps *panty liners*
sandalias ⓕ pl san·da·lyas *sandals*
sandía ⓕ san·dee·a *watermelon*
sandwich ⓜ san·weech *sandwich*
sangre ⓕ san·gre *blood*
santo/a ⓜ/ⓕ san·to/a *saint*
sarampión ⓜ sa·ram·pyon *measles*
sartén ⓕ sar·ten *frying pan*
sastre ⓜ sas·tre *tailor*
sauna ⓕ sow·na *sauna*
secar se·kar *dry*
seco/a ⓜ/ⓕ se·ko/a *dry*
secretario/a ⓜ/ⓕ se·kre·ta·ryo/a *secretary*
seda ⓕ se·da *silk*
seguir se·geer *follow*
segundo ⓜ se·goon·do *second (time)*
segundo/a ⓜ/ⓕ se·goon·do/a *second (place)*
seguro ⓜ se·goo·ro *insurance*
seguro/a ⓜ/ⓕ se·goo·ro/a *safe*
sello ⓜ se·lyo *stamp*
semáforos ⓜ pl se·ma·fo·ros *traffic lights*
semana ⓕ se·ma·na *week*
Semana Santa se·ma·na san·ta *Holy Week*
sembrar sem·brar *plant*
semidirecto/a se·mee·dee·rek·to/a *non-direct*
señal ⓕ se·nyal *sign*
sencillo/a ⓜ/ⓕ sen·see·lyo/a *simple*
sendero ⓜ sen·de·ro *path*

senos ⓜ *se*·nos *breasts*
sensibilidad ⓕ sen·see·bee·lee·*da film speed • sensitivity*
sensual sen·*swal sensual*
sentarse sen·*tar*·se *sit*
sentimientos ⓜ pl sen·tee·*myen*·tos *feelings*
sentir sen·*teer feel*
separado/a ⓜ/ⓕ se·pa·*ra*·do/a *separate*
separar se·pa·*rar separate*
ser ser *be*
serie ⓕ *se*·rye *series*
serio/a ⓜ/ⓕ *se*·ryo/a *serious*
seropositivo/a ⓜ/ⓕ se·ro·po·see·*tee*·vo/a *HIV positive*
serpiente ⓕ ser·*pyen*·te *snake*
servicio ⓜ ser·*vee*·syo *service • service charge*
— militar mee·lee·*tar military service*
— telefónico automático te·le·*fo*·nee·ko ow·to·ma·*tee*·ko *direct-dial*
servilleta ⓕ ser·vee·*lye*·ta *napkin*
sexismo ⓜ sek·*sees*·mo *sexism*
sexo ⓜ *sek*·so *sex*
— seguro se·*goo*·ro *safe sex*
sexy *sek*·se *sexy*
si see *if*
sí see *yes*
SIDA ⓜ *see*·da *AIDS*
sidra ⓕ *see*·dra *cider*
siempre *syem*·pre *always*
silla ⓕ *see*·lya *chair*
— de ruedas de *rwe*·das *wheelchair*
sillín ⓜ see·*lyeen saddle*
sillita ⓕ see·*lyee*·ta *child seat*
similar see·mee·*lar similar*
simpático/a ⓜ/ⓕ seem·*pa*·tee·ko/a *nice (person)*
sin seen *without*
— plomo *plo*·mo *unleaded*
— techo *te*·cho *homeless*
sinagoga ⓕ see·na·*go*·ga *synagogue*
Singapur seen·ga·*poor Singapore*
sintético/a ⓜ/ⓕ seen·*te*·tee·ko/a *synthetic*

SMS *e*·se *em*·e *e*·se *SMS*
sobre ⓜ *so*·bre *envelope*
sobre *so*·bre *about • over (above)*
sobredosis ⓕ so·bre·*do*·sees *overdose*
socialista ⓜ&ⓕ so·sya·*lees*·ta *socialist*
sol ⓜ sol *sun*
soldado ⓜ sol·*da*·do *soldier*
soleado/a so·le·*a*·do/a *sunny*
sólo *so*·lo *only*
solo/a ⓜ/ⓕ *so*·lo/a *alone*
soltero/a ⓜ/ⓕ sol·*te*·ro/a *single (unmarried)*
sombra ⓕ *som*·bra *shade • shadow*
sombrero ⓜ som·*bre*·ro *hat*
soñar so·*nyar dream*
sondeos ⓜ pl son·*de*·os *polls*
sonreír son·re·*eer smile*
sopa ⓕ *so*·pa *soup*
sordo/a ⓜ/ⓕ *sor*·do/a *deaf*
soroche ⓜ so·*ro*·che *altitude sickness*
sorpresa ⓕ sor·*pre*·sa *surprise*
su soo *his • her • their*
sostén ⓜ sos·*ten bra*
subir soo·*beer climb*
submarinismo ⓜ soob·ma·ree·*nees*·mo *diving*
subsidio ⓜ de desempleo soob·*see*·dyo de des·em·*ple*·o *dole*
subterráneo ⓜ soob·te·ra·*ne*·o *metro • subway*
subtítulos ⓜ pl soob·*tee*·too·los *subtitles*
sucio/a ⓜ/ⓕ *soo*·syo/a *dirty*
Sudamérica ⓕ sood·a·*me*·ree·ka *South America*
sudamericano/a ⓜ/ⓕ sood·a·me·ree·*ka*·no/a *South American*
sudar soo·*dar perspire*
suegra ⓕ *swe*·gra *mother-in-law*
suegro ⓜ *swe*·gro *father-in-law*
sueldo ⓜ *swel*·do *wage*
suelo ⓜ *swe*·lo *floor (ground)*
suerte ⓕ *swer*·te *luck*
suéter ⓜ *swe*·ter *jumper • sweater*
suficiente soo·fee·*syen*·te *enough*
supermercado ⓜ soo·per·mer·*ka*·do *supermarket*

superstición ① soo·per·stee·*syon*
superstition

sur ⓜ soor *south*

surf ⓜ soorf *surfing*
— **sobre la nieve** *so*·bre la *nye*·ve
snowboarding

T

tabaco ⓜ ta·*ba*·ko *tobacco*

tabla ① **de surf** *ta*·bla de soorf
surfboard

tacaño/a ⓜ/① ta·*ka*·nyo/a *stingy*

tajo ⓜ ta·kho *chopping board*

talco ⓜ *tal*·ko *baby powder*

talla ① *ta*·lya *size (clothes)*

taller ⓜ ta·*lyer* *garage (car repair)* •
workshop

tamaño ta·*ma*·nyo *size (general)*

también tam·*byen* *also*

tampoco tam·po·ko *neither*

tampones ⓜ pl tam·*po*·nes *tampons*

tapón ⓜ ta·*pon* *plug (bath)*

tapones ⓜ pl **para los oídos**
ta·*po*·nes *pa*·ra los *o*·ee·dos *earplugs*

taquilla ① ta·*kee*·lya *ticket office
(cinema, theatre)*

tarde *tar*·de *late*

tarjeta ① tar·*khe*·ta *card*
— **de crédito** de *kre*·dee·to *credit card*
— **de embarque** de em·*bar*·ke
boarding pass
— **de teléfono** de te·*le*·fo·no
phone card
— **SIM** seem *SIM card*

tarta ① **nupcial** *tar*·ta noop·*syal*
wedding cake

tasa ① **del aeropuerto** *ta*·sa del
a·e·ro·*pwer*·to *airport tax*

taxi ⓜ *tak*·see *taxi*

taza ① *ta*·sa *cup*

té ⓜ te *tea*

teatro ⓜ te·*a*·tro *theatre*
— **de la ópera** de la *o*·pe·ra *opera
house*

techo ⓜ *te*·cho *roof*

teclado ⓜ te·*kla*·do *keyboard*

tela ① *te*·la *fabric*

tele ① *te*·le *TV*

teleférico ⓜ te·le·*fe*·ree·ko *cable car*

teléfono ⓜ te·*le*·fo·no *telephone*
— **móbil** *mo*·bil *mobile phone*
— **celular** se·loo·*lar* *cell phone*
— **público** *poo*·blee·ko *public
telephone*

telegrama ⓜ te·le·*gra*·ma *telegram*

telenovela ① te·le·no·*ve*·la *soap opera*

teleobjetivo ⓜ te·le·ob·khe·*tee*·vo
telephoto lens

telesquí ⓜ te·le·*skee* *ski lift*

televisión ① te·le·vee·*syon* *television*

temperatura ① tem·pe·ra·*too*·ra
temperature

templado/a ⓜ/① tem·*pla*·do/a *warm*

templo ⓜ *tem*·plo *temple*

temprano tem·*pra*·no *early*

tenedor ⓜ te·ne·*dor* *fork*

tener te·*ner* *have*
— **hambre** *am*·bre *be hungry*
— **prisa** *pree*·sa *be in a hurry*
— **resfriado** res·*frya*·do *have a cold*
— **sed** se *be thirsty*
— **sueño** *swe*·nyo *be sleepy*

tenis ⓜ *te*·nees *tennis*

tensión ① **premenstrual** ten·*syon*
pre·mens·*trwal* *premenstrual tension*

tentempié ⓜ ten·tem·*pye* *snack*

tercio ⓜ *ter*·syo *third*

terible te·*ree*·ble *terrible*

terminar ter·mee·*nar* *finish*

ternera ① ter·*ne*·ra *veal*

terremoto ① te·re·*mo*·to *earthquake*

testarudo/a ⓜ/① tes·ta·*roo*·do/a
stubborn

tía ① *tee*·a *aunt*

tiempo ⓜ *tyem*·po *time* • *weather*

tienda ① *tyen*·da *shop*
— **de fotografía** de fo·to·gra·*fee*·a
camera shop
— **de provisiones de cámping**
de pro·vee·*syo*·nes de *kam*·peen
camping store
— **de recuerdos** de re·*kwer*·dos
souvenir shop
— **de ropa** de *ro*·pa *clothing store*
— **deportiva** de·por·*tee*·va *sports store*

Tierra ① *tye*·ra *Earth*

tierra ① *tye*·ra *land*

tijeras ① pl tee-*khe*-ras *scissors*
tímido/a ⓜ/① tee-mee-do/a *shy*
tío ⓜ tee-o *uncle*
típico/a ⓜ/① tee-pee-ko/a *typical*
tipo ⓜ tee-po *type*
— **de cambio** de *kam*-byo *exchange rate*
toalla ① to-*a*-lya *towel*
toallita ① to-a-*lyee*-ta *wash cloth* • *flannel*
tobillo ⓜ to-*bee*-lyo *ankle*
tocar to-*kar* *touch* • *play (an instrument)*
— **la guitarra** la gee-*ta*-ra *play the guitar*
tocino ⓜ to-*see*-no *bacon*
todavía (no) to-da-*vee*-a (no) *(not) yet*
todo to-do *everything*
todo/a ⓜ/① to-do/a *all (singular)*
todos/as ⓜ/① pl to-dos/as *all (plural)*
tofú ⓜ to-*foo* *tofu*
tomar to-*mar* *take* • *drink*
tomate ⓜ to-*ma*-te *tomato*
tono ⓜ to-no *dial tone*
torcedura ① tor-se-*doo*-ra *sprain*
tormenta ① tor-*men*-ta *storm*
toro ⓜ to-ro *bull*
torre ① to-re *tower*
torta ① tor-ta *cake*
tos ① tos *cough*
tostada ① tos-*ta*-da *toast*
tostadora ① tos-ta-*do*-ra *toaster*
trabajar tra-ba-*khar* *work*
trabajo ⓜ tra-*ba*-kho *work (occupation)*
— **a tiempo parcial** a *tyem*-po par-*syal* *part-time work*
— **a tiempo completo** a *tyem*-po kom-*ple*-to *full-time work*
— **administrativo** ad-mee-nees-tra-*tee*-vo *paperwork*
— **de limpieza** de leem-*pye*-sa *cleaning*
— **eventual** e-ven-*twal* *casual work*
traducir tra-doo-*seer* *translate*
traer tra-*er* *bring*
traficante ⓜ **de drogas** tra-fee-*kan*-te de *dro*-gas *drug dealer*
tráfico ⓜ *tra*-fee-ko *traffic*
traje ⓜ *tra*-khe *suit*
— **de baño** de *ba*-nyo *swimsuit*

tramposo/a ⓜ/① tram-*po*-so/a *cheat*
tranquilo/a ⓜ/① tran-*kee*-lo/a *quiet*
tranvía ⓜ tran-*vee*-a *tram*
tratar de ligar tra-*tar* de lee-*gar* *chat up*
tren ⓜ tren *train*
trepar tre-*par* *scale* • *climb*
tribunal ⓜ tree-boo-*nal* *court (legal)*
triste *trees*-te *sad*
tú too *you* sg inf
tumba ① *toom*-ba *grave* • *tomb*
tumbarse toom-*bar*-se *lie (not stand)*
turista ⓜ&① too-*rees*-ta *tourist*

U

uniforme ⓜ oo-nee-*for*-me *uniform*
universidad ① oo-nee-ver-see-*da* *university*
universo ⓜ oo-nee-*ver*-so *universe*
urgente oor-*khen*-te *urgent*
Uruguay ⓜ oo-roo-*gway* *Uruguay*
usted oos-*te* *you* sg pol
ustedes oo-*ste*-des *you* pl pol&inf
útil *oo*-teel *useful*
uvas ① pl *oo*-vas *grapes*

V

vaca ① *va*-ka *cow*
vacaciones ① pl va-ka-*syo*-nes *holidays* • *vacation*
vacante va-*kan*-te *vacant*
vacío/a ⓜ/① va-*see*-o/a *empty*
vacuna ① va-*koo*-na *vaccination*
vagina ① va-*khee*-na *vagina*
vagón ⓜ va-*gon* *train carriage*
— **restaurante** res-tow-*ran*-te *dining car*
validar va-lee-*dar* *validate*
valiente va-*lyen*-te *brave*
valioso/a ⓜ/① va-*lyo*-so/a *valuable*
valle ⓜ *va*-lye *valley*
valor ⓜ va-*lor* *value*
varios/as ⓜ/① pl *va*-ryos/as *several*
vaso ⓜ *va*-so *glass (drinking)*
vegetariano/a ⓜ/① ve-khe-ta-*rya*-no/a *vegetarian*

U

vegetariano/a estricto/a ⓜ/ⓕ
ve·khe·ta·*rya*·no/a es·*treek*·to/a *vegan*
vela ⓕ *ve*·la *candle • sail*
velocidad ⓕ ve·lo·see·*da speed*
velocímetro ⓜ ve·lo·*see*·me·tro
speedometer
vena ⓕ *ve*·na *vein*
vendaje ⓜ ven·*da*·khe *bandage*
vender ven·*der sell*
venenoso/a ⓜ/ⓕ ve·ne·*no*·so/a
poisonous
Venezuela ⓕ ve·ne·*swe*·la *Venezuela*
venir ve·*neer come*
ventana ⓕ ven·*ta*·na *window*
ventilador ⓜ ven·tee·la·*dor fan*
(machine)
ver ver *see*
verano ⓜ ve·*ra*·no *summer*
verde *ver*·de *green*
verdulero/a ⓜ/ⓕ ver·doo·*le*·ro/a
greengrocer
verdura ⓕ pl ver·*doo*·ra *vegetable*
verja ⓕ *ver*·kha *gate*
vestíbulo ⓜ ves·*tee*·boo·lo *foyer*
vestido ⓜ ves·*tee*·do *dress*
vestuario ⓜ ves·*twa*·ryo *changing
room • wardrobe*
vez ⓕ ves *time (occasion)*
viajar vya·*khar travel*
viaje ⓜ *vya*·khe *trip*
vida ⓕ *vee*·da *life*
— **nocturna** nok·*toor*·na *night life*
video ⓜ vee·*de*·o *video*
vidrio ⓜ vee·*dryo glass (material)*
viejo/a ⓜ/ⓕ *vye*·kho/a *old*
viento ⓜ *vyen*·to *wind*
vinagre vee·*na*·gre *vinegar*
viñedo ⓜ vee·*nye*·do *vineyard*
vino ⓜ *vee*·no *wine*
— **blanco** *blan*·ko *white wine*
— **espumoso** es·poo·*mo*·so
sparkling wine
— **tinto** *teen*·to *red wine*
violar vyo·*lar rape*

virus ⓜ *vee*·roos *virus*
visado ⓜ vee·*sa*·do *visa*
visitar vee·see·*tar visit*
vista ⓕ *vees*·ta *view*
vitaminas ⓕ pl vee·ta·*mee*·nas
vitamins
viuda ⓕ *vyoo*·da *widow*
viudo ⓜ *vyoo*·do *widower*
víveres ⓜ pl *vee*·ve·res *food supplies*
vivir vee·*veer live*
volado/a ⓜ/ⓕ vo·*la*·do/a *stoned
(drugged)*
volar vo·*lar fly*
voleibol ⓜ vo·*lay*·bol *volleyball*
volver vol·*ver return*
votar vo·*tar vote*
voz ⓕ vos *voice*
vuelo ⓜ *vwe*·lo *flight*
— **doméstico** do·*mes*·tee·ko
domestic flight

WAP ⓜ gwap *WAP*

y ee *and*
ya ya *already*
yip ⓜ yeep *jeep*
yo yo *I*
yoga ⓜ *yo*·ga *yoga*
yogur ⓜ yo·*goor yogurt*

zanahoria ⓕ sa·na·o·*rya carrot*
zapatería ⓕ sa·pa·te·*ree*·a *shoe shop*
zapatos ⓜ pl sa·*pa*·tos *shoes*
zodíaco ⓜ so·*dee*·a·ko *zodiac*
zoológico ⓜ so·o·*lo*·khee·ko *zoo*
zoom ⓜ soom *zoom lens*

don't just stand there, say something!

To see the full range of our language products, go to:

www.lonelyplanet.com

What kind of traveller are you?

A. You're eating chicken for dinner *again* because it's the only word you know.

B. When no one understands what you say, you step closer and shout louder.

C. When the barman doesn't understand your order, you point frantically at the beer.

D. You're surrounded by locals, swapping jokes, email addresses and experiences – other travellers want to borrow your phrasebook.

If you answered A, B, or C, you NEED Lonely Planet's phrasebooks.

- **Talk to everyone everywhere**
  Over 120 languages, more than any other publisher

- **The right words at the right time**
  Quick-reference colour sections, two-way dictionary, easy pronunciation, every possible subject

- **Lonely Planet Fast Talk** – essential language for short trips and weekends away

- **Lonely Planet Phrasebooks** – for every phrase you need in every language you want

'Best for curious and independent travellers' – Wall Street Journal

Lonely Planet Offices

Australia
90 Maribyrnong St, Footscray,
Victoria 3011
☎ 03 8379 8000
fax 03 8379 8111
email: talk2us@lonelyplanet.com.au

USA
150 Linden St, Oakland,
CA 94607
☎ 510 893 8555
fax 510 893 8572
email: info@lonelyplanet.com

UK
72-82 Rosebery Ave,
London EC1R 4RW
☎ 020 7841 9000
fax 020 7841 9001
email: go@lonelyplanet.co.uk

France
1 rue du Dahomey, 75011 Paris
☎ 01 55 25 33 00
fax 01 55 25 33 01
email: bip@lonelyplanet.fr
website: www.lonelyplanet.fr

www.lonelyplanet.com